Celtic Christianity
and Nature

Celtic Christianity and Nature

Early Irish and Hebridean Traditions

Mary Low

THE
BLACKSTAFF
PRESS

BELFAST

Elizabeth Stuart Farquhar
1924–77
in affectionate memory

First published in Ireland in 1996 by
The Blackstaff Press Limited
3 Galway Park, Dundonald,
Belfast BT16 0AN, Northern Ireland

Published simultaneously in Great Britain by
Edinburgh University Press
22 George Square, Edinburgh

Typeset in Monotype Ehrhardt
by Koinonia, Manchester, and
printed and bound in Great Britain

A CIP record for this book is available
from the British Library

ISBN 0-85640-579-5

Contents

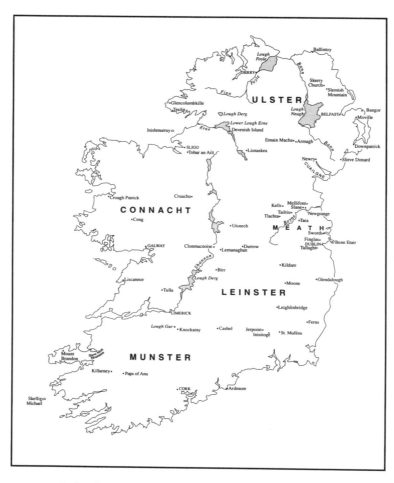

Ireland, with principal sites mentioned in the text

Acknowledgements

Permission to quote from the work of recent authors, editors and translators is gratefully acknowledged as follows: from the Governing Board of the School of Celtic Studies of the Dublin Institute for Advanced Studies for extracts from Ludwig Bieler, *The Patrician Texts in the Book of Armagh*, 1979, and from Denis Meehan, *Adomnan's De Locis Sanctis*, 1983; from Thomas Kinsella for extracts from *The Táin*, Oxford University Press, 1970, originally published by Dolmen Press, 1969; from T & T Clark Ltd for material from M. Herbert and M. Macnamara, *Irish Biblical Apocrypha*, 1989; from John O'Donohue for 'After the Sea' in his collection *Echoes of Memory*, Salmon Publishing Ltd, Dublin, 1994; from Routledge Ltd for 'St Columba's Island Hermitage' and the extract from 'St Brendan and the Harper', both translated by Kenneth Hurlstone Jackson in *A Celtic Miscellany*, revised edition, Penguin Books, 1971, original edition by Routledge & Kegan Paul Ltd, 1951; from Phillimore and Co. Ltd for extracts from A. B. E. Hood, *St Patrick, his writings and Muirchú's Life*, London, 1978. Material from John O'Meara, *Gerald of Wales: The History and Topography of Ireland*, Penguin, 1982, first published by the Dundalgan Press, 1951, revised edition by the Dolmen Press, 1982, is reprinted by permission of Colin Smythe Limited and John O'Meara whose recent editions of the *Navigatio Sancti Brendani* came to my attention too late for inclusion here. Extracts from Jeffrey Gantz, *Early Irish Myths and Sagas*, 1981, and from J. F. Webb's translation of *The Voyage of St Brendan* in J. F. Webb and D. H. Farmer, *The Age of Bede*, revised edition, 1983, are reproduced by permission of Penguin Books Ltd. Full citations and page references are given in the bibliography and in notes to the main text. While every effort has been made to contact copyright holders, not all have been traced successfully at the time of writing. I am none the less grateful to them and any omissions will be made good in subsequent editions. I acknowledge the influence of earlier translations in some of my own renderings of the texts, though most are simply revised for readability from archaising into modern English. Finally, I acknowledge permission from Dick Warren, Morebattle, Roxburghshire, to reproduce his fine set of pencil drawings.

St Columba's Island Hermitage

Delightful I think it to be in the bosom of an isle, on the peak of a rock, that I might often see there the calm of the sea.

That I might see its heavy waves over the glittering ocean, as they chant a melody to the Father on their eternal course.

That I might see its smooth strand of clear headlands, no gloomy thing; that I might hear the voice of the wondrous birds, a joyful tune.

That I might hear the sound of the shallow waves against the rocks; that I might hear the cry by the graveyard, the noise of the sea.

That I might see its splendid flocks of birds over the full-watered ocean; that I might see its mighty whales, greatest of wonders.

That I might see its ebb and its flood tide in their flow; that this might be my name, a secret I tell, 'He who turned his back on Ireland.'

That contrition of heart should come upon me as I watch it; that I might bewail my sins, difficult to declare.

That I might bless the Lord who has power over all, Heaven with its pure host of angels, earth, ebb, flood tide.

That I might pore on one of my books, good for my soul; a while kneeling for beloved heaven, a while at the psalms.

A while gathering dulse from the rock, a while fishing, a while giving food to the poor, a while in my cell.

A while meditating upon the Kingdom of Heaven, holy is the redemption; a while at labour not too heavy; it would be delightful.

Anon. Twelfth century. Translated by Kenneth Jackson, in *A Celtic Miscellany*, revd edn, Harmondsworth, 1971, 279–80.

Preface

On one of the islands in the Inner Hebrides there is a ruined monastic settlement dating from the ninth century. The place is remote and often inaccessible. Local people believe that St Brendan visited it on one of his voyages, and that St Columba, Colum Cille, landed here on his way to Iona and returned from time to time, using it as a place of retreat. I first heard of it from a friend who had lived and worked as a minister in the nearest mainland parish, but it was years before I finally visited the place. The idea was to test the beginnings of an interest in Celtic Christianity by spending a day on the island.

One morning at the beginning of June, we jumped from the boat on to a rocky ledge and picked our way through the bog cotton and the flag irises towards the ruins. Our boat was too big to land safely at the inlet where the monks drew in their curraghs. There is a path from the inlet and a spring dedicated to Colum Cille. We grazed our knees in the beehive cells, crouched in the souterrain, loitered in the roofless oratory, but what I remember most about that day was the breadth of the sky, the brightness of the sea, the seal who came up to look at us, and the skipper's concern for the tides. Whatever I had been looking for in that rather self-conscious pilgrimage of discernment, the experience was of a vibrant world of nature refusing to be ignored. Absurdly, this was not what I had expected.

I went home and re-read the twelfth-century Irish poem translated by Kenneth Jackson as 'St Columba's Island Hermitage'. Many people have remarked on the freshness and clarity of early Irish nature poetry and this is a fine example. With its casual juxtaposition of dulse and angels, it was unlike anything I had come across in the Continental Christianity of the same period. I found it approachable and refreshing and wanted to know more about that tradition which gave rise to it and about the beliefs of the people who worked and prayed in places like these. Love of nature is often said to be a characteristic feature of Celtic Christianity, but rather than setting out to prove a particular point, I simply decided to

explore the texts of the period, to see what they had to say. This book is
the result of that exploration. It traces the theme of nature and the Sacred
through a wide range of prose and poetry from medieval Ireland and Iona.
Some texts are obviously 'religious', others less so, but people do not
always present their beliefs in religious language. Indeed they may often
tell us more between the lines when speaking of other things or when
telling stories of Otherworld personages and events. It is also important
to understand the culture which gave Irish and Hebridean Christianity
its distinctive flavour, and the broad focus will help us to do that as well.

I have many people to thank for their help during the various stages of
this project. Professor James Mackey, Professor William Gillies, Dr Andrew
Ross and Dr Máire Herbert all read the whole of the manuscript in its
previous incarnation as a doctoral thesis. It has changed enormously since
then, but the time and care they took during its formative stages have been
invaluable. None of them are in any way responsible for mistakes in this
later version and I hope they are not too embarrassed by the result. In the
same way, I also want to thank   the University of Edinburgh Divinity
Faculty for sponsoring me through the first three years of my research. I
acknowledge a profound debt to Noel O'Donoghue who first introduced me
to Celtic Christianity and to several other people who directed me to relevant material, particularly in biblical studies and primal religions, notably
John Gibson, John Parrott and Jill Munro. Further afield, I am particularly grateful to the many scholars in Galway, Dublin and Maynooth
who took the time to speak to me with advice, suggestions and warnings
of possible pitfalls. A less formal thank-you is due to all the members and
former members of the Celtic Christianity post-graduate group at New
College, Edinburgh, for many good conversations over cups of coffee –
though I have to complain that the carry-out never materialised. Thanks
to all of them and also to Veronica Gordon-Smith, Muriel Wilson,
Martin Marroni, to Ian Clark for his tact, to John Goodall for his Latin,
and to the Revd Joe Brown for inadvertantly setting the whole project in
motion. Thanks also to my father, Jim Farquhar, for laying the foundations in so many ways, and to Thomas and Barbara Kerr and the rest of
my mother's family for all their kindness and hospitality over the years.
Dick Warren's beautiful drawings seem to me to be far more than just
illustrations and I hope readers will appreciate them as much as I do.
Finally, the book would never have been written without the good-
humoured practical support of my husband, Bruce, who willingly spent
hours looking for holy wells and sacred trees when he could easily have
been lounging on a sofa somewhere listening to Sibelius or John Coltrane.

9 June 1995   Gattonside

Chapter 1

Introduction

Long ago, before there were churches, it was normal for people to practise their religion out of doors. In the Hebrew Bible, Abraham meets his
God under an oak tree and Deborah prophesies under a palm. In the
New Testament, Jesus prays in the temple at Jerusalem, but also in the
hills of Galilee. Nature was an acceptable place of worship, as it still is in
many parts of the world. In Africa, for example, many people practise
highly localised traditional religions – primal religions – whose earth
shrines and sacred rivers are literally part of the landscape. Even in
cultures where people have long-since abandoned primal religion, they
may still frequent places of outdoor worship in fields and forests, on
mountains, riverbanks and islands, in caves, beside rocks and springs.
These are the old wild sanctuaries, the first places of worship.

Some of them are places of great natural beauty and people still seek
them out, for spiritual refreshment or simply for pleasure. Nature, in the
sense of landscape, is not always a comfortable place to be, but people are
still attracted to it and some feel nothing less than anguish at its destruction. Church buildings, temples, mosques and synagogues all represent
a retreat from this raw encounter with nature. In many parts of the world
it is simply assumed that proper worship needs a roof over its head.
Outdoor spirituality is seen as a fringe activity or a private affair, and on
Sundays throughout the year Christians turn their backs on nature to
worship its Creator in a house of their own making.

The reasons for this are rarely explored. One must surely be that we
seek protection from nature – from extremes of heat and cold, from rain,
wind, insects and all kinds of natural hazards. Also, there is a sense of
being held and protected by four strong walls, and some churches have
a prayerful atmosphere which might be dissipated outside. Some are also
very beautiful, and it could be said that in art and architecture people
offer their creativity back to God while making allowances for their
physical vulnerability and their limited capacity for the infinite. At the

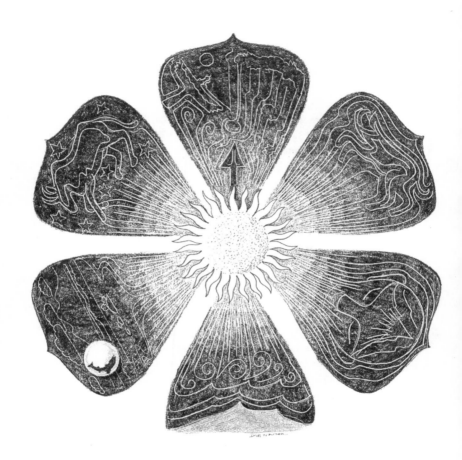

same time, any church building, no matter how beautiful, enc
idea that God and holiness, salvation and the christian life,
separate compartment from nature and that the two may even b
with each other. The expectation seems to be that God is mor
found indoors – in the space created by bricks and mortar or in the ᵤᵢner
space of human consciousness. Nature is not so easily dismissed, however. It reappears in carvings and stained glass windows, in Christmas
trees, daffodils and the produce at harvest festivals. Objections are raised
from time to time in some quarters, but most Christians enjoy these
reminders of fertility and the wider world. Few would do without flowers and none would baptise without water.

Outdoor spirituality is acceptable in most parts of Ireland and in some
Hebridean islands. This tradition goes back at least as far as the early
middle ages, as was brought home to me a few years ago as I was
travelling around Ireland looking for early christian sites and places of
pilgrimage. Unconsciously, I carried with me a mental image of Celtic
sites in Britain – Iona Abbey, Lindisfarne Priory – forgetting that the
imposing buildings which stand in these places today were built to re-
place – or at best, assimilate – Celtic Christianity, not to celebrate it. The
Cistercian ruins at Mellifont or Jerpoint are among their nearest Irish
equivalents, and very beautiful they are too, but early Celtic monasticism
is better represented by clusters of tiny churches like those at
Glendalough and Clonmacnoise. Even these, in their present form, tend
to be relatively late constructions dating back no further than about the
tenth century.

From the earlier period we find mainly crosses incised in stone, beehive cells, caves associated with hermit-saints, and place-names indicating where a church once stood. The earliest churches were commonly
made of wood and have not survived, but it would be a mistake to think
of any of them on the scale of the later Benedictine or Cistercian abbeys
(the earliest ones were small and simple) or even the size of a modern
parish church. In fact there is little sign of large communal places of
worship where clergy and laity, kings and tribespeople could all gather
together under one roof. Larger churches may possibly have existed, at
Kildare for example, where there was a double monastery for men and
women, but these were the exception rather than the rule.[1] Some of the
tiny churches seem to have been used only for the consecration of the
elements. Adamnán, for example, describes Colum Cille saying mass on
an outlying island, and apparently beginning the service out of doors,
going into the church only after the Gospel in order to celebrate the
sacred mysteries with some visiting priests. Presumably the rest of the

congregation remained outside.² Here the church is being used like the screened-off sanctuaries of the Orthodox tradition, while the first part of the celebration takes place in the open air.

It takes the visitor some time to notice that next to the abbeys and in other places throughout Ireland, there are often natural features such as rocks and wells, bearing the name of a patron saint or some other dedication which is often either obscure or ambiguous. Prayers are still offered in some of these places. Not all of them are ancient centres of worship – some may date only from penal times – but they belong to an ancient tradition of outdoor worship which continues to this day. St Patrick's memory of praying 'in the forests and on the mountain' would seem to represent a more ancient and enduring strand of Celtic spirituality than any abbey church.³

As the Roman empire collapsed and communications across Europe became difficult, the newly-christianised peoples of Ireland were increasingly thrown back on their own resources. They continued to use Latin to write, pray, sing and celebrate the mass. But they gradually also developed their own distinctive style and idiom, not out of any great desire to be different, but simply because like the Greek and Roman Christians before them, they had no choice. They could not somehow step outside their own mental and cultural horizons in order to receive and understand Christianity in exactly the same way as their continental neighbours, let alone in the same way as the first Jewish followers of Jesus. Irish culture was changed by Christianity certainly, but it would also be true to say that Christianity was changed by Irish culture. In order for it to take root at all, it had to be received and make sense in terms of what Irish people already held most dear, in other words, in terms of native values and belief-systems.

In post-missionary Africa, the appointment of native clergy was a decisive step in accelerating this process. In Ireland, there were native clergy and religious from the time of Patrick, if not earlier, and the emerging churches were not hampered by the presence of an imperial power as they were in Africa. By the late sixth and early seventh centuries Ireland was beginning to produce one of the first and finest bodies of vernacular literature in post-Roman Europe. This literature is a treasure house for anyone with an interest in Celtic Christianity. Most of it lay hidden in libraries and private houses till the middle of the nineteenth century, when renewed interest in Gaelic culture gradually brought it back into circulation. Many of the manuscripts were incomplete and the languages in which they were written – Archaic, Old and

Middle Irish – had to be carefully deciphered and reconstructed, a process which continues today. Most early Irish literature is now available in translation, even if much of it is still found only in specialist journals and out-of-print books.[4] In addition, there are the Hiberno–latin texts, like St Patrick's *Confession*, the Latin hymns, Lives of saints and so on dating from the fifth to the twelfth centuries and beyond. There is no strict segregation of Latin and Irish texts after the appearance of vernacular writing. Latin comments and phrases often appear in the midst of Irish-language works, as if the writer were equally at home in both.

As for a Celtic theology of nature, we shall certainly not find one ready-made. There is no major work or treatise on the subject. Attitudes and beliefs have to be pieced together from a wide variety of sources, though it is often possible to learn a great deal from careful attention to an individual text. Explicitly ecclesiastical material provides the obvious starting-point for research. There is no lack of liturgical texts, hymns, prayers, calendars of feast days, Lives of saints, penitentials, homilies, rules, biblical apocrypha and poems on the hermit life. Other works appear at first sight to be more 'secular' in character. These are the law tracts, annals, collections of place-lore, tales of kings, heroes, supernatural beings and so on. But the term 'secular' is misleading here and should certainly not be understood in the modern sense of free from religious presuppositions – a questionable definition even for today. Religion pervaded all areas of human activity in early Christian Ireland. It was accepted as a matter of course that cosmic order depended on there being a right relationship between the human world and the divine world and that everyone had a part to play in this, particularly the leaders of society: kings, scholars, poets, legal experts, artists, people in charge of the production and storage of food, even fighting men. Matters of belief are not confined to texts on explicitly ecclesiastical subjects, and many 'secular' writers sometimes composed works on religious subjects. It is of course notoriously difficult to tell the state-of-life of an anonymous author from his or her works.[5] We also find stories of clerics engaged in activities which are not always recognised as 'religious' because they lack a familiar ecclesiastical context, voyaging among mythical islands for example. And finally, since most of the literature of the time passed at some stage through the monastic scriptorium, there can be few texts which are untouched by Christianity.

A quick glance through any of the main twentieth-century anthologies of early Irish poetry illustrates how little we have really come to grips with this situation. A typical section on 'Religion' for example, would focus mainly on monastic poems like *St Columba's Island Hermitage* and others dealing with specifically ecclesiastical subjects. Under headings like 'Nature' or 'Description' however, we would find other poems in which religion plays a significant part, like *Marbhán's Hermitage* or *The Ivied Tree-Top*. Stories of Otherworld journeys by kings and clerics are sometimes classified as 'Celtic Magic' or even as 'Secular Poems' despite a large number of undisguised christian references. Since they also contain some beautiful nature imagery they will certainly have a claim on our attention. It seems to me that there are several sources of confusion at work here: one is an over-rigid and anachronistic view of the division between sacred and secular, another is a view of religion which is narrow even for our own time, and finally there is a difficulty over meeting Celtic Christianity on its own terms.

Lives of saints, monastic rules and so on, are perhaps less challenging in this respect than other kinds of literature. Some stories which might appear at first sight to be merely entertaining fantasies often contain religious elements as well. The late-seventh or eighth-century *Voyage of Bran / Immram Brain* for example, tells how a mysterious woman once appeared in the hall of a king called Bran, carrying a marvellous branch:

> I bring a branch of Evin's apple tree
> In shape like those you know:
> Twigs of white silver are upon it
> Buds of crystal with blossoms.[6]

She introduces herself as a visitor from a land 'without sorrow, without grief, without death, without sickness, without weakness' and goes on to sing about her island home where there is a huge tree, covered with blossom and singing birds (95). The word she uses for this tree is *bile* – the term for a sacred tree. This is not the garden paradise of Eden or the city paradise of the New Jerusalem, but it is certainly a paradise of some kind and the mysterious woman is clearly an Otherworld visitor, that is, someone from beyond the boundaries of everyday experience.

The religious character of the poem is even clearer when Bran sets off in search of the island paradise and encounters Manannán Mac Lir, generally acknowledged to be a pre-christian deity, who explains that the sea is in fact a delightful plain, and that his kingdom is untouched by original sin. He also prophesies the birth of Christ and the birth of Mongán, a sixth-century king who will 'delight the company of every fairy-mound' and be 'in the shape of every beast' – dragon, wolf, stag, salmon, seal, swan. Manannán himself would be Mongán's father, in union with a mortal woman. This is not exactly the conventional European description of a christian ruler, but there can be little doubt that the *Voyage of Bran* is in some way a religious text, touching on the reputation of a historical king and incorporating a paradise myth, several prophecies, an unfamiliar cosmology and a myth of divine fatherhood. So why do we not find it in the 'Religion' sections of the anthologies?

Part of the answer may be that many people still automatically equate religion with Christianity. This may help to explain why traditions about the Cross for example, are readily understood as 'Religion', whereas traditions about sacred trees are more often classified as 'mythology', 'folklore' or 'superstition'. Even the most conservative theologians would agree, however, that religion and Christianity are not synonymous. The world has seen many other religions and belief-systems, including of course, the pre-christian religions of Ireland. It follows that if some of the nature imagery in the *Voyage of Bran* should happen to be in conti-nuity with pre-christian religious imagery, it is still religious imagery since it touches on genuinely religious questions such as the nature of reality, the nature of time, the mystery of human identity and our rela-tionship to other beings, including sacred beings. At the same time it is important to remember that the *Voyage* is not a pre-christian text. It was composed by Christians for a christian audience.

Another factor is the tendency to recognise only one cultural expres-sion of Christianity: the Christianity which developed in and around the monasteries and teaching centres of western continental Europe in the post-Roman period, after the adoption of Christianity in Ireland. This Christianity, in either its Catholic or its Protestant form, was exported in the days of colonial expansion and has been dominant for so long that it is often mistaken for the only Christianity, but there have long been others, in Syria, Greece, Africa and India for example. The new enculturisation movements of the Third World remind us that in order for Christianity to take root and thrive in mission countries – as it certainly did in Ireland – it must express itself in terms which make sense to local people. We cannot assume, therefore, that Irish and Hebridean Christi-anity will present itself to us in wholly familiar forms, despite its strong ties with Christianity on the continent. It would be a mistake to over-emphasise these differences. Irish Christians were in full communion with their continental neighbours, read many of the same books and admired many of the same great spiritual leaders.[7] But they also had heroes and heroines of their own, and tended to express themselves differently: both in terms of church organisation and in their enthusiastic use of poetry and story for religious purposes.

As for the mythological features of the *Voyage of Bran*, these confirm rather than deny its religious character. Myths – the stories which we tell each other about the nature of reality – can be ancient or contemporary, christian and non-christian, treacherous or inspired. *The Voyage of Bran* tells us something about the world-view of the people who composed it. It incorporates a paradise myth and contains both familiar and unfamiliar religious imagery, some of which clearly relates to nature. I have no hesitation in including it in the book. Other voyage tales like *The Voyage of Máel Dúin* and *The Voyage of the Úi Chorra* also include religious motifs alongside descriptions of nature in the form of mysterious wooded islands and resplendent birds.[8] Again, most of the wonders and miracles in these tales are unfamiliar from a biblical or theological point of view, but there are also some recognisably christian elements. One of the islands visited by Máel Dúin and his companions is inhabited by a grey-haired priest living in a little church. He explains that he is the last of a group of fifteen men of the company of Brénainn (Brendan) 'who came on their pilgrimage in the ocean, until they arrived at this island'.[9] He shows them Brendan's writing-tablet and they cross themselves with it.

The Voyage of the Úi Chorra tells of three brigands who become disciples of St Finnian of Clonard. In the course of their voyage, they receive divine guidance from a bird with the soul of a woman, who explains that she comes from Ireland and is in fact a religious sister. She reassures them that they will not go to hell. She then shows them a number of bird-souls who have been less fortunate. They are in hell, she says, but they are let out on Sundays. Whatever we make of such stories today, there can be no doubt that they touch on genuinely religious themes: holiness, pilgrimage, providence, the soul, mercy, punishment, even the ten commandments. It comes as something of a surprise then, to find them in *A Celtic Miscellany* under the heading of 'Magic'.

The encounter of the Úi Chorra with a religious sister in the form of bird, highlights the difficulty of distinguishing between Otherworld texts and texts on explicitly christian subjects. It is not uncommon for both elements to be present in the same text, even in the same image, as they are here. The examples we have been looking at are all from a recognised genre of 'voyage literature' in which the Otherworld is located on a faraway island or group of islands. Other texts locate it under the ground, in the *síd* mounds or fairy mounds or under water, beneath springs and lakes, or in a far country which is reached only after a strange overland journey.[10] Visitors to the Otherworld may be kings or heroes, saints or penitents. Some voyagers meet biblical characters like Enoch, Elijah or even Judas Iscariot, indicating that their journeys were through time as well as through space.[11]

Given the strange character of so many Irish nature texts, some readers might be tempted to focus only on passages which deal with christian
themes in a familiar way, leaving the strange material to one side. This
might seem the safest approach in some ways, but it would result in a
very limited and false picture of attitudes to nature in early Christian
Ireland since unknown dimensions of meaning could be missed through
ignorance of the wider context. It would also be impractical since the
material is too well mixed within the texts. For all of these reasons, we
shall not be excluding any material simply on grounds of strangeness.

At least one attempt has been made to dismiss the voyage literature from
discussions of early Irish nature poetry on the grounds that it has more
to do with 'magic' than with nature itself.[12] Magic can of course be
understood in various ways. To children, magic is a wonderful thing,
and since they learn about it from parents and teachers, many adults
must also have a secret hankering after marvels and mysteries. Take us
away from children and our rationalism and suspicion come to the fore.
Sir James Frazer described magic as the ritual manipulation of impersonal forces in a primitive attempt to influence the world around us. He
also believed that modern science had rendered it obsolete, along with
the only slightly less primitive practice of praying to a personal god.
Theologians are often hostile to magic, either because they have adopted
a rationalistic point of view, or because they see it as involving the
manipulation of personal demons and spirits which may be antithetical
to God. The trouble with this last idea is that, in terms of results, it is
difficult to distinguish between christian miracles and non-christian
magic. The attitude of the practitioner would seem to be a key factor.
The questions arise: whom is he addressing? Is she being open or mani-
pulative? But unless the practitioner tells us the answers to these questions, we can never know. All of this makes 'magic' a difficult word to
use, particularly in relation to the beliefs and rituals of an unfamiliar
culture, and across a distance of several centuries.[13]

In what sense then, might the nature imagery of the voyage literature be
classified as 'magic'? Probably not in Frazer's sense, since medieval Irish
cosmology is full of personal rather than impersonal powers – God,
Christ, the saints, angels, 'fairies' and other supernatural creatures.
Weather-working might be thought of as a variety of impersonal 'magic'
and it is certainly a common motif in early Irish literature, but the most
expert weather-workers are certainly the saints who outdo the druids at
every turn (165–7). We should also be wary of assuming that the elements
were in fact thought of as impersonal powers. There is some evidence to

the contrary, as we shall see (169–75). As for magic in the sense of the manipulation of demons and spirits, Bran's Otherworld visitor might certainly be thought of as a spiritual being, but there is no obvious sense in which anyone is being manipulated.

The silver trees and islands of immortality in the voyage literature are more straightforwardly described as imaginative or visionary images than as instances of 'magic'. Similar images are found in the Bible, for example, in the vision of the new Jerusalem as a radiant paradise where the trees fruit all the year round.[14] Some Irish authors, including some authors of the voyage literature, were directly inspired by the Book of Revelation. In the *Voyage of St Brendan / Navigatio Sancti Brendani* for example, the 'Land of Promise of the Saints' is a place of perpetual day where 'dusk and darkness are unknown, for Christ himself is our light'.[15] Silver trees are 'magic' of course, in the sense of being marvellous, but I see no need to banish them from our study for that reason alone. We might as well banish the Tree of Life from the Book of Revelation.

Another group of texts which have previously been excluded from discussion are the famous Amairgen poems in *The Book of Conquests / Lebor Gabála*. The reason given is very similar: these are not nature poetry but 'wizardry', apparently.[16] *The Book of Conquests* is a mythological history describing the invasion of Ireland by successive tribes, from the time of Noah's flood to the time of the Milesians, these being the mythical ancestors of the present inhabitants. Amairgen is chief poet of the Milesians. As he steps ashore at the mouth of the Boyne to take possession of the land on behalf of his people, he chants the following famous poem:

> I am wind on sea
> I am ocean wave
> I am roar of sea
> I am bull of seven fights
> I am vulture on cliff
> I am dewdrop
> I am fairest of flowers
> I am boar for boldness
> I am salmon in pool
> I am lake on plain
> I am a mountain in a man
> I am a word of skill
> I am the point of a weapon
> I am God who fashions fire for a head.[17]

Is this simply a form of boasting or rhetoric, Amairgen expressing his delight at having brought the Milesians safely ashore and boasting of his prowess? Possibly, but the wind, the sea, the lake, the sun, and the pool all have numinous associations in early Irish literature. The bull, the salmon and the boar are closely associated with Otherworld beings in many tales and Amairgen identifies himself completely with these numinous entities, like a medium or ecstatic. He even says at one point, 'I am God' and asks a series of rhetorical questions in which his sphere of influence extends to time, creation and the heavenly bodies:

Who smoothes the ruggedness of the mountain?
Who is he who announces the ages of the moon?
And who, the place where the sunset falls?[18]

This certainly sounds like a divine utterance rather than simply the voice of a wizard or magician. It is also reminiscent of the theophany in Job 38, though it is not derived from it in any obvious way. 'I am' is also Yahweh's famous self-designation in the book of Exodus, and John's Gospel uses it several times to express the divine identity of Jesus.[19] Students of Comparative Religion will also be aware of another sacred text from the opposite end of the Indo-European world:

I am the Lion among beasts and the eagle among birds ...
I am the Wind among purifiers, the King Rama among warriors
I am the crocodile among fishes, I am the Ganges among rivers.[20]

This is an extract from 'The Divine Manifestations of Krishna', and together with the biblical parallels, it alerts us fully to the potential theological resonances of 'I am wind on sea'. Taken in isolation, they can be read as a divine utterance, but Amairgen is a poet and a mythological ancestor rather than a god in the conventional sense, so unless his words came originally from a different context, they should probably be understood as those of a medium or ecstatic, or else as a kind of hymn or Credo. The idea of non-duality – that all things are ultimately related to each other and to God – is present in a number of religious traditions, notably in Hinduism and Buddhism and in some of the Western mystics. A sense of kinship with nature is also one of the features of primal religions, as we shall see. All this suggests a world-view, either remembered or surviving well into christian times, in which a human being might declare a sense of universal belonging – both to nature and to the invisible worlds of language ('I am a word of skill') and divine creativity ('who fashions fire ... who smoothes the ruggedness of the mountain'). It also presents a world in which the Sacred takes many forms, pervading

the natural world and acting upon it. Whatever the origins of this powerful declaration, its inclusion in *The Book of Conquests* adds to the
evidence that traditional world-views were still at work in early Irish
attitudes towards nature.

Gerard Murphy suggests that early Irish nature poetry was a direct
response to monotheism and the doctrine of creation.[21] The poems are
written in non-traditional verse forms as he rightly observes, but this
tells us more about technical literary innovations than about why the
poets chose to write about nature in the first place. He also claims that
the nature theme is generally absent from the 'early pagan sagas'. Now,
it would be true to say that poetry about nature is uncommon in texts
like the famous epic *Táin Bo Cuailgne / The Cattle-Raid of Cooley*. But
nature is subtly present none the less, and sometimes plays a decisive
role in the action. Consider the strange behaviour of the rivers in the
opening sections of the *Táin*.

The background to this episode is that Medb, queen of Connacht,
covets a great brown bull known as the Donn of Cuailgne whose owner
lives in the neighbouring territory Ulster, home of the Ulaid tribe. When
he refuses to lend it to her, she musters an army to carry it off by force.
As the army is ravaging Cuailgne, looking for the Donn, they find themselves obstructed by three of the Ulster rivers:

> The river Cronn rose up against them to the height of the tree tops
> and they had to pass the night by the edge of the water. In the
> morning, Medb ordered some of her followers across it. The famous
> warrior Ualu tried it. To cross the river he shouldered a big flagstone
> so that the water wouldn't force him backward. But the river
> overwhelmed him, stone and all, and he drowned ... So they went
> upward along the river Cronn until they reached its source ... Next
> day they travelled to the river Colptha. Recklessly they tried a
> crossing, but it too rose against them and bore off a hundred of their
> charioteers toward the sea ... They had to move along the river
> Colptha up to its source ... After this they went across Glen Gatlaig,
> but the river Gatlaig rose up against them also.[22]

Later at a ford in the Cronn, Cú Chulainn, the leading champion of the
Ulaid, prepares to meet the enemy in single-combat. He invokes earth,
air and water to help him, reserving a special prayer for the river in
which he is standing:

> 'I summon the waters to help me,' Cú Chulainn says. 'I summon
> air and earth; but I summon now above all the Cronn river:

And the water rears up to the tree tops.[23] The rivers of Cuailgne are not inanimate water-courses to Cú Chulainn. They are personal divine powers, to whom one may pray for help, but they also act independently to protect their territory and its inhabitants, as we saw in the earlier passage. Rivers play a decisive role again in *Togail Bruidne Da Derga / The Destruction of Da Derga's Hostel.* In the closing paragraphs of this tale, the major rivers and lakes of Ireland withhold their water to the battle-weary king, thereby contributing to his death.[24]

Murphy was rightly suspicious of racial theories about 'the Celtic love of nature' but his own proposal, that this was mainly the result of missionary teaching, is not entirely convincing. Certainly there are stories in which saints are portrayed as having a special relationship with birds and animals:

> This was the Máel Anfaidh who saw a certain little bird wailing and sorrowing. 'O God,' said he, 'what has happened there? I will not eat food until it is explained to me.' While he was there he saw an angel coming towards him. 'Well now, priest,' said the angel, 'let it not trouble you any more. Molua son of Ocha has died, and that is why the living things bewail him, for he never killed a living thing, great or small'.[25]

Earlier examples would include Colum Cille's care for the exhausted crane and Columbanus's friendship with the animals.[26] The question is, were these attitudes entirely new? Christianity is not the only religion which encourages a respect for all living creatures, if indeed it can be said to do this in any serious way. Hinduism and Buddhism show a much more practical respect for the animal kingdom. How do we know then, that Molua's compassion is entirely due to Christianity and not to some earlier value-system? It would also be interesting to know, if love of nature really was the result of missionary teaching, where they got it from, since it is so untypical of the rest of Europe at this time, certainly as far as written texts are concerned. We should at least be open to the possibility that some of these values were present in Ireland before the adoption of Christianity.

Another scholar who saw a christian impetus behind early Irish attitudes towards nature was Robin Flower, who linked the nature poetry of the eighth and ninth centuries with the contemporary *Céli Dé* movement. The word *Céli Dé* (sometimes anglicised as 'Culdees') means 'clients' or 'companions of God'. This movement within Irish monasticism is thought to have been characterised by asceticism and an interest in the hermit life, though there were also *Céli Dé* communities notably at Tallaght and

Finglas on the outskirts of Dublin.[27] Because of their association with the
hermit life, the nature poetry which Flower ascribed to them came to be
known as 'hermit poetry'. He outlines his theory in a famous passage:

> It was because they brought to that environment an eye washed
> miraculously clear by a continual spiritual exercise, that they first
> in Europe had that strange vision of natural things in an almost
> unnatural purity ... The best of these poems are all fire and air, praise
> and dedication of the heart, touching little upon dogma or miracle
> but content and eager with a new joy and a young revelation [28]

Robin Flower wears his heart on his sleeve in a way which is quite
unfashionable today. I find this almost as refreshing as the poems themselves. Ireland's earliest nature poems predate St Francis of Assisi's *Canticle
of the Sun* by some four or five centuries, so that they often come as a
pleasant surprise to readers who have previously know only the predominantly urban and abstract theologies of later tradition. As for their being
'first in Europe', this may well be true. If continental parallels exist for
the same period, they have yet to be identified. But they are probably not
the earliest nature poetry in Ireland and one might question whether
their visionary quality is necessarily the result of christian discipline
alone. Comparisons have been made with Japanese nature poetry, some
of which is connected with Zen and probably also with Shinto.[29] This
serves to remind us, if any reminder were necessary, that Christianity is
not the only religion capable of producing beautiful nature poetry. The
influence of pre-christian Irish culture and religion remains an unknown
quantity, but a number of Irish medieval texts describe rituals performed
by the traditional poets – the *filid* – in preparation for their work, part of
which involved divination. These 'spiritual exercises' were still remembered in christian times and at least one of them may still have been
practised as late as the ninth century.[30] It seems likely, therefore, that the
tradition of preparing for poetic inspiration in a religious way was not
something which Irish people had to learn for the first time from the
missionaries.

   Flower's idea that a large number of early nature poems were written
by hermits has rightly been challenged in recent years.[31] The monastery
rather than the hermitage seems to have been the normal source for most
of them, and if hermits ever did compose nature poetry in their huts and
caves, there is nothing in the surviving literature which can definitely be
ascribed to them. Some poems explicitly state that the speaker is not
currently living the hermit life – but would very much like to. This need
not mean, however, that these poems are nothing more than wishful

thinking by desk-bound scholars. The hermit life need not be understood as a permanent condition, but could in fact be undertaken for limited periods, by men and women who eventually returned to community life.

This was certainly the case in African and continental traditions: St Antony of Egypt, St Martin of Tours and St Benedict are all said to have lived in solitude for an extended period at the beginning of their religious lives. Martin apparently continued living in a hermitage after he was made bishop, though he ate with his disciples and even undertook a number of missionary journeys. Martin and Antony were both favourite figures in medieval Ireland. Not surprisingly then, a similar pattern emerges from some of the Lives of Irish saints: Colmán Mac Duaich, for example, lives as a hermit in the Burren for seven years and forty days, emerging on Easter Sunday; and Coemgen (Kevin) of Glendalough spends several years as a hermit at the start of his ministry, and in later life retires to a solitary hut during Lent.[32] Some 'hermit poems' may therefore be more than just descriptions of an imagined ideal. They could also be memories – or anticipations – of an experience which took place only intermittently, at certain times in a person's life, for purposes of formation or renewal or for some other reason. Be that as it may, our main interest here is not in the precise circumstances of the poets' lives, but in the attraction which they felt for the world of nature.

A few words of caution now about pre-christian Irish religion. Celtic scholars have always been interested in both christian and pre-christian influences in early Irish literature. At times, the search for pre-christian and Indo-European ideas has been carried on so enthusiastically that the thoroughly christian context of the texts has been overlooked. Recently, however, there has been a strong revival of interest in the influence of the Bible and other christian and literary sources, though the search for earlier ideas continues. It is important to understand that there are no pre-christian Irish documents dealing with religion, or indeed any other subject. Before Christianity, the only form of writing was ogam script, a system of notches carved in wood or stone. Surviving examples are plentiful, but they rarely amount to more than a few words: usually people's names. Even the sagas set in the pre-christian period and recounting the exploits of kings, heroes and deities, come to us from the pens of monks and scholars of the christian period. Pre-christian Irish mythology in its original form has gone for ever.

The image of the scribe faithfully recording tales without adding or subtracting anything of his or her own is certainly open to question, though at least one such person protested at having to copy out stories which he found ridiculous or even dangerous.[33] Against this we must set the fact that most Old and Middle-Irish texts were written long after the adoption of Christianity; that many include clear references to scripture or continental writings; and that some criticise or condemn pre-christian practices in the strongest terms. The relevance of both a popular and a scholarly oral tradition, contributing to parts of the written tradition, is still discussed,[34] and is not seriously in doubt, and oral delivery would still have been the main way of communicating even written material. However, the tradition was continually evolving and changing at the hands of people who were not so much scribes as apologists or myth-makers, skilfully re-working old materials into new patterns of meaning.

Some of what they wrote about the religion of their ancestors may be pure invention, but where comparative religion provides us with parallels from primal religions in other parts of the world, and where foreign literary parallels are less than exact, the very accuracy of such 'inventions' calls them into question. They could, of course, be new products of the primal imagination, as discussed below, but we would then have to ask how likely it is that such ideas occurred to Irish people for the first time only after the adoption of Christianity. Borrowing from imported sources certainly took place and should always be considered as a possibility, but if Irish primal religion vanished without trace, it was unusual in that respect, and many people will find it easier to believe that it survived in fragmentary form and was incorporated creatively into the medieval texts.

Outcrops of primal-looking material occur throughout early Irish literature. *I am wind on sea* and Cú Chulainn's prayer to the rivers show little or no sign of christian influence. Other authors fused traditional material with recognisably christian ideas. P. L. Henry and Noel O'Donoghue both detect a 'pre-christian savour' in the famous fourth stanza of *St Patrick's Breastplate*, known in Irish as *Fáeth Fiada*, which is usually translated as *The Deer's Cry*. John V. Taylor also notes parallels between this eighth-century hymn and traditional African world-views in which the universe is alive with visible and invisible presences. In *St Patrick's Breastplate*, he writes, all the spiritual awareness of the primal vision is lifted into the fullness of Christ.[35] This is a missionary's perspective, and one which clearly acknowledges that spiritual awareness does not begin with Christianity as day follows night. A better image might be new growth on an old tree or the grafting of a new scion onto a compatible rootstock.

St Patrick's Breastplate opens with a series of invocations to the Holy Trinity, Christ, the angels, patriarchs, prophets, apostles and so on.[36] But in the fourth stanza the singer goes on to invoke various natural phenomena – or more accurately various inherent characteristics of these phenomena – as additional protection against the powers of evil:

> I arise today
> Through the strength of heaven:
> Light of sun
> Radiance of moon
> Splendour of fire
> Speed of lightning,
> Swiftness of wind
> Depth of sea
> Stability of earth
> Firmness of rock.

These are what give the singer confidence to live boldly in a dangerous world. At some stage a preface was added, explaining that this was the hymn which Patrick sang as he and his companions journeyed towards Tara in the form of deer, to confront their religious and political opponents. There are resonances between this hymn and Cú Chulainn's plea to earth, air and water, but it would be a mistake to think of *St Patrick's Breastplate* as a momentary lapse into 'paganism'. Indeed parallels have been drawn between this verse and the biblical canticle *Benedicite*, as if the inspiration behind it were wholly christian.[37] Most of the same elements are indeed mentioned in the *Benedicite* but in a different order and for purposes of praise rather than protection. The idea that the *Breastplate* drew on a list of elements derived from the *Benedicite*, seems rather a complicated route by which to arrive at the stuff of everyday experience. The encounter with the elements is so basic that it may in the end be impossible to distinguish between christian and pre-christian influences in this hymn. Both may well be present, but there is no doubt as to the christian intentions of the singer who deliberately aligns him or herself with christian orthodoxy against druidry, 'the false laws of heresy' and 'the deceit of idolatry'. Other explicitly Christian documents invoke the elements in a similar way. One famous example invokes them in support of a new piece of christian legislation.

Nature is plainly regarded as a source or vehicle of spiritual power in many of the beautiful prayers and blessings which Alexander Carmichael collected from the men and women of the Western Isles during the nineteenth century. Examples include the splashing of a child with water in 'Bathing prayer', the turning of the face to the sun in 'Invocation for justice' and the anointing of the palms in 'Invocation of the Graces':

> I bathe thy palms
> In showers of wine
> In the lustral fire
> In the seven elements
> In the juice of the rasps
> In the milk of honey.[38]

This property of nature might be called its sacramentality. Such a word would never have been used either by Carmichael's islanders or by the early Irish Christians, but in each of the above examples nature becomes a visible means of invisible grace, a source of God's blessing and protection. This idea has biblical and theological parallels in the incarnational theology of the New Testament and in Teilhard de Chardin's vision of the Cosmic Christ. At the same time, the sacramentality of the universe is one of the chief characteristics of primal religions throughout the world, together with the belief that the physical can be a vehicle for the spiritual and that there is no sharp distinction between the two.

A few years ago in Glendalough, I met a young medical student who warned me gently that most of what I was researching was not Christianity at all but 'paganism'. 'Paganism' or primal religion is still a relatively unexplored area of Religious Studies though this is changing at last. One of the first scholars to take an interest in the subject was probably Sir James Frazer whose monumental work *The Golden Bough* contains literally thousands of examples of primal religion from all over the world. True, he regarded them as primitive products of 'the savage mind', but he was oddly fascinated by them none the less. The limits of Frazer's outlook are perhaps becoming clearer to us today, as morality and meaning struggle to keep up with advances in technology. At the same time, primal cultures are seen by many people as a source of energy and new ideas: for artists and dancers, writers and musicians, as well as for people disenchanted with modern Western ideologies and Christianity. This could be just a passing fashion and it has done little to protect indigenous peoples from violence and exploitation. Spiritual imperialism is also alive and well. In fact, one reason why primal religions are better understood today is that missionaries in search of converts have entered into dialogue with living primalists in the hope of winning them over.

There is cause for scandal here, if dialogue is backed by economic and military muscle. But as Christians begin to learn about primal world-views from the people who still inhabit them, they may also find themselves challenged as the common ground between Christianity and primal religion comes to light. The idea that Christianity has any common ground at all with primal religions makes some people uneasy. But comparative religion and missionary training are both based on the assumption that such common ground exists, since without it there could be no communication at all between people of different faiths. Religious concepts and experiences would simply not translate from one language to another.

Harold Turner, in his seminal article on primal religions, describes them as the most basic or fundamental religious forms in human experience, and as the common religious heritage of humankind.[39] In other words, primal religions are the bedrock of all other religious systems. Not only that, but they contribute to them in such a fundamental way that any attempt to eliminate them from subsequent faiths could be compared to knocking down the load-bearing walls of a house. This is not intended to imply that later religions are the same as primal religions, or that all primal religions are the same, or that they are fragments of some shattered original belief-system – rather that, historically and psychologically, they are the first religious forms to arise in human culture and consciousness.

Turner describes six features which primal religions exhibit to varying degrees. Only some of these concern nature, but the common ground between Christianity and primal religion can be seen in all six so it is worth presenting them all. They can be summarised as follows:

1. A sense of kinship with nature – of relatedness to the earth and to plants and animals which have their own spiritual existence and place in the universe.

2. A sense of creaturehood – a realistic humility about the human condition and a sense of standing in need of a power other than our own.

3. A belief that we are not alone in the world, but live in a personalised universe surrounded by friendly and unfriendly transcendent beings and spirits more powerful and ultimate than ourselves.

4. A belief that we can enter into relationship with the benevolent spirit-world, and so share its powers and blessings and receive protection from evil forces.

5. A sense that this relationship between human beings and the gods continues beyond death, so that in the majority of primal religions the ancestors remain united in affection and mutual obligations with the living.

6. The belief that we live in a sacramental universe where the physical acts as a vehicle for the spiritual and there is no sharp dichotomy between the two.[40]

With minor adjustments, most of these points could also describe certain kinds of Christianity: for gods, read God; for friendly and unfriendly transcendent beings, read saints, angels and demons; for ancestors, read family members who have died and gone to heaven. This illustrates some of the ways in which primal religions have contributed to Christianity. Not all forms of Christianity retain all of these beliefs, but where they do not, some hefty theological buttressing has been necessary to keep people from drifting away.

Scholars like John V. Taylor, Andrew Walls and Kwame Bediako use such terms as 'primal vision', 'primal world-view' or 'primal imagination' to express the element of continuity between the primal religions and Christianity.[41] The outlook from within a primal religion is obviously a primal world-view, but primal world-views are also discernible in the scriptures and ceremonies of the world religions, just as the primal imagination plays an active role in the faith of many perfectly orthodox Christians, Jews, Moslems, Hindus, Buddhists and so on. Christianity necessarily connects with, and builds upon, certain essential features of the primal tradition, even as it transforms and rejects others.

Primal world-views are common in early Irish literature and nowhere more so than in texts relating to nature. The invocation of the elements in *St Patrick's Breastplate* for example, shows a belief in the sacramental universe, a sense of kinship with nature, a realistic humility about the human condition, and a sense of not being alone in the universe. It also calls on a host of benevolent spiritual powers for help. If it shares some of these characteristics with Cú Chulainn's prayer to the river and Amairgen's *I am wind on sea*, this does not make it any the less christian. It simply means that within its Christianity, it is still in touch with the building blocks of religious experience, as these arise in human minds whatever creed they use to interpret that experience. No doubt people will continue to ask whether certain actions and attitudes to nature are christian or 'pagan', but if Turner is right, then some are inevitably both, and an oversimplified model of religious development will not help us to distinguish between them.

Scripture was a passion in medieval Irish monasteries and explicit biblical references are extremely common. When it comes to nature however, parallels may not always be what they seem. Alongside the familiar Hebrew polemic against idolatrous worship, there is also a clear tradition of sacred trees, wells, rivers, mountains and so on. These were often places where God, or an angel, is said to have appeared to one of the ancestors or prophets of Israel. This tradition is carried forward into the New Testament where mountains are still places of prayer and where Jesus reveals his identity to a woman at a well. Nature sanctuaries give rise to nature imagery and New Testament writers, like the prophets and psalmists before them, often use the imagery of trees, water, the sun and other aspects of nature when speaking about God or Christ. This means that some Irish nature texts might be attributed to biblical influence when in fact they are connected only at the level of the primal imagination. It also means that Irish and Hebridean Christianity was not unique or aberrant in its relationship to primal religion. A similar relationship exists, inevitably, between biblical tradition and Semitic primal religion.

Most of the material in this book was written between the seventh and twelfth centuries, but Patrick's *Confession* goes back to the fifth and I have included some late-medieval material as well, from the bardic tradition and the later Finn Cycle, for example. Most chapters begin with a contemporary example, to show the resilience of the primal imagination through changing circumstances and patterns of belief within Christianity. For the same reason, I have drawn in occasional examples from the Irish and Hebridean folk-tradition, but only where it illuminates the earlier material in an interesting way. The dating of the texts is a specialised task and I have relied on the work of people who are better equipped in this area than I am. Texts are constantly being reassessed and in some cases there is no general agreement.

During the twelfth century, a series of 'reforming' synods set out to bring Irish Christianity more into line with continental norms. At the same time, the first of the continental religious orders were establishing themselves in Ireland. The Anglo-Norman invasion of 1169 began a process which would drastically reduce the power of the old Irish aristocracy and with it their patronage of the older monasteries. Despite an intense burst of literary and cultural activity leading up to and including these events, the twelfth century is often referred to as the end of the Celtic period. This is slightly misleading since Celtic culture not only survived but even had an influence on the invaders. Celtic Christianity did not die out either – the bardic period was to see some of its most interesting ideas – but it did lose some of its old vigour and self-confidence.

'Nature' is an enormous subject, ranging from the elements of fire and water to the hills, mountains, rivers and woods of the landscape, and so to the creatures – including heroes, holy men and women and ourselves – who live and move amongst it all. The following chapters focus only on representative aspects of nature (animals deserve a book on their own!) and there are endless possiblities for further exploration into this fascinating world of experience and half-forgotten insights.

This is not a theological study, though it may be a useful source-book for theologians as well as others. Nor should it be read in isolation from other aspects of Celtic Christianity: the Celtic understanding of Jesus for example. I have focused primarily on the early Irish and Hebridean litera- ture, leaving aside the Welsh, Manx, Breton and Cornish tradition. The Welsh tradition of nature poetry is particularly rich and beautiful, and uses many of the same images and themes as its Irish counterpart. Unfortunately, it has not been possible to include it here, or to explore the links between nature and the Sacred in other parts of Europe. Such links are not confined to Celtic areas, being primal and therefore cross- cultural, but they do seem to have been expressed in Celtic Christianity at a particularly early date, and in the work of scholars and religious leaders, rather than simply in the folk tradition.

I hope you will enjoy reading this book as much as I have enjoyed writing and researching it. There is much here that will be familiar to Irish readers, though most of these texts are more usually seen from a literary or historical point of view, so the perspective may be new. Read- ers who come to it from the gentler climes of *Carmina Gadelica* or Alistair Maclean's *Hebridean Altars* or some of the more reconstructed kinds of Celtic spirituality, may find parts of it disconcerting, even shocking. To you I would say, if you really want to know more about Celtic tradition, read on, and try not to be put off by the very different character of these texts. The views which they reflect are those of medi- eval high society rather than the world of nineteenth-century crofting communities, but the two are closely related, and there is much to delight as well as challenge.

Chapter 2

The Land

Early Irish writers make frequent asides about place-names. These are often accompanied by stories of people who lived or died there, long ago. Large collections of such lore exist, both in verse and prose. Certain poets and scholars were expected to know the land intimately, and through the recitation of such place-lore to be able to pass on this knowledge to the listening audience. No doubt the land was often the subject of tribal and ancestral claims centred upon particular natural features, but the land has not always been simply an inanimate object. Indeed, there was still an acknowledgement that it had, in a very real sense, a life of its own, which could make or break the people who depended on it. The myth of sacred kingship remained powerful throughout this period, though some kings were now ordained by the clergy. At the same time, Ireland's plains, hills, mountains and rivers, retained the memories and the on-going myths of gods, goddesses and Otherworld beings who were said to have inhabited them. Stories about such figures were usually set in the mythical past, but often they remained present to the imagination through festivals, pilgrimages and other customs, as well as through the stories themselves. Most of these belong to the Middle-Irish period, which is frustrating if you are interested in Irish primal religion, but Christianity had to be fairly well-established in Ireland before the learned orders could begin their positive reclamation of the past, modifying it at the same time to serve the needs of the present.[1]

For many biblical writers, the land was also full of divine and angelic presences. This is often overlooked by modern readers of the Bible, but it provided one of the bridges by which the peoples of early medieval Ireland were able to make the transition from primal religion to Christianity. The idea that divine or supernatural beings were active in the landscape, and could occasionally be encountered there, was common to both traditions. In Ireland, tales of the old gods and goddesses continued

to be told, with modifications, rather in the same way as the first followers of Jesus retained and reinterpreted the Hebrew Bible. The old myths enshrined values and world-views which could not simply be discarded without threatening all that held the community together. Instead they were collected, modified, and reinvented in an on-going myth-making process.

ÉRIU, BANBA AND FÓTLA

The name Ériu – Ireland – is one of the most striking examples of the sacredness of the land. Ériu is the island, but like Banba and Fótla, it is also a goddess-name. The following passage comes from *The Book of Conquests* or *Lebor Gabála*, which is a mythological history of the 'takings' or conquests of Ireland by successive groups of people from before Noah's flood to the time of the Milesians. These were supposedly the ancestors of contemporary ruling families, and were said to have come from Spain. Having defeated the former rulers, the *Tuatha Dé Danann*, at the battle of Slieve Mis, they approach three leading women of the island to discuss terms:

> The sons of Míl had a colloquy with Banba in Sliab Mis. Banba said to them: 'if you have come to conquer Ireland, not right were the good fortune in which you have come.'
> 'It is by necessity', said Amairgen Gluingel, the poet.
> 'A gift from you to me then', said she.
> 'What gift?' said they.
> 'That my name may be on this island', said she.
> 'What is your name?' said they.
> 'Banba', said she.
> 'Let that be a name for this island', said Amairgen.
> (The *Book of Druim Snechta* says that Amairgen enquired after her race. 'I am of the children of Adam,' said she. 'Which race of the sons of Noah do you belong to?' said he. 'I am older than Noah,' said she; 'I was on a peak of a mountain during the Flood' ... but the foregoing is a surprising extract.) ... They had a colloquy with Fótla in Eblinne. She spoke to them in the same way, and desired that her name should be upon the island. Said Amairgen: 'Let Fótla be a name upon this island.' They had colloquy with Ériu at Uisnech. She said to them: 'Warriors,' said she, 'welcome to you. Long have soothsayers had [knowledge of] your coming. This island shall be yours for ever; and to the east of the world there shall not be a better island. No race shall be more numerous than yours.'
> 'That is good', said Amairgen; 'it is a good prophecy'.

'It is not right to thank her,' said Eber Donn, eldest of the sons of Míl. 'Thank our gods and our own might.'

'It makes no difference to you', said Eriu; 'you shall have no profit of this island, nor shall your children. A gift to me ...' said she; 'that my name shall be on this island.'

'It shall be its principal name,' said Amairgen.[2]

The *Tuatha Dé Danann* – or 'People of the Goddess Dana' – are generally understood to be old gods and goddesses of Irish primal religion, though they are sometimes given a mortal pedigree, as Banba is here, in order to euhemerise them, that is to say reduce them to the status of human beings. The editor notes, in an aside, that in the *Book of Druim Snechta* Banba claims descent from Adam and seniority to Noah, and explains how she survived the Flood. This is a good example of euhemerisation and also of 'synchronisation' – the process by which Irish and biblical traditions were boldly and freely combined into a new understanding of Ireland's place in the world.

After the battle of Slieve Mis, Banba, Fótla and Ériu, three women of the *Tuatha Dé Danann*, hold colloquies with the invaders. The hill of Uisnech, where Ériu meets them, was one of the principal sanctuaries of Irish primal religion. Amairgen the poet, whose task it is to negotiate with the Otherworld powers, answers her with gratitude and respect. But Donn, the king, treats her with contempt, she curses him and he subsequently drowns. Donn is presented as failing to give the Otherworld its due. He refuses to acknowledge that Ériu retains her power of life or death over kings and conquerors, and that the land can refuse its gifts even when taken by force.

THE THREE MACHAS

Ériu, Banba and Fótla illustrate the sacredness of the land on a rather grander scale than is usual. In the various place-lore collections known individually as *Dindshenchas*, the interest is far more local, so that a typical entry recounts the traditional lore of a particular hill, plain, river or lough. The main place-lore collections, compiled between the tenth and twelfth centuries, were often from much older material. Their meaning is wearing thin in places and parts of them have been revised and elaborated by medieval editors. But they still provide a fascinating glimpse of the Otherworld associations of the land in early Christian Ireland.

Armagh or Ard Macha was, and still is, one of the most powerful and prestigious ecclesiastical centres in Ireland, being the see of Patrick and his successors. The nearby fort of Emain Macha was once the headquarters of the powerful Ulaid tribe whose name attaches to the ancient kingdom of Ulster and whose exploits are recounted in the famous Ulster Cycle of tales, including the *Táin*. However, the place-lore of Ard Macha and Emain Macha focuses not on Patrick or any of the Ulster heroes, but on a group of female figures, all called Macha. Here is the entry for Ard Macha in the *Rennes Dindshenchas*:

> Ard Macha. Macha wife of Nemed son of Agnoman died there [on Mag Macha] and was buried, and it is the twelfth plain which was cleared by Nemed, and he bestowed it on his wife so that it might bear her name. Whence *Mag Macha* – 'Macha's Plain'.
>
> Otherwise: Macha daughter of Aed the red, son of Badurn – it is by her Emain was marked out – was buried there when Rechtaid of the red fore-arm killed her. To lament her, *Oenach Macha* – 'Macha's fair' was established. Whence *Mag Macha*.
>
> Otherwise: Macha wife of Crund son of Agnoman went there to race against king Conchobar's horses, for her husband had said that his wife was swifter [than they]. Thus then was the wife big with child: so she asked a respite till her womb should have fallen, and this was not granted to her. So then the race was run and she was the swiftest. And she said that the Ulaid would abide under feebleness of childbed whensoever need should befall them. Wherefore the Ulaid suffered feebleness for the space of a *nomad* from the reign of Conchobar to the reign of Mál son of Rochraide 'Great Heart'. And men say that she was Grian Banchure 'the Sun of Womanfolk', daughter of Mider of Bri Léith. And after this she died, and her tomb was raised on Ard Macha, and her lamentation was made, and her gravestone was planted. Whence *Ard Macha* – 'Macha's Height'.[3]

The reader – originally, the listener – is offered a short version of several traditions here. First, we hear of a Macha who is associated with a plain and with her husband's agricultural activities. Another source makes her a visionary, who foresees the bloody events of the cattle-raid of Cooley and dies of grief.[4] In the *Book of Conquests*, her husband Nemed is one of the earliest invaders of Ireland, so she is probably supposed to be understood as the oldest Macha.

Macha daughter of Aed is presented here as the founder of Emain Macha, the earthwork now known as Navan Fort which was once the headquarters of the Ulaid tribe. Like the first Macha, she is said to be buried on *Mag Macha*, Macha's Plain. Her *óenach* or fair was one of several such events held in different parts of the country at Lughnasad, the harvest festival at the beginning of August. Lughnasad, one of the old Celtic quarter-days, was named after the pre-christian Celtic male deity, Lug, but fairs or tribal assemblies held at this time were often traced back to female figures like Macha and others. In a moment we shall read a longer and more colourful version of the story of Macha daughter of Aed, as it appears in the *Dindshenchas* of Emain Macha.

The fair of Emain Macha is the setting for the story of Macha, wife of Crund.[5] Horse-races seem to have been an important feature of this fair and Macha's extraordinary swiftness marks her out at once as an Otherworld being. In another version of the story, she dies giving birth to twins immediately after the race, but not before she has cursed the Ulaid for forcing her to run in such a condition. Her curse results in their famous 'debility' – five days and four nights in which pangs like those of a woman in labour come over them at the time of their greatest need. This is their condition when Medb launches the cattle-raid of Cooley against them. Macha wife of Crund has links with kingship through the fair, which is a royal assembly, and also through her contest with the king's horses; but kingship or sovereignty is a much more dominant theme in the longer story of Macha daughter of Aed, also known as Macha Mong-ruad – Red-haired Macha.

In this version of the story, her father enters into an agreement with two other kings that they will rule jointly, each taking the kingship for seven years. This arrangement works well until Aed dies, whereupon the two survivors refuse to surrender the kingship to a woman. Macha goes to war against the kings and defeats them. She then rules the kingdom for seven years. At the end of that time, another of the kings dies, leaving five sons who claim the kingship, but Macha will not surrender it to them. They ask her to stand down but she refuses, defeats them in battle and takes Cimbáeth, the surviving king, to be her husband and leader of her armies. The five brothers are banished, but Macha follows them disguised as a leprous old hag. She finds them cooking a wild boar over a fire. They ask her for news, give her food and embark on a plan to rape her one by one in the forest. Macha overcomes each of them in turn, ties them up and brings them back to Ulster, where the outraged people urge her to put them to death. That would be for me 'a violation of prince's truth' she replies. This a reference to the kingly virtue of delivering true and fair judgements in disputes between clanspeople. Instead of killing them, she enslaves them and sets them to work building the ramparts of Emain Macha.[6]

The Machas of the place-lore have a clear association with the land, agriculture, child-birth, sexuality and kingship, but the name Macha also appears in the so-called 'war goddess' tradition. This is a group of tales and vignettes in which unpleasant Otherworld women reduce warriors to a state of terror, often on the battle-field. Macha's curse on the Ulaid and the binding of the five brothers by a leprous old hag may also be fragments of this tradition. In the *Book of Conquests* and the earlier *Battle of Moytura / Cath Maige Tuired*, Macha is the name of one of the three daughters of Ernmas, her sisters being Badb and a formidable figure known as the Morrígan (66) – or in another version, Badb and Anann. Badb is the 'battle raven', a shrieking woman who appears mainly on the battle-field. The Morrígan has a similar side to her character and sometimes forms a duo with Badb, but like Macha she has links with the land as well and some medieval scholars identified her with Ana or Anu who gives her name to the Paps of Anu in Kerry.[7]

In view of all this, it seems likely that a goddess called Macha, probably in triple form, was once worshipped in the Armagh area. She has been called variously a 'land goddess', a 'mother goddess', a 'war goddess', even a 'solar deity' but like many Irish goddesses and Otherworld women, she is extremely difficult to categorise.

CARMUN, TAILTIU AND THE 'LAND OF GODDESSES'

The Dindshenchas of Carmun is another place-lore text describing the establishment of a fair – óenach – in memory of an Otherworld woman.[8] It is worth reading the text in full for its wonderful description of an Irish medieval fair. This is the beginning:

> To bewail queens and kings
> to lament revenges and ill deeds,
> there came many a fair host at harvest time
> across the noble smooth cheek of ancient Carmun.
> Was it men, or a man of mighty prowess
> or woman with passionate jealousy
> that brought the market a title not unreputed
> and gave its proper name to noble Carmun?
> Not men it was, nor wrathful man
> but one fierce marauding woman –
> bright was her precinct and her fame –
> from whom Carmun got its name at the first ...

We are told how Carmun came from the East with her three sons, ravaging the fruit-trees of every land they pass through. When they arrive in Ireland, they do the same:

> Carmun, by means of every spell and fame
> destroyed all sap of swelling fruit
> after strife waged with all arts unlawful
> and the sons through battle and lawlessness.

The *Tuatha Dé* manage to expel the sons, leaving Carmun as a hostage. When she dies in violent circumstances 'among the oaks of the strong graves', the *Tuatha Dé* prepare her funeral:

> Thither came for the delight of her beauty
> To keen and raise the first wailing over her
> the *Tuatha Dé* over this noble plain eastward:
> it was the first true fair of Carmun.

There are a number of difficulties with this story. Carmun is said to come from abroad, but unlike the pan-Celtic deities (Lug, Brigit et al.) her name attaches to one particular place as if she were a local deity rather than an incomer. The poet describes how people arrive for the fair 'across the noble smooth cheek of ancient Carmun'. This identifies her very closely with the earth. Her associations with fertility are indicated by the timing of the festival – Lughnasad – and by its expected results: 'Corn, milk, peace, happy ease … full nets, oceans' plenty'.[9] If Carmun was always a destructive force, it is easy to see why a festival of fertility such as a harvest festival might celebrate her death. But the celebrations are not the straightforward exultation at the death of an enemy. There is admiration, respect, even some regret. Lughnasad is referred to in one text as *Brón Trogain* – 'when the earth sorrows under its fruits' – as if the earth was in labour but had not yet given birth.[10] Other place-lore traditions associate it with the death of a mother, e.g. Macha wife of Crund. Carmun remains something of an enigma, but she clearly demonstrates the ambivalence which some people felt towards the Otherworld powers who could bring death as well as life, destruction as well as fertility.

'Heaven, earth, sun, moon and sea, fruits of the earth and sea-stuff' are given as pledges of good behaviour at Carmun fair, and a few lines later Patrick, Brigit, Coemgen and Colum Cille are invoked for the same reason.[11] The fair ends with 'mass, genuflection, chanting of psalms' and a prayer for fertility:

> May there be given them from the Lord
> the earth with her pleasant fruits.

The *óenach* of Tailtiu or Teltown was held on a hillside near the confluence of the Boyne and the Blackwater.[12] Tailtiu is said to have been the daughter of a woman called Mag Mór – Great Plain. Like

Macha wife of Nemed, she and her mother both have strong agricultural connections and were said to have been in Ireland before the Milesians and even before their gods. Tailtiu is widowed when the newcomers arrive and becomes the wife of the new chief, who keeps her in captivity. She spends her time clearing trees with an axe and reclaiming meadowland till it becomes 'a plain blossoming with clover.' She is also named as one of the fosterers of Lug, as if she were in some way his senior. Tailtiu is eventually worn out by her labours. Before she dies, she asks that funeral games be held to lament her and promises that as long as she is remembered and accepted, blessings will follow: 'corn and milk in every house, peace and fair weather for the feast'.

Tara was said to be the burial mound of Tea, who had hills dedicated to her all over Ireland.[13] There was of course a famous gathering at Tara – the *feis* – held to inaugurate a new king. This may have been a different kind of festival[14] but like the others it has a goddess name and a hillside location. The *Dindshenchas* also tells the story of a woman called Tlachta who dies giving birth to triplets. The site of her *óenach* was a hill near Athboy, not far from Tara.[15] There was also a fair at Cruachu, named after a little known figure called Crochen, said to be a handmaid of Étaín, mother of Medb.[16]

The place-lore collections give the clear message that all these women (they are never called goddesses) were dead and buried. But they did not immediately disappear from consciousness. Their fairs were remembered and their stories continued to be told, after a fashion. A passing reference in *The Death of Crimthainn / Aided Crimthainn* mentions a female figure called Mongfinn 'to whom women and the common people still offer their prayers', in the eleventh century or later. This happened at Samain, the Celtic fore-runner of Hallowe'en / All Saints Day.[17] In the folk tradition this festival was particularly associated with the dead, and in many Catholic countries people still visit the family graves at this time of year. Mongfinn was dead – or more accurately perhaps, had died – but people still prayed to her, a custom which is, after all, no more paradoxical than the normal christian practice of praying to Christ throughout the year or – in some traditions – to the saints, particularly on All Saints' Day at the beginning of November.

Towards the end of the ninth century, fairs at ecclesiastical sites gradually became more common than the traditional fairs. However, the fair of Tailtiu was revived several times between the ninth and the twelfth centuries by the kings of the Southern Úi Néill, probably to mark an extension of their authority.[18] According to another report, the fair of Carmun was revived by the king of Leinster in the early eighth century and continued to be held till the eleventh.[19] A transitional stage between fairs named after goddesses and ecclesiastical fairs – between tutelary deities and patron saints – is found in the ninth-century *Triads of Ireland*, which lists the three *oenaig* of Ireland as the *óenach* of Tailtiu, the *óenach* of Cruachu and the *óenach* of St Colmán of Lann Ela.[20]

THE 'SOVEREIGNTY GODDESS'

Irish kings were traditionally required to be on good, indeed intimate, terms with the Otherworld. The institution of *hieros gamos* or sacred marriage between a deity and a human being is a well-known feature of primal religions in many parts of the world. In pre-christian Ireland, kings were ritually married to the 'sovereignty goddess' on the day of their inauguration. The exact form of the ceremony is unknown and probably varied from place to place, but it generally happened out of doors, in front of the assembled tribe, on a traditional site – often a mound under a sacred tree. Inauguration ceremonies persisted into christian times though there is evidence of clerical influence, particularly after the ninth century.[21] The mythology of kingship as sacred marriage survived, however, and remained an important way of legitimising dynastic power. Some of the most striking sovereignty narratives come from the eleventh and twelfth centuries, among them the story of Lugaid Láigde. Lugaid is not a major dynastic figure, but I have chosen his story because it is so enjoyable and because so rarely told.

Lugaid and his five brothers (all called Lugaid) outstrip the other men of Ireland in hunting a golden fawn. Lugaid Láigde eventually brings it down and kills it. The brothers sit down to an enjoyable feast, but instead of going home afterwards, they continue their hunt in unfamiliar territory:

> After that they hunt in the wilderness. A great snow fell upon them, so that it was labour to hold their weapons. One of them goes to look for a house, and he finds a wonderful house with a great fire in it, and ale, and abundance of food, and silver dishes, and a bed of white bronze. Inside he discovers a huge old woman, wearing a frontlet [?], and her spears of teeth outside her head and great old foul faded things upon her. She said to the youth, even Lugaid Corb: 'What do you ask?', said she. 'I seek a bed', he answered. 'If you come and lie with me' said she 'you would have one.' 'No', said the youth. He went back to his brothers and told them that he had not found a house, and the same reply was got from all of them. At last went Lugaid Láigde. The hag said the same to him. 'I will sleep alone with you' says Lugaid. The hag entered the bed, and Lugaid

followed her. It seemed to him that the radiance of her face was the sun rising in the month of May. A purple, bordered gown she wore, and she had beautifully coloured hair. Her fragrance was like to a perfumed herb garden. Then he mingled in love with her. 'Auspicious is your journey' said she. 'I am the Sovereignty, and the kingship of Ireland will be obtained by you.' Lugaid went to his brothers and brings them to the house and there they get the freshest of food and the oldest of ale. [22]

A similar and much more famous story is told of Níall Nóigíallach ('Níall of the Nine Hostages') who meets a hag (*cailleach*) by a well. When he yields to her advances, she too changes into a beautiful woman, and declares that he will be king of Tara.[23] Níall's story comes from the eleventh century, as does *The Vision of the Phantom / Baile in Scáil*, which tells how Conn Cétchathach ('Conn of the Hundred Battles') also met the sovereignty woman. After an Otherworld journey (*echtra*) across a misty plain, he comes to a king's *rath* or ring-fort, with a golden tree at the door. Inside, he sees a young woman sitting on a crystal chair by a golden vessel with a gold cup in front of her and a golden crown on her head. She is accompanied by a mysterious figure, 'the phantom himself on his throne'. This 'phantom' introduces himself as the god Lug and instructs the woman to pour a cup of red ale for Conn and all the kings of Tara who will come after him.[24] This offering of a cup of wine or ale is a typical feature of the sovereignty myth and seems to be the sign and seal of the king's relationship with the goddess.

Earlier versions of the sovereignty myth are more fragmentary. Tomás Ó Máille was perhaps the first to realise that Medb of Cruachu, with her many husbands and jealous suitors, was not a shamefully promiscuous mortal, but a goddess whose suitors are rivals for the kingship, and whose husbands are successive generations of kings.[25] Cruachu was once a major centre of Irish primal religion. It is mentioned variously as an inauguration place, a royal residence, a place of assembly, one of the three chief burial grounds of Ireland, the site of a fair and the site of a cave – the 'cave of the cats'. One early ninth-century story describes the cave of Cruachu as the entrance to Hell. Various destructive animals emerge from it – 'three-headed creatures', pigs, birds. Medb gets the better of the pigs and they run off to some other part of the country.[26] The Morrígan also emerges from the cave and a warrior called Nerai disappears into it never to be seen again. Cruachu was also occasionally portrayed as a place of healing. In *The Cattle Raid of Fraích / Tain Bo Fráich*, a wounded youth whose mother is a 'fairy woman', is taken to the *sid* of Cruachu and emerges next day 'completely healed, without spot or blemish'.[27] Like Tara, Emain Macha and Uisnech, Cruachu was not christianised, presumably because its associations with primal religion were too powerful. By the turn of the ninth century, its sanctuaries had all but vanished.[28]

The name Medb is thought to mean 'she who intoxicates'. This is usually seen as a reference to the cup of kingship. Medb is known throughout the *Táin* and elsewhere as queen of Connacht, but she also had a namesake in Leinster – Medb Lethderg – who 'tolerated no king in Tara without his having herself as a wife'. These two Medbs may ultimately be one and the same, but there were other 'sovereignty goddesses' as well. Sovereignty motifs can be identified in the stories of Ériu, Étaín, Eithne, Mór Muman, Macha Mong-ruad and many others.[29] The association of these Otherworld women with particular territories or kingdoms shows that the land was absolutely central to the sovereignty myth.

Most scholars still distinguish between 'land goddesses' and the 'sovereignty goddess' but this is not an easy distinction to maintain, since there was believed to be a direct link between the king's relationship with the 'sovereignty goddess' and the peace and fertility of the land. A tribe whose king was in the right relationship with the Otherworld powers through his union with the 'sovereignty goddess' could expect good harvests, fine weather, health, fertility and peace. But if he abused his position by giving false or unfair judgements, all kinds of disasters were expected to follow: famines, invasions, bad weather, war. The just king was said to exercise *fír flathemon* or 'prince's truth' – the virtue of truth and justice which appears in the Old Irish *Testament of Morann / Audacht Morainn*, a seventh-century document containing advice to a young king, and is still going strong in the story of Conaire Mór which illustrates the same principle in narrative form.[30]

THE FERTILE REIGN OF CONAIRE MÓR

The tragic story of Conaire Mór appears in *The Destruction of Da Derga's Hostel / Togail Bruidne Da Derga*. Sacred marriage does not figure in the story of Conaire, though the 'three crowns of Ériu' and the hag who appears on the night of his death can perhaps be read as sovereignty motifs.[31] Conaire's first relationship with the Otherworld is of a different kind. He is portrayed as the son of an Otherworld father – a bird-man who enters his mother's hut secretly through the skylight, leaving his 'feather hood' on the floor.[32] Later Conaire meets another bird-man – king of his father's bird-troop – who helps him to become king of Tara (109). At first all goes well and his kingdom becomes a model of peace and abundance. One of his foster-brothers describes the situation in glowing terms:

Since he became king, no cloud has obscured the sun from the
middle of spring to the middle of autumn. Not a drop of dew falls
from the grass until noon; no gust of wind stirs a cow's tail until
evening. No wolf takes more than one bull calf from every enclosure
during the year, and seven wolves remain by the wall of his house
as a guarantee of this agreement ... Each man's voice seems to his
neighbour melodious as the strings of harps, and that because of the
excellence of law and peace and goodwill throughout Ériu. It is in
Conaire's reign that we have the three crowns of Ériu: the crown
of corn, the crown of flowers and the crown of acorns. May God
not bring that man here tonight.[33]

The image of the seven wolf-hostages by the wall makes an interesting
picture, but since brigands are often 'wolves' in early Irish literature, the
intention may be more serious than playful.[34] Conaire's foster-brother is
a brigand, but he is not under any such restrictions. On the contrary, he
belongs to a raiding party which is about to attack Da Derga's Hostel
where Conaire happens to be spending the night. Conaire's reign is no
longer as perfect as it once was. He has broken the laws of kingship by
giving unfair judgements in favour of his murderous foster-brothers. He
has also just broken his *geassa*, the taboos placed on him by his
Otherworld teacher, and a hideous hag has appeared in the doorway of
the hostel, prophesying carnage. By morning he will be dead. During the
night, Conaire suddenly wakes and recites a poem in which he foresees
the coming destruction. Not only is he overwhelmed by enemies, but
nature turns against him as well: 'a cold wind across a dangerous blade
... a fearful wind ... destruction of corn'. Similar disasters befall other
kings (176) though not always in such dramatic circumstances. No grass,
leaves or corn grow for a year in Tara after Lugaid Mac Con gives a false
judgement. His people finally expel him 'because he was an unlawful
ruler.'[35]

THE LAND OF ISRAEL

The relationship between God and the land in the Hebrew Bible is
usually that of Creator and upholder:

In his hands are the depths of the earth
The heights of the mountains are his also
The sea belongs to him for he made it
And the dry land, shaped by his hands.[36]

The image of the Creator, shaping the contours of the land, suggests
both an intimate connection and a certain distance between Yahweh and

his work. The judeo–christian tradition often emphasises God's otherness, but the Creator was nevertheless believed to be intimately involved with creation, moulding it like a potter or a sculptor, sending or witholding rain, making the crops grow and so on.

The God of Abraham, Isaac and Jacob does not commonly give his name to lands or settlements. Where this does occur, it is usually part of a wider description and the divine name in question is El, rather than Yahweh. Thus we find Beth'el, 'house of El', and Isra-el, explained by one of the redactors of Genesis, not as a place-name but as a personal name – 'he who strives with El'. Only Peni'el ('face of El') approaches the sort of physical identification we find in Ireland.[37] The land is, however, immensely important in the Hebrew scriptures. The call of Abraham is not to kingship or prophecy, but to 'a land that I will show you.' The call of Moses is to 'a land flowing with milk and honey', a phrase which is repeated constantly throughout the Hebrew Bible.

Like Judaism today, the Hebrew experience of God was intimately bound up with the land of Israel. Fine weather, good harvests, peace and security were all ascribed to the favour of Yahweh. Harvest festivals were held twice a year in his honour. Leadership was vested in a king who was believed to hold his mandate from a divine source. Sacred marriage was common in the Middle East, but a different sort of family relationship was claimed for the Davidic kings. Their investiture is believed to have included a rite of adoption by which they became sons of God. In the reign of a good king, the land would flourish. His ability to give true and fair judgements was crucial for the prosperity of the kingdom:

> Give the king your justice, O God
> And your righteousness to the royal son
> May he judge your people with righteousness
> And your poor with justice
> let the mountains bear prosperity for the people
> and the hills righteousness.[38]

The converse of this belief is expressed with particular clarity in the book of Amos, where the prophet claims that the injustice and hypocrisy of Israel's leaders have brought famine, drought, and pestilence to the land.[39] The prophets of Israel, like the myth-makers of Ireland, saw blessings and disasters as signs of divine favour or disfavour. Every now and then, their denunciations give way to a longing for some future time when peace and prosperity would be restored. They hoped for a return to the golden age of the Davidic kingship in the coming of the Messiah, when the land would flourish in response to his righteous rule:

And in that day the mountains shall drip with sweet wine
And the hills shall flow with milk
And all the stream beds of Judah shall flow with water.[40]

There is an obvious parallel between the kingly virtues of 'righteousness and justice' in Israel and the Irish virtue of 'prince's truth'. Indeed, one might reasonably ask whether the ideal of *fir flathemon* might not have been adopted from the Bible in order to promote a christian ideology of kingship. There is, however, little sign of ecclesiastical influence in the seventh-century *Testament of Morann*, where *fir flathemon* is expounded in such detail. The biblical virtues of 'righteousness and justice' could have reinforced existing ideals of kingship, but there is no evidence that such leadership values had to be imported. Differences between the two traditions can also be noted. For example, Ireland retained an active interest in the sovereignty myth even after the adoption of Christianity, whereas one has to go back to the Ras Shamra texts to discover that El once had a female partner.[41] Secondly, the religious duty of Israel's rulers towards widows, orphans and the poor is rarely urged on their Irish counterparts. This concern does find its way occasionally into the Lives of saints, but does not feature prominently among the ideals of the Irish warrior aristocracy.

CORMAC IN THE LAND OF PROMISE

There is a parallel at some level between the 'land flowing with milk and honey' which is realised in the future reign of the Messiah and the Irish 'land of promise' which is realised in the everyday world during the reign of a true king. It has been pointed out that the name – *Tír Tairrngiri* – 'Land of Promise' – can be seen as a direct translation from the Latin *terra repromissionis* – a New Testament term for Abraham's Promised Land.[42] But Irish journeys to the Land of Promise often describe a thoroughly Celtic paradise with no obvious borrowings from the Bible. The following passage describes the arrival of Cormac in the Land of Promise. Cormac mac Airt was a legendary king of Tara who lost his wife and family to an Otherworld being in exchange for a silver branch. He sets off in search of them, travelling through a desolate plain where people do impossible tasks, till he reaches his destination:

> He sees a fortress, vast and royal, and another wall of bronze around it. There were four houses in it. He entered the fortress. He sees a vast palace with its beams of bronze, its wattling of silver, and its thatch of the wings of white birds. Then he sees in the garth a

shining fountain, with five streams flowing out of it, and the hosts
in turn drinking its water. Nine hazels of Buan grow over the well.
The purple hazels drop their nuts into the fountain and the five
salmon which are in the fountain bite them open and send their
husks floating down the streams. Now the sound of the falling of
those streams is more melodious than any music that humans sing.
He entered the palace. There was one couple inside awaiting him.
The warrior's figure was distinguished owing to the beauty of his
shape and the comeliness of his form and the wonder of his coun-
tenance. The girl along with him, blooming, yellow-haired, with a
golden helmet, was the loveliest of the world's women. Her feet are
washed without being observed. There was bathing on the partition
without anyone in attendance, but the heated stones went in and out
of the water by themselves.[43]

What Cormac sees is in fact a heightened version of an Irish royal
residence. Its wattles are made of silver instead of willow or hazel, its
well is the mythical well of wisdom (68) and it also has a miraculous self-
heating bathing pit. There is no sign of 'milk and honey' or any other
biblical delights in this *Tír Tairrngiri*. Nor are they common in the other
paradise places of early Irish literature – *Tír na n'Óc* – 'Land of the
Young', *Mag Mell* – 'The Delightful Plain', or *Tír na mBéo* – 'Land of
the Living'. True, the 'Land of the Living' also occurs in the Psalms and
other parts of the Hebrew Bible, but there it tends to mean here and
now, the everyday world, as opposed to 'the Pit', the destination of the
dead. Even if it could be proved that the 'Land of the Living' and 'Land
of Promise' are imported terms, they have brought little with them apart
from their names. Other tales in the voyage and journey traditions show
a greater degree of synthesis between native and christian imagery (94–
101) but there can be little doubt that the Land of Promise in *Cormac's
Journey* draws heavily on a native paradise myth which continued to
impress and entertain people for centuries, as well as influencing their
cosmology and spiritual landscape.

Chapter 3

Mountains and Hills

A fine April morning, and a party of German students spill out into the car park at the base of Croagh Patrick, Ireland's best-known holy mountain. They are on pilgrimage in honour of St Kilian, an Irish monk who became bishop of Würzburg during the seventh century and was eventually martyred there, one of the few Celtic saints to suffer 'red martyrdom' in addition to the 'white martyrdom' of voluntary exile. The students are celebrating his thirteen-hundredth anniversary. I watch them set off, equipped mainly with cameras and woolly jumpers. The weather stays fine for them, fortunately, though a puff of white cloud hangs around the summit like a wisp of smoke. Most pilgrims wait till later in the year.

The last Sunday in July is the traditional day for the pilgrimage. People used to get up before dawn and climb in the dark, but this was changed during the 1970s to reduce the risk of accidents on the scree-covered slopes. People of all ages and backgrounds make the ascent, some in bare feet, some leaning on sticks. Some stop to pray at three 'stations' along the route: at *Leacht Benain* or 'Benen's monument' named after a disciple of St Patrick, at *Leaba Phádraig* or 'Patrick's bed' on the summit, and finally on the way down at *Roilig Muire*, named after Mary. Round each of the stations is a well-worn path from the *dessel* or right-handed / sunwise circuits (149) which people make while saying their prayers. Many of them hope to reach the summit in time for the first mass of the day, held in the open-air at eight o'clock; others will take longer over it, stopping to rest every hundred feet or so, and talking to other pilgrims along the way. Some people climb the mountain every year, others only once in a while for a particular intention.

Mountain pilgrimages occur in many parts of the world as part of an ancient and continuing tradition. Examples spring to mind from India and Japan, South America and the Middle East. Mount Zaphon was sacred for the Canaanites, as Olympus was for the Greeks and Mount Zion for the Jebusites, the early inhabitants of the area around Jerusalem

(144). Abraham meets Melchizedek, the priest-king of Zion, in the early chapters of Genesis and Solomon's temple, built on the same rocky outcrop, was a major centre of pilgrimage in ancient Israel. This tradition continued after the exile, through the time of Jesus and beyond, so that even today, Jews, Christians and Moslems still flock to the holy places on the Temple Mount. In many parts of Europe, churches are commonly built on hilltops. In Provence for example, every hilltop village has its tiny church, usually on the highest piece of ground.

Early Irish literature is full of encounters with Otherworld beings on mountains or hills. Some of the most developed examples come from the Finn Cycle, a collection of stories about the warrior-seer Finn mac Cumaill. Others involve saints such as Patrick, and we begin this section with an extract from the *Confession* in which the ageing missionary looks back on his spiritual awakening in Ireland as a young man.

THE SLAVE BOY ON THE MOUNTAIN

After I reached Ireland, well, I pastured the flocks every day and I used to pray many times a day; more and more did my love of God and my fear of him increase, and my faith grew and my spirit was stirred, and as a result I would say up to a hundred prayers in one day, and almost as many at night; I would even stay in the forests and on the mountain and would wake to pray before dawn in all weathers, snow, frost, rain; and felt no harm and there was no listlessness in me – as now I realise, it was because the Spirit was fervent within me.[1]

This autobiographical passage shows beyond doubt that Patrick's primary place of prayer was the world of nature – in the fields as he herded the animals, or in the forests and on the mountain, surrounded by the elements in all their moods. Later he would build churches, but his first experience of God was nurtured by an outdoor spirituality which he never seems to have regretted or revoked. There is a note of nostalgia in his voice, as if this sort of prayer still had special significance for him, though he was no longer able to practise it quite so eagerly. It is hard to imagine such a man simply permitting outdoor worship, as a sort of missionary tactic. Patrick's nature spirituality was not an outsider's attempt at enculturation. It was based on experience. He firmly believed that the Holy Spirit had prompted him to seek God on the mountain, and in the woods and fields.[2]

By the time Muirchú wrote his latin *Life of Patrick*, towards the end of the seventh century, Patrick's experience had been elaborated and other traditions added.[3]

An angel used to come to him regularly on the seventh day of every week, and as one man talks to another, so Patrick enjoyed the angel's conversation. Even when, at the age of sixteen, Patrick had fallen into captivity, the angel came thirty times to meet him, and he enjoyed the angel's counsels and their conversations before he went from Ireland to the Latins.[4] He used to pray a hundred times during the day and a hundred times during the night. One day while tending swine, he lost them and the angel came and showed him where the swine were. One day after the same angel had talked to him about many things, he placed his foot on the rock of Scirit opposite Slíab Mis and ascended in his presence, and the footprint of the angel can be seen in the rock to the present day. And it is that place where the angel had spoken with him thirty times, and that place is a place of prayer, and there the faithful obtain most happily the things for which they pray.[5]

The angel is Victor or Victoricus, a frequent figure in Patrician hagiography. Patrick himself mentions a Victoricus in the *Confession*. The context is different and the word 'angel' is not used, but his function is clearly that of an angel or messenger of God. According to Patrick, Victoricus came to him one night in a dream after he had returned to Britain.[6] If Victoricus ever figured in Patrick's waking consciousness, he makes no mention of the fact in his writings and there is no way now of distinguishing between Patrick's mysticism and the myth-making tendency of the hagiographer.

However, this passage clearly preserves and elaborates the outdoor spirituality of the *Confession* and recommends it for Patrick's followers. The rock of Scirit is proudly advertised as a christian holy place, a threshold between heaven and earth where prayers are certain to be answered. Another version of this story says that the rock of Scirit was on the summit of Slíab Scirit, 'a mountain beside Slíab Mis' where the angel, Victor, visited Patrick in his dreams.[7] This Slíab Mis has been identified as Slemish Mountain in Co. Antrim, the only significant mountain in the area. Five miles away, among the ruins of Skerry church, is a stone said to bear the imprint of the angel's foot.[8] Rocks with 'footprints' on them are in fact found all over Ireland and the west of Scotland. The 'footprint' is more often said to be that Patrick himself, or some other saint, or occasionally the footprint of a king. Later in this section, we shall be looking at an even more elaborate story in which Patrick converses with an angel on a mountain-side, but first here are some mountain traditions of a different kind.

FINN ON THE PAPS OF ANU

At that time there was a very beautiful girl in Bri Éle, that is to say, in the fairy mound of Bri Éle, and the girl's name was Éle. The men of Ireland were feuding about that girl. One man after another went to woo her. Every year at Samain the wooing used to take place; for the fairy-mounds of Ireland were always open about Samain; for at Samain nothing could ever be hidden in the fairy-mounds. Every time a man went to woo her this used to happen: one of his people was killed. This was done to mark the occasion, nor was it ever found out who did it.

Like everybody else, the poet Cethern went to woo the maiden. However, Finn did not like the poet's going on that errand ... As they went towards the fairy-mound, one of their company was killed; and it was not known who had killed him. Oircbel the poet was the name of the man who was killed there ... However, Finn thought it a grievance and a great disgrace. He went till he came to the house of the champion Fiacail mac Conchinn, at Slievemargue. It is there that his dwelling was at that time. To him then, Finn made his complaint, and told him how the man had been killed among them in the fairy-mounds. Fiacail told him to go and sit down by the two Paps of Anu behind Luachair. So he went and sat down between the two strongholds which are between the two Paps of Anu.

Now when Finn was there between them, on Samain night, he saw the two fairy-mounds opened around him, even the two strongholds, the ramparts in front of them having vanished. And he saw a great fire in each of the strongholds; and he heard a voice from one of them which said; 'Is your sweet food good?'

'Good indeed!' said a voice from the other fairy-mound.

'Question: shall anything be taken from us to you?'

'If you give something to us, something will be given to you in return.'

While Finn was there he saw a man coming out of the fairy-mound. A kneading trough was in his hand with a ... pig upon it, and a cooked calf and a bunch of wild garlic upon it. That was their Samain feast. The man came past Finn to reach the other fairy-mound. Finn made a cast with the spear of Fiacail mac Conchinn. He hurled it southward from him towards Slievemargue. Then said Finn: 'If the spear should reach any one of us, may he escape alive from it. I think this was revenge for my comrade.'[9]

It was indeed. By fate, miracle, or a sort of poetic justice, his spear hits the right man and Oircbel is avenged. This story comes from a twelfth-century collection called *The Boyhood Deeds of Finn / Macgnímartha Finn*. The Paps of Anu is also the setting for a similar but gentler story from another twelfth-century work from the Finn Cycle, *The Colloquy of the Ancients / Acallam na Senorach*. Here Cáel, a king's son, successfully woos a formidable Otherworld woman called Créide, but not before he has proved himself in a lengthy outdoor ordeal. He must wait on the Paps of Anu 'exposed to difficulties for four days and half a week' before he can offer his bridal gift – a magnificent praise-poem in her honour.[10]

The Oircbel story refers to a belief that at certain times of year the fairy-mounds or *síd* mounds are open, so that it is possible to see into them and even encounter their inhabitants. Samain was one such time and we are given a glimpse of the Samain feast in the *síd* mounds, with dishes being exchanged between two households. Cethern and his companions go to the *síd* mound at Samain seeking Éle, since that is the appointed time for courting her. Finn goes to the Paps of Anu at Samain, but he is seeking justice rather than love. In a later paragraph, Fiacail tells him that he might have to wait another whole year if he misses this opportunity, so it would seem that Finn's enterprise was also well-suited to the season.

Are these stories based on a tradition of Samain pilgrimages to hill shrines and burial mounds? Cethern's 'courtship' can certainly be seen as a metaphor for approaching the goddess and Cáel's exposure as a form of initiatory ordeal. Finn's spear-cast is also an approach to the Sacred, though in rather a different spirit.

The death of Oircbel takes place on Éle's fairy-mound. Finn's vengeance is enacted miles away on the Paps of Anu or Ana, who is described in *Cormac's Glossary / Sanas Cormaic* as 'mother of the Irish gods'.[11] The Paps are near Killarney in County Kerry while Cruachan Brig Éle is the hill of Croghan in County Offaly. Both belong to a tradition which clearly associates hills and mountains with Otherworld women, many of whom we have already met in the *Dindshenchas*:[12] Macha, Carmun, Tailtiu, Tea, Crochen – and Buí, 'the Hag of Beare', whose name attaches to Cnoc Búi, the burial mound at Knowth in the Boyne valley.

Many of the 'fairy hills' were in fact prehistoric burial mounds. The compiler of the place-lore collections knew that these mounds were graves and says as much: Carmun, for example, is described from the outset as the burial ground of kings, where people came at harvest time to lament the nobles of the tribe, not just Carmun herself. Games or races were a central part of proceedings, and in the *Dindshenchas* of

Tailtiu such races are explicitly described as funeral games. We are told elsewhere that Tailtiu was one of the three chief burial places in Ireland, another being Cruachu, where there was also a fair.[13] Was the cult of the ancestors simply on the same site as the cult of the gods – or were the *síde* ('fairies') once in fact ancestors, as some scholars have suggested?[14] Irish medieval authors gave no consistent explanation of the *síde*. Some distinguish between them and *Tuatha Dé Danann*,[15] others do not. The distinction between ancestors and deities is often blurred in primal religions.

Some of the hills of Otherworld women in the place-lore collections were inauguration places as well as forts and *síd* mounds – Cruachu and Tara for example. This suggests a relationship between some of these women and the 'sovereignty goddess'. Irish kings were normally inaugurated on earth platforms, many of which would have been *síd* mounds. Tomás Ó Cathasaigh sees this as symbolic of the Otherworld support offered by the *síde* to the king through his marriage with the goddess. Literally and figuratively, the people under the hill can been seen as the 'mystical support' of kingship and a potential source of peace *(síd)* and fertility for the tribe.[16] The stories of Finn and Cáel indicate a belief that such peace is not easily won and that the approach to the Otherworld is fraught with difficulties and dangers.

HOLY MOUNTAINS OF ISRAEL

And after six days, Jesus took with him Peter and James and John, and led them up a high mountain apart by themselves; and he was transfigured before them, and his garments became glistening, intensely white, as no fuller on earth could bleach them. And there appeared to them Elijah with Moses; and they were talking to Jesus. And Peter said to Jesus, 'Master, it is well that we are here; let us make three booths, one for you and one for Moses and one for Elijah'. For he did not know what to say, for they were exceedingly afraid. And a cloud overshadowed them, and a voice came out of the cloud, 'This is my Beloved Son; listen to him.' And suddenly looking around they no longer saw anyone with them but Jesus only.[17]

Biblical writers also thought of mountains as places of power where the Divine presence might be felt, heard or even seen; and many of Israel's holy mountains were sacred long before the Bible was written.[18] They were centres of semitic primal religion, sacred for the Canaanites, Hittites, Phoenecians and Hebrews alike. Such sites belong to the bedrock of religion in the Middle-East. Intuitions which formed here nourished the imagination of the prophets, even as they struggled to dissociate themselves from the 'high places' in favour of a single holy mountain in Jerusalem.

At an early period in their history, the Israelites thought of Yahweh as dwelling in or on a sacred mountain in the 'Wilderness' or perhaps in a cave on that mountain. There they would go to await the theophany, the voice or vision of God.[19] According to one tradition, this mountain was Horeb where Moses saw the burning bush and later received the covenant.[20] Horeb was also associated with Elijah, who spends the night in the cave there, hears the voice of God, and goes out to stand on the mountain for the theophany of the 'still small voice'.[21] Mount Sinai – 'the mountain of God' – is the setting for another version of the covenant story. Yahweh descends upon it and Moses goes up to meet him, together with a number of other people, and 'they beheld God and ate and drank'.[22] Other holy mountains in the area were Tabor, Carmel and Hermon. All three were sacred to several different semitic cults. Hermon is sometimes identified with Mount Zion.[23]

The 'high places' – *bamôth* – were not always natural features. We also read of 'high places' being built or in some cases 'cast down'. De Vaux describes them as mounds or knolls for the purpose of public worship. He notes a series of such mounds on the crest of a hill near Jerusalem, and the discovery of a large oval platform dating from the third millenium BC, roughly contemporary with Newgrange (139).[24] This circular heap of stones, fourteen yards across, would in Ireland be called a cairn. *Bamôth* were often adorned with a standing stone (*massebah*) which recalled a theophany and a continuing divine presence. Jacob sets up his pillow as a *massebah* in the 'house of god', Beth'el. Such cairns and standing stones were also sometimes memorials to the dead.[25] Later writers denounced the high places as inimical to the true worship of Yahweh. This has tended to obscure the fact that from earliest times to the end of the monarchical period, these knolls were not just legitimate but favoured holy places of Israel, where Samuel and Solomon went to offer sacrifices.[26]

New Testament and early christian traditions looked favourably on the tradition of holy mountains. Mount Tabor is traditionally the mountain of Transfiguration, in a story modelled to some extent on the theophany at Horeb.[27] Mountains are among Jesus' favourite places of prayer in the gospels, particularly mountains at night.[28] He also teaches and prophesies on various hills, including in the temple on Mount Zion.[29] He spends his last night on the Mount of Olives and dies on the hill of Calvary, which becomes in its own way a powerful place of theophany: 'Truly this was the son of God'.[30]

IONA'S HILL OF ANGELS

In both Irish and Biblical tradition, mountains seem to be thought of as one of those remote liminal places where God or the Otherworld was very near and where an encounter with the Sacred might be deliberately sought out.[31] Moses is summoned to the mountain and returns with the covenant. Finn goes to the Paps of Anu seeking justice and eventually receives it. Elijah goes to Horeb in despair and returns with renewed courage. Patrick of the *Confession* goes to the mountain to pray, as does Colum Cille in this early tradition from Iona:

> Another time also, when the blessed man was living on Iona, he made this known to the assembled brothers with very great earnestness, saying, 'Today I wish to go alone to the western plain of this island; let none of you therefore follow me'. They obeyed and he went alone as he desired. But a brother, who was cunning and of a prying disposition, proceeded by another road, and secretly placed himself on the summit of a certain hill which overlooked the plain, because he was very anxious to learn the blessed man's motive for going out alone. While the spy on top of the hill was looking upon him as he stood on a mound in the plain, with arms extended upwards and eyes raised to heaven in prayer, then strange to tell, behold a wonderful scene presented itself ... for holy angels, the citizens of the heavenly country, clad in white robes and flying with wonderful speed, began to stand around the saint while he prayed; and after a short converse with the blessed man, that heavenly host, as if feeling itself detected, flew speedily back again to the highest heavens ... Hence even to this day, the place where the angels assembled is called by a name which bears witness to the event which took place in it; this may be said to be in Latin *Colliculus Angelorum* and in Irish, *Cnoc Angel*.[32]

Adamnán here portrays Colum Cille as someone who needed time alone in prayer, like Jesus in the Gospels. The saint goes off to the western side of Iona, nowadays called the *machair*, to a little hill or mound called the Hill of Angels. He is secretive about his prayers, just as Jesus is secretive about many of his miracles and his Transfiguration. But of course, they are both found out, and in the next paragraph, Adamnán invites us to consider how many more times, when Colum Cille was unobserved, angels approached and spoke to him. Adamnán does not explain exactly what the angels are doing as they stand around him. Are they guarding him while he prays? Are they providing a retinue for a 'prince' among Christians? Are they simply attracted by his holiness? These are all possibilities, but the main aim is to show that Colum Cille was in frequent communication with the shy messengers of God and that one of the places where this happened was on the Hill of Angels. This is pointed out to modern visitors as the hummock on the left, just beyond the gate into the *machair*. This unremarkable feature appears on Reeves's nineteenth-century map as *Sithean mór* – 'great fairy mound' – though it is unclear exactly how and when this piece of primal-christian substitution came about. According to Richard Sharpe, the identification of *Sithean mór* with the Hill of Angels is first found in accounts by eighteenth-century travellers, so Adamnán may have been thinking of a different hill. On the other hand, we may be looking at a long-standing local tradition which goes back to the time of Adamnán and beyond.[33] As for the survival of the name *Sithean mór*, there is evidence to suggest that even after the Reformation, the protestant clergy of the Highlands were more tolerant towards the traditional belief in fairies than they were towards catholic devotion to the saints.[34]

ST PATRICK ON THE REEK

The story of St Patrick on Croagh Patrick, also known as the Reek, makes some people uncomfortable today. It is certainly not a gentle spirituality. The saint's audacity is breath-taking and perhaps deliberately shocking, but God's response to it in the end is favourable – a wry back-handed compliment, so we should probably allow for an element of humour in our judgements. The main aim of the story is not to describe the nature of God, but to celebrate Patrick's achievements. It also provides a good example of how Irish and biblical traditions could meet and merge around a common experience of nature, in this case the holy mountain, in order to celebrate the greatness of St Patrick and his death-defying commitment to the Irish people. Tírechán wrote an earlier version of this story in Latin towards the end of the seventh century. He relates how Patrick climbed the mountain in order to fast for forty days and forty nights following the example of Moses, Elijah and Jesus, how the birds were troublesome to him, and how God commanded all holy people to climb the mountain.[35] Tírechán's narrative is short and relatively unadorned. The version below is much more elaborate. It comes from the so-called *Tripartite Life of Patrick* or *Bethu Phátraic* which was written in Irish during the tenth century.[36] Croagh Patrick is here referred to by its medieval name, Cruachan Aigle:

> Then Patrick went to Cruachan Aigle on the Saturday of Whitsuntide. The angel came to commune with him and said to him: 'God does

not give you what you are demanding because it seems to him excessive and obstinate and great are the requests.'

'Is that his pleasure?' says Patrick.

'It is,' says the angel.

'Then this is my pleasure', says Patrick, 'I will not go from this Reek till I am dead or till all the requests are granted to me'.

Then Patrick remained on Cruachan in much displeasure, without drink, without food, from Shrove Saturday to Easter Saturday, after the manner of Moses son of Amra, for they were alike in many things. To both God spoke out of the fire. Six-score years was the age of them both. The burial-place of each of them is uncertain.

Now at the end of those forty days and forty nights the mountain was filled with black birds, so that he could see neither heaven nor earth. He sang maledictive psalms at them. They did not leave him because of this. Then his anger grew against them. He strikes his bell at them, so that the men of Ireland heard its voice, and he flung it at them, so that its gap broke out of it and that is 'Brigit's Gapling'.[37] Then Patrick weeps till his face and the chasuble in front of him were wet. No demon came to the land of Ireland after that till the end of seven years and seven months and seven days. Then the angel went to console Patrick and cleansed the chasuble and brought white birds around the Reek and they used to sing sweet melodies for him.

'You shall bring that same number of souls out of pain, and all that can fill the space which your eye reaches over the sea'.

'That is not a favour to me' says Patrick. 'My eye does not reach over the sea very far'.

'Then you shall have both sea and land,' says the angel.

Patrick said:

'I fear to go into the round Reek
Troops without godliness ahead of me
Fear has seized me ...
Ten hundred heads contending against me.
Dark men with hideousness of teeth
With the colour of death ...
Thirteen sure thousands
Ten hundreds in every thousand are they.'

'Is there anything else that he grants me besides that?' says Patrick.

'There is', says the angel. 'Seven people every Saturday from now till Doom are to be taken out of hell's pains'.

'If he should give anything to me', says Patrick, 'let him give me twelve men.'

'You shall have them' says the angel, 'and now get down from the Reek.'

'I will not get down' says Patrick, 'since I have been tormented, till I am blessed. Is there anything else that will be given to me?'

'There is,' says the angel, 'you shall have out of hell's pains, seven people every Thursday and twelve every Saturday; and now get down from the Reek.'

'I will not get down,' says Patrick, 'since I have been tormented, till I am blessed.'

'Is there anything else that you would demand?' says the angel.

There certainly is. Patrick continues with his demands, bargaining to get more and more people out of hell, till eventually he asks that he himself should be judge over Ireland on the last day. At this point, even the angel's patience comes to an end:

'Assuredly,' says the angel, 'The Lord will not give you that.'

'Unless it is got from Him,' says Patrick, 'departure from this Reek shall not be got from me, from today till Doom; and what is more, I shall leave a guardian there'.

The angel went to heaven. Patrick went to mass. The angel came back at nones.

'How is that?' says Patrick.

'Like this,' says the angel. 'All creatures, visible and invisible, including the twelve apostles, besought the Lord and they have obtained your request. The Lord said, "There has not come, and there will not come, after the apostles, a man more admirable, were it not for your hardness." What you have prayed for, you shall have. Strike your bell,' says the angel, 'and there will be a consecration of the people of Ireland, both living and dead.'

Says Patrick, 'A blessing on the bountiful King who has given this; and now I shall get down from the Reek.'

There are a number of biblical allusions in this passage. The comparison between Patrick on the Reek and Moses on Mount Sinai is quite explicit. Patrick's attitude – 'I will not get down ... till I am blessed' – is reminiscent of Jacob's refusal to release the angel (or is it Yahweh himself?) who wrestles with him all night at Peni'el: 'I will not let you go until you bless me.' There are also echoes of Abraham bargaining with God over the number of just men required to save the city of Sodom. The number is gradually reduced from fifty down to ten. In a similar way, Patrick haggles over the number of souls who will be freed from hell through his intercession, and as the numbers rise steadily, he adds a number of other conditions as well. Like the widow pestering the unjust judge, he pursues his case relentlessly, and is rewarded for his persistence.

However, there is another source of inspiration at work here as well. The writer uses the Bible very boldly and freely, mixing several stories together and presenting Patrick as a figure greater than Abraham – who failed after all, to save Sodom from destruction – and equal to Moses and a number of other biblical figures. There is no mention of fasting in the story of Moses, either on Sinai or Horeb. On the contrary, in one version of the event, we read that Moses and his companions 'beheld God and ate and drank'. The fasting motif could have been derived from the temptation of Jesus in the wilderness (this may be where the guardian angel comes from) but there is no bargaining with God in that story. The most likely source would seem to be the Irish legal tradition of fasting for redress.[38] This sort of fasting was generally undertaken against a high-ranking person by a person of lesser nobility who felt themselves to have been wronged. Patrick was not the only saint to be portrayed engaging in this activity. Adamnán was also said to have fasted against God in order to obtain a better lot for the women of Ireland.[39]

Patrick's attitude is a far cry from either Augustinian guilt or mystical self-abandonment, but it is not so very different from Abraham's bargaining on behalf of Sodom, Jacob's wrestling with the angel or Luke's parable of the importunate widow.[40] The idea that God has to be coerced into showing mercy is repellent to modern ears, but the *Tripartite Life* is less interested in the nature of God than in the bold single-mindedness of Patrick and his comforting determination to save as many people as possible. He is presented here as a sort of spiritual champion, facing hunger, thirst, supernatural terrors and even death, on behalf of the people of Ireland. The story turns on the reality of hell, but the fear of it is mitigated by Patrick's achievement and by his role on the Day of Judgement. The 'hardness' of the saint is acknowledged with a touch of humour towards the end and it seems likely that the story is intended to shock and amuse, as well as to impress and reassure.

The Croagh Patrick story is thus a fusion, sometimes an uncomfortable fusion, of biblical and native elements. But it is unlikely to be the original reason for the pilgrimage which thousands of people still make every year. The timing of it coincides with the old Celtic festival of Lughnasad, and this together with the large number of megaliths in the area suggests that the Croagh Patrick area was a religious centre long before the adoption of Christianity.[41] The day of the pilgrimage was formerly named after an obscure mythological figure known as Crom Dubh, and the pilgrim path now known as *Tóchar Phádraig* or Patrick's Causeway, from Aughagower, predates the time of Patrick himself.

COLUM CILLE ON THE HILL OF HOWTH

A gentler experience of the mountain is found in the opening lines of the following poem in which an anonymous author, probably from the twelfth century, imagines the sixth-century abbot, Colum Cille, sitting on the Hill of Howth looking out to sea:

> Delightful to be on the Hill of Howth
> Before going over the white-haired sea:
> The dashing of the wave against its face,
> The bareness of its shores and of its border.
>
> Delightful to be on the Hill of Howth
> After coming over the white-bosomed sea;
> To be rowing one's little coracle
> Ochone! On the wild-waved shore.
>
> Great is the speed of my coracle
> And its stern turned upon Derry
> Grievous is my errand over the main
> Travelling to Alba of the beetling brows.
>
> My foot in my tuneful coracle,
> My sad heart tearful
> A man without guidance is weak
> Blind are all the ignorant.
>
> There is a grey eye
> That will look back upon Erin
> It shall never see again
> The men of Erin nor her women.[42]

The Hill of Howth or Benn Étair, as it is called in Irish, is the rocky headland on the north side of Dublin Bay, looking south towards the Wicklow hills and north towards the Mournes. To the west it looks inland and to the east, out to sea. It seems quite appropriate that a poem in which exile is such an important theme should be set in a place where the traveller could see so much of the land he was about to leave behind, and the prospect of the sea before him. The poem then goes into a long sequence of compliments and blessings directed towards people and places throughout Ireland.

Melodious her clerics, melodious her birds
Gentle her youths, wise her elders,
Illustrious her men, famous to behold,
Illustrious her women of fond espousal.

It is in the West sweet Brendan is
And Colum son of Criffan,
And in the West fair Baithin shall be
And in the West shall be Adamnán ...

Colum Cille was famous for his prophetic powers and in this last verse he names people and monastic foundations of the future as well as those of the sixth century. In effect, the poem is pronouncing a posthumous blessing on the native monastic tradition at a time when influences from the Continent were in the ascendant. It matters little whether the saint ever visited Benn Étair in person. Adamanán tells us that he once visited 'the midland part of Ireland' including Durrow and Clonmacnoise.[43] These are both further west, but Benn Étair would certainly have been familiar to many of his twelfth-century followers and there were important Columban monasteries nearby at Swords and Kells, both of which are mentioned later in the poem. Kells was in fact the headquarters of the Columban league from the ninth century onwards and an important synod was held there in 1152.

Benn Étair was also rich in non-ecclesiastical associations, most of them rather sombre. One exception would be the story of Lugaid Láigde (32–3). There it is the place where the magical mist separates Lugaid and his brothers from the rest of the hunters as they pursue the golden fawn. Shortly afterwards Lugaid meets the 'sovereignty woman' who promises him the kingship of Ireland. Most other traditions of the place are tragic however. In *The Hiding of the Hill of Howth / Uath Beinn Étair*, the fugitive lovers Diarmuid and Gráinne are betrayed there by a hag, who sings doom-laden verses at the mouth of their cave while shaking her briny cloak. Another pair of lovers, Deirdre and Noisiu, begin their exile to Scotland from Benn Étair after being pursued all over Ireland by Conchobar. As for the place-lore collections, the first place-lore of Benn Étair tells of a drowning and the second of a death in exile.[44]

The present poem may be related in some way to the place-lore traditions. It uses the same type of body-imagery for the headland: 'The dashing of the wave against its face' parallels Benn Étair 'forehead to the flood' and 'the grey sea [roaring] against his shoulder' in the *Dindshenchas*. The associations with danger and exile are also repeated here, as Colum Cille weeps and worries about the journey, not to mention the peculiar-looking people of Alba, whom he later describes in even less complimentary terms:

> Many in the East are lanky chiels
> Many the diseases there and distempers
> Many they with scanty dress
> Many the hard and jealous hearts.

By contrast, he feels at home on Benn Étair and he is delighted to be there. Amidst all the sadness and upheaval of his life, the hill is a rocky refuge where he experiences stability and a strong sense of belonging to a particular place and people. He also feels safe, temporarily, from the the perils of the sea and from the strain of having to live always among foreigners. The hill is a sanctuary for him, a secure retreat, and perhaps for that reason, it is also a place where he can pour out his heart. At the same time it is a place of blessing and vision, and a place to take stock. His vision is partial of course, but probably not in a way which would have worried his twelfth-century followers.

MOUNT BRANDON AND SKELLIG MICHAEL

Near the summit of Mount Brandon, above Dingle, there is a cluster of early monastic ruins associated with Brendan of Clonfert, alias 'the navigator'. A community of ascetics or penitents used to live there in beehive cells, praying in the oratory and drinking from the spring. Every year on 29 June, pilgrims make the ascent from the ancient burial ground at Currauly, using the old saints' road. Tradition has it that St Brendan / Brenainn climbed the mountain before setting off on his famous voyage and saw the Land of Promise from the summit:

> Brenainn returned to bishop Eirc and received ecclesiastical orders from him. There he heard the Gospel: 'Every one that hath forsaken father or mother or sister or lands for my name's sake shall receive a hundredfold in the present and shall possess everlasting life.' After that then, for love of the Lord grew exceedingly in his heart and he desired to leave his home and his country and his parents and his land, and he urgently besought the Lord to give him a land secret, hidden, secure, delightful, separated from human company. Now after he had slept on that night, he heard the voice of the angel from heaven, who said to him 'Arise, Oh Brenainn,' he says, 'for God has given you what you were seeking, even the Land of Promise.'
>
> Then Brenainn arose and his mind was glad at that answer, and he goes to Sliab Daidche, and he saw the mighty intolerable ocean on every side, and then he beheld the beautiful noble island, with

trains of angels rising from it. After that he remains there for the space of three days, and again he fell asleep. So then the angel of the Lord came to commune with him and said, 'I will be with you,' says he, 'from now on, for ever and ever, and I will teach you how to find the beautiful island which you have seen and which you desire to reach.' Brenainn then wept exceedingly, because of his delight at the angel's answer to him, and he renders thanks to God. After that, Brenainn went from the mountain and comes to his family.[45]

Soon afterwards he sets sail for the Land of Promise. This passage is reminiscent of the story of Moses at the end of his life, climbing Mount Nebo and seeing the Promised Land in the distance.[46] But the biblical Promised Land has a geographical location, whereas Brendan at some stage crosses the threshold into a different world, of shining incorruptible bodies and the souls of the righteous; and though Moses dies, he never enters the land of Canaan, whereas Brendan does finally reach his island paradise. Like Cáel and Patrick, he spends several days on top of the mountain. Like Colum Cille and Patrick, he meets an angel there, but there is no hard bargaining, no hostile birds, no fasting for forty days. On the contrary, the land is given to Brendan as a gift, and the angel freely offers his companionship and instruction. Like Colum Cille on the Hill of Howth Brendan glimpses the future from his mountain, a happy future this time, but not without its 'intolerable ocean' on the way.

Another parallel which springs to mind is that of St Antony of Egypt who also hears the Gospel being read and withdraws from society, in his case to become a hermit.[47] Brendan, with his love of God and his desire for solitude, is in some ways Antony's spiritual descendent, though his island, when he gets there, is not a place of testing and renunciation, but an island paradise. Perhaps we should think of his boat as his hermitage and the ocean as his desert. Certainly, it is often said that the Irish hermit tradition has its roots in the desert spirituality of the East. Skellig Michael, off the Waterville Peninsula in Kerry, can be seen as an Irish version of the Egyptian Thebaid, a 'desert in the ocean' and a variation on the holy mountain tradition.[48] With its jagged peaks rising straight out of the sea, it has none of the utopian qualities of Brendan's Land of Promise though it may once have been thought of as a route to eternal bliss. It is, by all accounts, a hard dangerous beautiful place, completely exposed to the elements, where some time between the sixth century and the Viking raids a community of monks built a cluster of beehive cells. These may have been intended for seasonal retreats only, but it is possible that people once lived on Skellig Michael all the year round.

There are occasional reports of people taking refuge from their enemies on the rock, but it ceased to be a place of safety when the Vikings came. Later, from the sixteenth to the nineteenth centuries, pilgrims came from all over Ireland and even from the Continent, to perform a set of dangerous penitential exercises along the ridge leading to the summit. On a summer's day the Skellig must seem like a perfect place for meditation, but people who lived there for extended periods must either have been extremely tough and determined or must have felt that ultimately they had no choice. Hermitages and churches on the tops of very high mountains were in fact comparitively rare in Ireland. Although there was at least one other, on Slieve Donard in the Mournes.[49]

Concluding this chapter, we might say that high places are places of power in a very practical way. They are easily defended and important as places of refuge and observation. If the deity is believed to be one who protects his or her people, then the mountain can sometimes be seen as embodying this protective function, as it does for Colum Cille on Benn Étair. But Finn goes armed to the mountain, and Cáel is tested rather than protected as he woos the goddess. In the Croagh Patrick legends, the mountain is a place of heroic confrontation, and in the Gospels, Jesus faces three of his most terrible moments on mountains – the Mount of Olives, the Hill of Calvary, and according to tradition, the Mount of Temptation outside Jericho.

To visit the mountain or the *síd* mound was to encounter in a very real way the visible and invisible forces at work in the universe. To the primal imagination, many of these forces are personal, with no sharp dichotomy between matter and spirit. The experience of sacred presences on the mountain might happen spontaneously, as on the rock of Scirit, or it might be deliberately sought out as on Mount Brandon.

Mountains and hills were seen as places of theophany where sacred beings had once appeared and might appear again. Explanations for these beliefs might be sought from various authorities in psychology, psychiatry, theology of language or literary criticism, but the reality of an externally-existing Otherworld or spirit-world was taken for granted in rural Ireland at this time and to some extent is still with us today.[50]

Chapter 4

Water

The well of *Tobar an Ailt* spills out into a wood on the shores of Lough Gill, County Sligo. I first visited it one weekday afternoon and met no less than seven other pilgrims in the space of about twenty minutes: two students, a man in his thirties, an older woman and a father with two teenage sons standing in the river up to their knees, filling up bottles of it to take home. Old photos show the trees beside the well, festooned with rags and strips of cloth, like prayer-flags or votive candles. These were given in exchange for healing, as 'riddances' through which an illness or trouble might be left behind. A few loose threads still cling to the hollies at the edge of the wood, but most people nowadays light candles. Some also throw coins into the well, though this is also discouraged. In some ways, *Tobar an Ailt* is a rather modern version of a holy well. Prayers for peace are said there every week and the two healing sacraments, reconciliation and anointing, are celebrated during the annual three-day pilgrimage on 'Garland Sunday' at the end of July. There is also a dawn mass at which the local bishop presides, reminding people that in penal times their forebears gathered here for the very same purpose, by a rock under an oak tree.

No one seems to know how long people have been coming to *Tobar an Ailt*. At one time the pilgrimage seems to have been a lay-devotion, with an all-night vigil and dancing as well as 'stations'. There are also rumours of visits by Patrick and Colum Cille, and local place-names like Church Island and Cloghermore might indicate that there was once an important monastery nearby.[1] Garland Sunday coincides with the old Celtic festival of Lughnasad and even today, when the official celebrations are over, people still queue up to drink and fill their bottles at the well. Water continues to be a focus of faith for them, as well as a cherished part of their Catholic heritage.

During the nineteenth century there was an enormously popular pilgrimage to Struell Wells near Downpatrick. The pilgrims set off from

'St Patrick's grave' in the town, heard mass at a house nearby, climbed barefoot up Struell hill, sat on a rock known as 'St Patrick's chair', walked sunwise (149) round a group of cairns and finally washed or bathed at the wells themselves. There was a bath-house with a deep stone tank for those who could afford it. Poorer people would strip in the open air and bathe next door in the 'limb-well'. Some would go on to the eye-well and the drinking well further upstream. P. D. Hardy, a protestant visitor who described the pilgrimage in 1836, seems to have been both exasperated and impressed by one young man who intended to perform the stations fasting every morning, on behalf of a dead man whom he had never met. Hardy also voiced his disapproval of the drinking, dancing and fighting which went on in the vicinity of the wells during the evenings of pilgrimage.[2]

Tradition has it that the Struell wells were blessed by St Patrick, but it was not his feast day which drew the crowds.[3] The main pilgrimages were at the summer solstice and the old festival of Lughnasad, suggesting some degree of continuity with the pre-christian past. The sacramentality of water is a feature of primal religions in many parts of the world including Ireland. Water deities figure in the mythologies of India, Egypt, Babylon, Greece, Rome and many other cultures. This widespread reverence towards water also found its way into the Hebrew Bible, via semitic primal religion, and in time would become one of the central symbols of Christianity, its sacramentality preserved in baptism. In early Christian Ireland, springs, wells, rivers and loughs often had strong associations with saints or Otherworld beings. The tradition does not usually distinguish between a well and a spring. Some holy wells are simply springs in their natural state; others are surrounded by some kind of structure, but we are not generally talking about pitched-roofed wellhouses with shafts and buckets.

TWO PRE-CHRISTIAN HOLY WELLS

There are no contemporary descriptions of pre-christian holy wells or springs, but christian writers occasionally give us glimpses of them. Adamnán, ninth abbot of Iona, wrote in Latin during the seventh century about a pre-christian holy well in Pictish territory. Liberal-minded readers may be discomfited by Adamnán's intolerance towards 'the heathen' and by the confrontational attitudes which he describes. He is in fact less intolerant than many of his continental contemporaries who cheerfully depict the destruction of 'pagan' shrines and the killing of their religious leaders, usually by supernatural means. Valerie Flint describes this as 'the heroic approach' and argues that it was eventually modified because it actually confirmed the power of the non-christian supernatural (by showing what tremendous efforts were required to overcome it) and because like any form of bullying, it failed to produce lasting respect or lasting conversions. It is particularly common in sixth and seventh-century Lives of saints from continental Europe.[4] The Irish tradition certainly has its 'heroic' moments. Druids are struck dead in at least two confrontations with St Patrick (84, 148) but there are very few tales in which we see the destruction of pre-christian shrines. Usually, we find a more subtle approach in which the shrines are adapted to christian use and saints outshine non-christian leaders by performing beneficial miracles rather than harmful or ostentatious ones. Such is the case in Adamnán's story:

> Again, while Colum Cille was stopping for some days in the province of the Picts, he heard that there was a well famous among the heathen populace, which foolish people, having their senses blinded by the devil, worshipped as a god. For those who drank of this well, or purposely washed their hands or feet in it, were allowed by God to be struck by demonic art, and went home either leprous or half-blind or at least suffering from weakness or other kinds of infirmity. By all these things the pagans were seduced and paid divine honour to the well. Having ascertained this, the saint one day went up to the well fearlessly; and on seeing this, the druids [magi] whom he had often sent away from him in confusion and defeat, rejoiced greatly thinking that he would suffer like others from the touch of that baneful water. But he, having first raised his holy hand and invoked the name of Christ, washed his hands and feet; and then with his companions, drank of the water which he had blessed. And from that day, the demons departed from the well; and not only was it not allowed to injure anyone, but even many diseases among the people were cured by this same well, after it had been blessed and washed in by the saint.[5]

Adamnán's intention here is to show Colum Cille's courage and influence as well as Christ's protection and his power over the elements, in this case, water. There was – and still is – a tradition of baneful holy wells as well as life-giving healing ones, and Adamnán wishes to show that Colum Cille could 'exorcise' the noxious properties of the water by blessing it in the name of Christ. Significantly, he does not denounce the well or drive the people away from it. Instead, he converts it from a harmful place to a place of healing. Wells of Colum Cille are found in many parts of Scotland: on the islands of Barra and Colonsay for example, and at Invermoriston near

Inverness. In Ireland, Durrow, Swords, Rosaveel, Glencolumbkille and Kilmacrennan all have wells of Colum Cille, to name but a few. Many of them are still places of pilgrimage.

Tírechán mentions pre-christian worship at a well in his seventh-century *Life of Patrick*. We are told that 'Patrick came to the well of Findmag, which is called Slán, because he had been told that the druids honoured the well, which they called "king of the waters", and offered gifts to it "as to a god"'.[6] Local people apparently believed that the bones of a wise man were contained in a casket beneath the capstone of the well. According to Tírechán, Patrick expected to find gold and silver in it 'from their wicked sacrifices', but when the capstone was lifted, there was nothing in the well but water – the pure element itself. The alternative name of the well of Findmag – *Slán*, i.e. 'whole, sound, healthy' – suggests that at some stage it had a reputation as a healing well.

As for the report that druids offered gifts to the well of Findmag, this is probably a half-truth. In primal religions, gifts and worship are indeed offered at certain wells, but they are offered to the deity of the well, not to the well itself, if such a distinction can be made in primal religions, one of whose characteristics, according to H. W. Turner, is the belief that the physical acts as a vehicle for the spiritual and there is no clear division between the two. The custom of throwing offerings into water is in fact very ancient. Four beautifully-crafted bronze trumpets recovered from Loughnashade, near the old Ulster capital of Emain Macha, are unlikely to have been deposited by accident and were almost certainly votive offerings. Other pieces of fine metalwork – bowls, weapons, bridle-bits, items of jewellery – have been recovered from loughs, rivers and bogs throughout Ireland. In other parts of northern Europe, human beings may once have been sacrificed in lakes, and at least one archaeologist thinks that an Iron-Age bog body from County Galway could have been the subject of a ritual killing.[7] In the tenth-century *Life of Mochta*, some druids demand that a human victim be thrown overboard to calm the sea, but as Charles Plummer points out, this could well be modelled on a biblical human sacrifice – that of Jonah.[8] Human remains have been recovered from Loughnashade, but only in the form of skulls. There was a custom at one time of throwing the heads of one's enemies into loughs and wells. The less gruesome practice of throwing pieces of food or clothing into certain loughs is recorded in the folk tradition.

To throw something into the water was probably to deliver it into the lap of the god or goddess in the hope that this voluntary sacrifice or tribute would help to foster a good relationship with him or her. Payments to human leaders, in money or in kind, were part of the social system of many early cultures. In return, the overlord was supposed not only to refrain from harassing his vassals, but actively to protect them. It is possible that the throwing of objects into loughs and wells was seen as establishing an equivalent contract with the Otherworld powers. Certain loughs and wells may once have been seen as orifices of the earth, as caves were to dry land. There are occasional tales of journeys to a land under the waves, this being an Otherworld location like the land under the hill.[9]

CAOILTE'S WELL

Christian baptisms were also performed in wells and springs. Some of these were formerly sacred to primal gods and goddesses, and the following passage from the twelfth-century *Colloquy of the Ancients / Acallam na Senórach,* is an imaginary account of the transfer of such a well to Christianity. The *Colloquy* describes how Caoilte, a former companion of Finn Mac Cumaill, travels sadly across Ireland, with a number of faithful companions, making for the *rath* or fort of Drumderg, one of Finn's old haunts. When he gets there, he finds Patrick saying mass and pronouncing a blessing on the place. The clerics in attendance are frightened because Caoilte is plainly a visitor from a bygone age, and because he and his companions are so enormous. Patrick, however, sprinkles him with holy water (to dispel the demons which are floating around his head) and the following conversation takes place:

> 'Good now,' Patrick said to Caoilte, 'what is your name?'
> 'I am Caoilte, son of Crunnchu, son of Ronan.' For a long time the clergy marvelled greatly as they gazed on them; for the largest man of them reached only to the waist or else to the shoulder of any given one of the others, even when they were sitting.
> Patrick said ... 'Caoilte, I would like to ask you a favour.'
> He answered, 'If it is within my strength or power, you shall have it. At all events, tell me what it is.'
> 'To have in our vicinity here, a well of pure water, from which we might baptise the people of Bregia, of Meath and of Uisnech.'
> 'Noble and righteous one,' said Caoilte, 'that I have for you,' and crossing the rath's circumvallation they came out. In his hand he took Patrick's and right in front of them they saw a well, sparkling and clear. The size and thickness of the cress and of the brooklime that grew on it was a wonder to them. Then Caoilte began to tell its fame and qualities, in the doing of which he said:
> 'O well of *tráig dá bhan,* ['strand of two women'] beautiful are your luxurious-branching cresses ... from your banks your trout are

to be seen, your wild pigs in your wilderness; the deer of your fair hunting cragland, your dappled and red-chested fawns. Your mast all hanging on the branches of your trees; your fish in estuaries of your rivers; lovely the colour of your purling streams, you who are azure-hued, and again green with reflection of surrounding copse wood.'¹⁰

The name of the well, 'strand of two women', together with its lough-side location, suggest at once that this is probably no ordinary well, but one with sacred associations. When Caoilte goes down to the well and addresses it directly with a praise-poem in its honour, we begin to see that this is in fact a hymn rather than simply an outbreak of romantic feeling. He begins by praising its cresses and its trout, but the scope of his eulogy soon widens to include a much wider territory. The deity of this well is not just a minor water-sprite. The beasts of the forest belong to her – the wild pigs and the deer. The produce of the forest is hers, as is the whole wilderness area with its trees and crags. She owns the rivers, as one might expect, and the fish in the rivers, but notice that these rivers are plural and that she also presides over estuaries (plural) and therefore in different parts of the country. This eulogy is not just to a local deity who is somehow confined to this particular well. It becomes possible to compare her with Áine who is associated with wells, rivers and hills, or with the hag of Beare (*cailleach bhéarra*) with her hill and forest connections, or indeed with the 'sovereignty' woman whom Níall meets by a well in the wilderness.¹¹ Whatever her identity, the deity of Caoilte's well is, in a very practical and indispensable way, a source and giver of life, comparable also with the God who is the 'fountain of life' in the Bible. A similar comparison seems to occur to Caoilte when he offers the waters of *tráigh dá bhan* to Patrick as waters suitable for baptism. The author of the *Colloquy* clearly thinks this is quite appropriate and chooses to emphasise the continuity when he could so easily have disguised it.

Notice too that it is Caoilte, the representative of the old order, who makes the theological link, matching one image of God with another through the symbolism of the water of life. This is not of course a historical account, and the *Colloquy*'s obvious affection for the primal past contrasts sharply with the attitudes of Tírechán and Adamnán five centuries earlier. But Caoilte's action may still represent one of the ways in which the old sacred places became christian sanctuaries – by consent rather than by conquest. There were after all no imperial armies or District Commissioners waiting in the wings.

The contrast in religious attitudes between the seventh and the twelfth centuries is interesting. At first sight it is curious that later texts should be more tolerant towards primalism than earlier ones. Was this because in the seventh century, Christianity was still young and insecure in Ireland, still feeling the need to establish itself vis-à-vis primal religion? Was it that by the twelfth century writers felt strong enough to recreate and idealise a past which they still needed for cultural reasons? Was there also perhaps a genuine pang of regret for something lost, something in danger of being forgotten?

Later in the *Colloquy*, Ossian takes a more protective attitude towards the old sacred places. When he goes to his sacred spring, he is careful to go alone. He returns with some of its water, marvellous cresses and eight beautiful salmon. A share of these is offered to Patrick, who accepts, but the well is not christianised and its location is not revealed.[12] The spring in question is the well of Uisnech on the hill of Uisnech, which was one of the most important cultic centres in pre-christian Ireland. The author of the *Colloquy* may have felt obliged to 'lose' this particular well with its powerful primal associations, but in the process, whether deliberately or not, he creates another myth – that somewhere out there, like treasure hidden in a field, the supremely beautiful, white-rimmed well of Uisnech lies waiting to be rediscovered.

The author of the *Colloquy* did not invent Patrick's predilection for holy wells. The *Tripartite Life* had already claimed numerous wells for him including one at Magh Slecht, a powerful pre-christian site, and another at Uaran Garad which Patrick 'loved greatly'.[13] Traditions like these can be traced back at least as far as the seventh century. Tírechán, for example, prefaced the well of Findmag episode with a brief statement that Patrick baptised thousands of people at the well of Sine and founded three churches there. The well here functions like a sort of baptistery, an open-air version of the special buildings which were often constructed over baptismal pools beside the grander churches of the Mediterranean world. Tírechán also situates one of Patrick's most famous encounters beside a well, that of Clébach, where he meets and baptises the two daughters of Loegaire, king of Tara.[14] This well was apparently on the slopes of Cruachu (33) and may therefore have been a sacred site before it was associated with Patrick. No doubt some of these stories are invented, and there is no proven link between the historical Patrick and any particular well, but when he mentions in the *Confession* that he baptised people in remote districts where 'no one had ever penetrated', it is difficult to imagine that he was baptising them in a font.[15]

FINDCHOÉM'S BABY

Findchoém, Cathbad's daughter, Amairgen's wife, suffered from 'hesitation of offspring', so that she bore no children. But a certain druid met her and said, 'If my fee were good,' he said, 'you would bear a noble son to Amairgen.' 'That will be true' said she, 'I shall pay you well.' So the druid said: 'Come to the well tomorrow and I will go with you.' So next day the two go off to the well, and the druid sang spells and prophecies over the spring. And the druid said, 'Wash yourself with it and you will bring forth a son, and no child will be less respectful to his mother's kin, that is, to the people of Connacht'. Then the young woman drank a draught out of the well … When Cet mac Magach, heard this, that his sister would bear a child that would slay more than half the Connachtmen, he continued protecting his sister till she should bring forth her boy. The young woman's time arrived and she bore a son. Druids came to baptise the child into heathenism, and they sang the heathen baptism over the little child.

This passage comes from the entry for Conall Cernach in the twelfth-century text *On the Fitness of Names / Cóir Anmann*.[16] Conall Cernach was known from earlier tales as an Ulster champion who boasted that he never slept without the head of a Connachtman under his knee. Gentler readers of today might take this to be the story of an aggressive man spawned from an evil well.[17] But the modern aversion to head-hunting was not necessarily shared by the story's original listeners and the intention may have been rather different. It was probably to explain Conall's awesome success as a champion that he was given these mysterious, but not necessarily sinister origins. Indeed, the well's life-giving properties are clearly illustrated.[18]

This story of Findchoém's baby is set in pre-christian times, but Celtic Christianity did not reject fertility wells as part of the primal past. One medieval author includes them in a list of things created by God at the beginning of the world, and fertility wells survive to this day, along with eye wells, wart wells and others whose purpose is less benign.[19] In a variation of the fertility well tradition, *On the Fitness of Names* also describes how St Finnian of Moville cured the infertility of Mugain daughter of Concrad by giving her holy water to drink. She gives birth first to a lamb, then to a salmon, and finally to a son, after bathing in the water as well as drinking it.[20]

As for 'the heathen baptism', very little is known about this, though Eleanor Hull collected a number of interesting allusions to it.[21] Circumcision is referred to as 'the heathen baptism' in one early-modern commentary on the births of Isaac and Ishmael, so it is possible that the word could be applied loosely to other rites of initiation.[22] But water is clearly envisaged in the birth ritual of Ailill Ólom, the mythical king of Munster, who was said to have been baptised 'in druidical streams'.[23] As late as the nineteenth century, Hebridean islanders performed what they called 'birth baptism' soon after the baby was delivered. The midwife or a member of the family washed the child or sprinkled him or her with water, prayers were said, and he or she was given a temporary name. Later the child would also be baptised by a priest.[24]

OTHERWORLD WOMEN AND WATER

Rivers were often associated with Otherworld women in early Christian Ireland. Many were almost certainly the old 'river goddesses' of Irish primal religion, though they constantly defy such neat categorisations and are often involved in other areas of activity as well. Boand and Sinann (69) are closely tied to the rivers which bear their names, but consider also the example of the Morrígan: usually associated with war and sometimes with the land (29) she also has clear associations with water in parts of her tradition. In the ninth-century *Battle of Moytura / Cath Maige Tuired*, the Dagda arranges to meet her in a northern glen and finds her washing herself astride a river. They immediately have sexual relations, after which she offers him various predictions, promises and advice about the coming battle. Later she meets the rest of the army at a place called the 'Ford of Destruction' on the same river.[25] In the *Táin*, she courts Cú Chulainn by another ford, as he engages the champions of Connacht in single combat. He rejects her love and her offer of help, and she avenges herself by coming against him in various forms during the next battle. One of her transformations is as an eel.[26]

    The Book of Conquests / Lebor Gabála, 'explains' a number of rivers as commemorating women who died during the Milesian invasion. For example, the harbour and the estuary at Inber Scéne was said to be named after Scéne the satirist, while the river Fial apparently gets its name from an unfortunate woman who should perhaps have taken a few lessons from the Morrígan:

> Lugaid son of Íth was bathing in Loch Luigdech; Fial wife of Lugaid bathed in the river that flows out of the lake. Her husband went to her naked, and she saw the nakedness of her husband, and died for shame. Whence it is named Loch Luigdech and Fial and Inber Féile.[27]

A greater contrast to the more rumbustious world of the saga literature could hardly be imagined. Intentional humour certainly exists in early Irish literature, but this is probably not an example of it. The distinctly biblical overtones of the fatal moment suggest a monastic origin for Fial's terminal modesty.[28]

In the placelore collections, Liffe (Liffey) gives her name to a plain as well as to the famous river. Centuries later, she would become Anna Livia Plurabelle in Joyce's *Finnegan's Wake*. The fairs of Tailtiu and Carmun both took place on hillsides above water. At Tailtiu it was the river Blackwater. Carmun's 'hallowed water' has not been identified. Wells called *tobar na caillighe* – 'well of the hag' – are reminiscent of Níall's encounter with the 'sovereignty goddess' and Étaín, one of the classic sovereignty figures of early Irish literature, is transformed at one stage into a pool.[29] Wells called *tobar Áine* in Derry and Tyrone were sacred to a figure called Áine who is also associated with hills and possibly fire and the sun (155–6). In the folk traditions of County Limerick she is sometimes a mermaid-like figure associated with Lough Gur and the little river Camóg nearby.[30]

In Donegal, fishermen used to ask a blessing and lower their sails in the direction of a well near Teelin Bay.[31] The well was called *Tobar na mBan Naomh* – well of the holy women – and was said to be named after three sisters who grew up in the vicinity of the well and became nuns. This explanation fails to disguise a resemblance to the old triple goddesses. An all-night gathering was held at this well on the eve of the summer solstice. A number of wells dedicated to the Holy Trinity may also have been dedicated to pre-christian triple deities. One of these is at the source of the Boyne. It is impossible to say whether the many wells of Brigit or Bride were originally dedicated to the goddess or the saint, if indeed these two can be distinguished. Brigit's well at Cliffony, Co. Sligo, holds its pattern day (festival of the patron saint) on the old Celtic festival of Imbolc – Bride's Day.

Most holy wells are nowadays associated with male saints: Patrick, Colum Cille, Moling, Brendan, Colman. When Charles Plummer was editing his Latin and Irish Lives of saints, he noticed that water miracles are particularly common in the Lives of saints Abban, Ailbe, Bairre and Declan. He attributed this to the influence of 'the Celtic water-god'.[32] Plummer's idea of one single male deity solely in charge of water, looks more and more questionable these days. The evidence is now more in the direction of several 'water-deities', mostly female, whose influence extends into other areas as well. The predominance of female figures in the place-lore could of course be due to other causes, such as the need to recount the death-tales of a large number of pre-christian goddesses.

THE WELL OF WISDOM

Sinann, daughter of Lodan Lucharglan, son of Ler, out of the Land
of Promise, went to Connla's well, which is under the sea, to behold
it. That is a well at which are the hazels and inspirations of wisdom,
that is the hazels of the science of poetry, and in the same hour their
fruit, and their blossom and their foliage break forth, and these fall
on the well in the same shower, which raises on the water a royal
surge of purple. Then the salmon chew the fruit, and the juice of
the nuts is apparent on their purple bellies. And seven streams of
wisdom spring forth and turn there again. Now Sinann went to seek
the inspiration, for she wanted nothing save only wisdom.[33]

Cormac saw this well on his journey to the Land of Promise (37–8). Here
Sinann, the eponymous goddess of the Shannon, goes in search of it, with
tragic consequences as we shall see. References to the hazels, salmon and
well of wisdom appear in various texts, from the ninth century onwards.[34] The details vary, but the core image is that of an Otherworld
well, surrounded by hazel trees whose nuts fall into the water, where
they are eaten by salmon. The waters of the well, the salmon and/or
some of its produce, then flow out into the world where its wisdom could
be acquired in a number of ways – by eating the salmon, or the husks of
the hazels, or by ingesting mysterious bubbles known as *imbas*, 'great
knowledge'. These were said to float down or upstream from the well at
certain times of year. This may account for the tradition that the water's
edge was believed to be a place of inspiration for poets.[35] One tenth-
century text says that the springs of Segais could distinguish between
guilt and innocence and that 'whosoever approaches them with a lie ...
goes not from them in like guise'.[36] This is particularly relevant to the
place-lore traditions of Boand which we shall be examining in a moment.

The 'poetry' mentioned in the third line was *filidecht*, which encom-
passed a wide range of scholarship and skills, including praise-poetry and
satire, story-telling, music, place-lore, knowledge of the past – and divination, knowledge of the future. Poets *(filid)* were often seers in early
Irish literature, and their wisdom had a mystical dimension. The myth of
the well of wisdom plainly shows that the *filid*'s wisdom was believed to
have an Otherworld source. In other words it was seen as a divine
wisdom. Eating or drinking of the produce of the well can be interpreted
as a sacramental act by which the initiate joined the company of sages.
Readers may be surprised to find the religious dimension of *filidecht* surviving in the monastic culture of early Christian Ireland, but examples
are found into the late-medieval and early-modern period as well.[37]

In the passage above, the well is said to be under the sea and is called Connla's well, otherwise known as the Well of Segais. This well appears again in the *Dindshenchas* of Boand (the Boyne) but there it rises in a *síd* mound, rather than under the sea. There was agreement, however, that the source of the well was in the Otherworld (under the hill and under the sea were both Otherworld locations) and that it flowed out as a certain number of rivers, two of which were the Boyne and the Shannon.

THE BOYNE AND THE SHANNON

The largest entries for rivers in the place-lore are undoubtedly those for the Boyne (Boand) and the Shannon (Sinann). Here is the beginning of the first *Dindshenchas* of Boand:

> Síd Nechtain is the name that is on the mountain here
> the grave of the full-keen son of Labraid,
> from which flows the stainless river
> whose name is Boand ever-full.

> Fifteen names, certainty of disputes
> given to this stream we enumerate,
> from Síd Nechtain away
> till it reaches the paradise of Eden.

> Segais was her name in the Síd
> to be sung by thee in every land:
> River of Segais is her name from that point
> to the pool of Mochua the cleric.

Síd Nechtain was named after Boand's husband, Nechtan son of Nuadu.[38] Notice that the river flowing from the *síd* is called Segais, and that Segais is said to be the first of Boand's fifteen names. Segais was also of course the name of the well of wisdom (68). Links between Boand and wisdom appear in other texts as well. In the *Cauldron of Poesy*, for example, where we are told that bubbles of *imbas* ('great knowledge'), from the hazels of Segais, float upstream on the Boyne every seventh year. And in *The Boyish Exploits of Finn*, Féc's pool on the Boyne is the place where Finn Mac Cumaill (literally 'son of hazel') serves his apprenticeship as a poet. This is also where his master catches the famous salmon of wisdom, and Finn, tasting it before him, receives the prodigious gifts of poetry and prophetic insight.[39] These fragments bring Boand very close to the metaphors of divine wisdom in the Bible, where 'the fountain of wisdom is a gushing stream' and 'the teaching of the wise is a fountain of life.'[40] Wisdom is also of course a female figure in the Hebrew Bible and the Septuagint.

If the authors of the place-lore knew of the wisdom traditions of
Boand, they decided to ignore or even obscure them. They also present
a strikingly different picture of the famous well:

> Nechtan son of bold Labraid
> whose wife was Boand, I aver
> a secret well there was in his stead
> from which gushed forth every kind of mysterious evil ...
>
> Hither came on a day white Boand
> (her noble pride uplifted her)
> to the never-failing well
> to make trial of its power.
>
> As thrice she walked round
> about the well heedlessly
> three waves burst from it
> whence came the death of Boand ...

Boand walks round the well, as people still do at holy wells today, and it
bursts out over her, disfiguring and eventually drowning her (149–50). In
the second *Dindshenchas* of Boand, she drowns after hurrying guiltily to
wash at the well after committing adultery with the Dagda. In both place-
lore traditions, however, the memory of Boand's other identity is preserved
in a number of praise-names: she is still 'white Boand', 'Boand ever-full',
'white-bellied Boand', 'gentle Boand', and even 'bright honour'.

The traditions of Boand and Sinann are closely related, indeed one is
probably derived from the other. Sinann's death-tale is told as follows:

> One night the maiden bethought her –
> the sweet-voiced red-lipped maiden –
> that every sort of fame was at her command
> save the mystic art alone.
>
> The maiden – fair was her form –
> came on a day to the river
> and saw – it was no paltry matter –
> the lovely mystic bubbles.
>
> The maiden goes on a lamentable venture
> after them into the green-flowing river:
> she is drowned yonder through her venture
> so from her is Sinann named.[41]

The poet lingers over Sinann's beauty and even sounds a note of regret, but the main point is to emphasise her folly and presumptuousness in desiring, more than anything else, the 'mystic art' (*imbas*) conferred by the well of Segais. As she reaches into the water for it, she drowns. On the whole, the story of Sinann is slightly more sympathetic than that of Boand, but there is more than a hint that in reaching for the *imbas* – 'great knowledge' – of the well, she is reaching for the forbidden fruit. The comparison with Eve is surely deliberate.

Stories about floods and dangerous waters are very ancient and no doubt had a traditional place in Irish mythology. I have not found death-tales of Boand or Sinann in any earlier texts, but two of Boand's alternative names, 'Arm of Nuadu's wife' and her 'Leg', are reminiscent of much older stories in which natural features are created from the bodies of dismembered people and animals. Whatever the age of the tradition, its recitation here distances the goddesses from the river and conveniently 'sweeps away' two important pre-christian deities. The well of wisdom probably survived because even in christian times it was important to the men of learning. The goddesses were more difficult to assimilate.

There was, however, a bold imaginative attempt by the author of the first *Dindshenchas* of Boand, to reassert the sacredness of the river by creating a new myth for it. We have already noted his idea that Boand has fifteen names. He takes us down through each of them, 'Arm of Nuadu's wife', 'Great Silver Yoke', 'White marrow of Fedlimid', 'Stormy wave', 'River of white hazel'. Then suddenly we are into different rivers, and even different countries:

Banna is her name from faultless Lough Neagh:
Roof of the ocean, as far as Scotland:
Lunnand she is in blameless Scotland –
The name denotes her according to its meaning.

Severn is she called through the land of the sound Saxons
Tiber in the Roman's keep:
River Jordan thereafter in the east
and vast River Euphrates.

River Tigris in enduring paradise
long is she in the east, a time of wandering
from paradise back again hither
to the streams of this Síd.

Something very interesting is going on here. The primal imagination of this author is still fired by the idea of sacred rivers and he recognises, consciously or instinctively, a widespread tradition of them running right across Europe to the Middle East. In this way, Boand remains a bearer of Otherworld wisdom, encircling the world from the Irish paradise of the *síd*, to the biblical paradise of Eden, and back again. The sacred waters of Ireland are not just compared to those of the Bible, they are fully identified with them. Tigris and Euphrates are two of the rivers of Eden in Genesis.[42]

The implication is that there is wisdom in both traditions, that native and biblical wisdom connect, that they flow out to meet each other, and that both have their origin and destination in paradise. By linking the Boyne with the rivers of Eden, the poet re-asserts the holiness of the river and christianises it, making it a contemporary means of grace rather than an embarrassing survival from the past. The first *Dindshenchas* of Boand was clearly designed to be spoken on the spot – 'on this mountain here'. Listeners were invited to experience, in the spring at their feet, the life-giving waters of Eden and the healing waters of Jordan, where Naaman washed and Jesus was baptised. No doubt some readers will feel that the price for all this was too high. Others will note that there was an opportunity for a different synthesis to be made, based on the figure of Wisdom in the Hebrew Bible. For whatever reason, this opportunity was not taken.

THE FOUNTAIN OF LIFE

From the holy wells of Genesis to the water of life in Revelation, the christian scriptures contain a lively tradition of sacred waters. Water sanctuaries were part of semitic primal religion, from which early Hebrew religion emerged. In the Bible, water sanctuaries were often places where people were believed to have heard or seen God or an angel of God, the distinction between the two often being blurred.

Hagar, wandering alone in the desert, meets an angel by a spring.[43] The spring-water saves her life and she names it Beer-la'hai-roi – 'well of the Living One who sees'. This was obviously a well of some significance. The author gives precise directions as to its location, and it is mentioned later in Genesis as the well where Rebecca meets Isaac and where they settle down to live.[44] Islamic tradition identifies it with the well of Zamzam in the great mosque in Mecca.

Beersheba was another well with sacred associations. Isaac goes there one evening after a series of disputes over watering rights. Yahweh appears to him, blesses him and passes on to him the covenant with Abraham.[45] Beersheba was clearly a religious centre of some importance. Far from disowning it, the Genesis traditions are keen to assert Hebrew ownership and to promote it as a holy place frequented by the patriarchs and visited by Yahweh himself.

Fifty miles south of Beersheba, was the oasis of Qadesh with its 'spring of judgement' or 'of the oracle'. The waters of Massah and Meribah at Qadesh were the traditional site of the miracle in which the children of Israel complain against God because they have no water to drink, and Moses strikes the rock and water flows out. Adamnán tells a rather similar story about Colum Cille.[46] Qadesh seems to have been a judicial centre of some kind, where people put their complaints before a sacred authority. It is sometimes said that the Levites, with their practice of divination by lots, were descended from the priests of Qadesh.[47]

The site chosen for the tent of the ark of the covenant in Jerusalem was beside the spring of Gihon. David sends Solomon to Gihon to be made king, and later Solomon's temple was built on the same site. Gihon was also the name of one of the rivers of Eden in Genesis.[48] If this association is deliberate, then the spring of Gihon in Jerusalem was seen as containing the pure water of paradise, capable of nurturing a new Eden.

From the practical experience of sacred waters came a rich tradition of water imagery. One particularly striking example is Ezekiel's vision in which he sees water welling up inside the temple on Mount Zion and spilling out over the threshold. It soon becomes a stream, then a deep river with trees on either side, bringing life and fruitfulness even to the Dead Sea.[49] The Law is a river for one of the Psalmists and this may be part of its meaning in Ezekiel's' vision.[50] On the other hand, the Spirit of God is 'poured out' like water in Isaiah, and again in Joel, so this might be part of Ezekiel's meaning as well.[51] The 'fountain of life' is often used as a metaphor for God's presence and activity in the world, by the Psalmists and also in the Wisdom traditions, where Divine Wisdom is a 'fountain of life' pouring from the mouth of the righteous and the teaching of the wise.[52] Even Jeremiah, for all his hostility towards primal religion, adopts the language of sacred waters to describe Israel's apostasy: 'for they have forsaken the Lord, the fountain of living water.'[53] For all these writers, water has come to represent something which begins with the material necessities of life but extends far beyond them. They know that to be fully alive means something more than merely to exist, and they choose the imagery of water to describe these invisible necessities and their divine source.

In John's Gospel, water imagery is used constantly of Jesus. 'If anyone is thirsty let them come to me and drink', is both typical and eloquent, given the role of water imagery in the Hebrew Bible. Significantly, Jesus is also presented as the giver of life, 'life in all its fullness'.[54]

He is depicted offering 'living water' to a Samaritan woman, healing a
man at a holy well – the pool of Bethesda – and healing a blind man at
the pool of Siloam.[55] There is no sign that Jesus disapproves of Bethesda,
indeed the evangelist freely attributes the well's healing power to 'the
angel of the Lord'. First-century votive offerings have apparently been
found at this pool.[56] The pool of Siloam was a water reservoir for Jerusalem, fed by a canal from the spring of Gihon. Water drawn from
Siloam on the feast of Tabernacles apparently symbolised the blessings
of the messianic age.[57]

But water can be just as awesome and destructive as any other aspect of
nature, and the biblical tradition does not gloss over this uncomfortable
fact. The waters of Genesis are the raw material of creation, but they are
also part of the primeval chaos. Danger waters are represented by the Flood,
and by the drowning of the Egyptians in the Red Sea.[58] Symbolically,
they can be seen as washing away sin and evil, waters of purification writ
large. John the Baptist stands in this tradition, as does St Paul with his
baptismal theology of passing through death to life.[59] It is perhaps more
difficult to come to terms with the Psalmist's strange and rather terrible
experience of drowning in God – 'all your waves, all your breakers pass
over me'.[60] This starts out with the gentle image of a hind longing for
running streams, but it soon becomes the prayer of all people swept
along by forces beyond their control. There was little sentimentality in
these ancient people. They knew that water was life–giving and sacramental, and dangerous, and deserving of total respect.

THE MONSTER IN THE RIVER NESS

The earliest example of a water monster in early Irish literature probably
comes from Scotland. Adamnán tells how Colum Cille came upon the
funeral of a man who had been fatally mauled while swimming in the
river Ness. Colum Cille, who was intending to cross the river, asks for a
volunteer to swim over and collect the boat:

> But the monster, which so far from being satiated was lying at the
> bottom of the stream, and when it felt the water disturbed above by
> the man swimming, suddenly rushed out and, giving an awful roar,
> darted after him, with its mouth wide open, as the man swam in the
> middle of the stream. Then the blessed man observing this, raised
> his holy hand, while all the rest, brethren as well as strangers, were
> stupefied with terror, and invoking the name of God, formed the
> saving sign of the cross in the air, and commanded the ferocious
> monster, saying, 'Go no further, nor touch the man; go back with
> all speed.' Then at the voice of the saint, the monster was terrified,

and fled more quickly than if it had been pulled back with ropes, though it had just got so near to Lugne, as he swam, that there was not more than the length of a spear shaft between the man and the beast. Then the brethren, seeing that the monster had gone back, and that their comrade Lugne returned to them in the boat safe and sound, were struck with admiration, and gave glory to God in the blessed man. And even the barbarous heathens, who were present, were forced by the greatness of this miracle, which they themselves had seen, to magnify the God of the Christians.[61]

However we view the reality of this experience today, water-monsters were certainly seen as one of nature's hazards by the Christians of medieval Ireland. The glossator of the *Eulogy of Colum Cille / Amra Choluimb Chille* repeats the story of a sea monster which was envisaged as some sort of spouting creature, possibly a whale: 'When it spews with its face towards land, poverty and scarcity in that country during seven years …'.[62] Another sea-monster ('the daughter of Crimthand of Cualu') causes the drowning of a young man in the first *Dindshenchas* of Benn Étair and in *The Colloquy of the Ancients* a monster rises out of a lough and kills a hundred hounds and a hundred men. Not until the time of Patrick could it be subdued, apparently.[63] In other parts of the tradition, saints were often credited with power over water-monsters, and when St Brendan meets a monster in the sea it declares its respect for St Brigit and agrees to honour Brendan as well.[64]

There is perhaps a propagandist element to some of these stories. In a fragment of place-lore with apocalyptic overtones, St Fursa confronts 'a dragon of fire in a salmon's shape' which bursts out of the earth and is consigned by Fursa to the bottom of Lough Bél Dragon. We are warned that on St John's Day at the end of the world, it will rise again to afflict Ireland.[65] This could be a reference to the summer solstice / Birthday of John the Baptist which, in the folk tradition, was a traditional date for bonfires and fire ceremonies (156). However, in the scholarly tradition of medieval times, the feast of the Beheading of John the Baptist (29 August) seems to have been associated in Ireland with apocalyptic-type disasters such as fire, lightning and plague.[66] If Fursa's dragon is intended to recall the dragons and beasts of Revelation, then this seems the more likely reference. Its salmon-form is puzzling given the honoured place of the salmon in Celtic tradition, including in christian prayers of the bardic period (78). If this is anti-primal propaganda in the 'heroic' mode, it is an unusual manifestation of it. Perhaps we should understand it simply as a cunning disguise – an Irish version of the wolf in sheep's clothing.

The water-monster can be seen as a manifestation of the demonic, but there is no reason to suppose that it was purely the invention of christian propagandists in Ireland. The Hebrews remembered myths of how Yahweh cut Rahab the sea monster in pieces, and in Greek and Roman mythology Perseus saves Andromeda from a sea monster to whom she has been offered in sacrifice.[67] Early Irish literature is full of frightening natural phenomena, including destructive Otherworld animals, which are subdued not by saints, but by warriors, kings and even by fellow-Otherworld beings. This would hardly be the case if all monsters were demonised gods and goddesses.[68]

Stories of the water monster remained popular in late-medieval and modern times. One thirteenth-century poem tells how Goll Mac Morna boasted that he 'left no hideous monster in lough or linn, no spectre, no phantom but was slain by me'.[69] A female *píast* – beast or monster – appears in a piece of sixteenth-century place-lore, where a monster from Lough Derg kills two thousand of Finn's companions and continues to demand a tribute of fifty cows and fifty horses a day.[70] In a slightly earlier poem, Finn and his comrades cut their way out of a 'great beast' which comes up out of the lough and eats them alive. The poet goes on to list some twenty-seven other supernatural creatures killed by Finn, fourteen of them from loughs, five from rivers and fords, five from glens, and three from mountains.[71] These are exactly the sort of numinous places which are associated elsewhere with Otherworld beings, saints and devotional practices. The use of the definite article ('the beast of Lough Neagh', 'the beast of the Shannon' etc.) suggests that such myths were both well-known and widespread. Their popularity and tenaciousness is evident in a modern folk tale from the Galway area, where it is Patrick who is swallowed by a monster, fighting his way out with his crosier.[72]

To fear the water monster is to acknowledge the destructive power of nature, in this case water and the unknown terrors of the abyss. To enjoy the victory of the saint or hero, is to believe that there are friendly as well as unfriendly powers abroad in the universe, and that our friends can deliver us from the destructive power of the others. The fate of the monster varies, but it is interesting that neither Fursa nor Colum Cille attempt to destroy it completely. Their achievement is to limit its destructiveness and to keep it in its place. This is enough of a miracle for Adamnán, who sees in it a clear demonstration of God's saving help.

CHRIST THE SALMON

The story is told of a man, blind from birth, who regained his sight at *Tobar an Ailt*. The parallel with the pool of Siloam is fairly clear,[73] and the christian character of the man's experience is plain enough, but it is mixed with inspiration from a different source. 'Oh look at me', he cries, 'I was blind from birth, and saw no light till I came to the blessed well; now I see the water and the speckled trout down at the bottom, with the white cross on his back'.[74] The fish is of course, a well-known symbol of Christ,[75] and this is made explicit here by the sign of the white cross. But the fish may also have belonged to the world of Irish primal religion, preserved here through the primal imagination of the folk tradition.

It was almost part of the definition of a holy well to have fish in it, particularly trout, salmon, or occasionally eels. This has parallels in other cultures, and several examples have been noted from the ancient world as well as from China, Mexico and Africa, including Tripoli where, in 1902, there was still a 'convent of the sacred fish' where the souls of moslem saints were said to inhabit the fish of a certain pool.[76]

Salmon and eels in early Irish literature have been described as 'mediating creatures' because they (or figures associated with them) come and go between this world and the Otherworld bearing various kinds of power and intelligence.[77] It is easy to see how this came about, given the migratory habits of actual salmon, and eels, which have the extraordinary ability to migrate overland. The salmon of the well of Segais come and go between the river and Connla's well under the sea, or the river and *Síd Nechtain*, but there are also tales in which fish seem to be Otherworld personages in a different form.

Wells with sacred eels recall the Morrígan's transformation at the ford. T. F. O'Rahilly associated salmon with the Dagda and also with Fintan Mac Bochra, a one-eyed shape-shifting figure who was said to have lived for thousands of years, part of the time in salmon form.[78] The memory of a shape-shifting goddess may underlie a folk tale about a man who went to fish in the 'Pigeon Hole' near Cong, between Lough Corrib and Lough Mask. The Pigeon Hole is a deep natural shaft overhung by trees. Last time I was there it was completely dry at the bottom, but the story describes an underground river in which there were sacred fish. We are told how the man caught one of these fish, but as he was attempting to roast it over a fire, it changed into a beautiful woman and disappeared.[79] Fish in holy wells were commonly believed to be immortal or indestructible, as if they were at least as holy as the wells themselves. In St Ciarán's well, Castlekeeran, there were traditionally believed to be three trout who were visible only at midnight on the first Sunday in August. This Trinitarian-sounding event may also be an echo of an old triadic theophany connected with the festival of Lughnasad and transferred to the christian saint.

It is against this background that we should read Giolla Brighde Mac Con Midhe's beautiful protection prayer to Christ, as 'the salmon of the well of mercy':

> Between me and the pitch-black abyss,
> may He stand, the great Virgin's child,
> the fresh nut of a cluster in our break,
> the salmon of the well of mercy.[80]

This is primarily a prayer for protection, for Christ to stand between us and the abyss, the dark unknown, which for Giolla Brighde is the pit of hell. Then there is the poignant and humbling image of the child, where one might have expected a powerful angel or at least an adult to stand on the frightening outside edge of eternity. Then suddenly we are into praise poetry, with the homely metaphor of the nut, the mysterious metaphor of the salmon – 'the bright blessed beautiful salmon' as Giolla Brighde calls him elsewhere.[81] The first carries a sense of discovery, the fresh nut in the familiar hedgerow – and the second a sense of wonder, the wild salmon shimmering in the pool. Readers will recognise without difficulty the hazel nuts of knowledge and the salmon of wisdom, fully incorporated here into Christianity. As images for Christ and probably also eucharistic images, they are perfectly enculturated and awaken a desire to taste or pluck or catch or maybe just to gaze. Here is a holy well whose deity is the christian God, and whose medial salmon is Christ, the wisdom and inspiration of his people.

Chapter 5

Trees

Trees at holy wells often had strips of cloth tied to their branches and small objects pushed into their bark such as coins, nails, pins, even rosary beads. Similar trees can still be found at crossroads, in churchyards, on top of earthworks, in the corners of fields or even in the middle of the road. They are traditionally subject to a large number of taboos. Cutting them down or taking parts of them for firewood was considered particularly dangerous. On the other hand, splinters or pieces of bark from such a tree, if carried in the pocket, were sometimes believed to have protective properties.[1] The sacredness of the tree is often explained by association with a particular saint, who is said to have lived beside it or founded a church, or planted his staff there so that it struck root. Moling's Tree – *Crann Moling* – for example, near Inistioge, is associated with St Moling who is believed to have had a hermitage nearby. There is a spring beside the tree and a stone font brought from the ruins of Mullennakil church. The altar, which faces the tree itself, is covered with stones, statues, crosses and other votive offerings. *Crann Moling* cannot be the actual tree where Moling worshipped in the seventh century, but it is in continuity with a strong tradition of sacred trees in early Christian Ireland, and indeed with a tradition which is older than Christianity and common to many cultures, including that of the Hebrew Bible and the New Testament.

According to Tacitus, the druids of Anglesey worshipped in sacred groves.[2] Lucan also mentions druidical groves, and Strabo refers to a Celtic assembly place called 'Drunemeton' – a sacred grove, possibly of oaks, somewhere in Galatia.[3] Maximus of Tyre reports that the Celts worshipped a large oak tree as a symbol of Zeus, though the Greeks and Romans did the same, so he could be interpreting in the light of his own traditions.[4] Trees are however an ancient and apparently universal symbol of the Divine. They figure in the art and spirituality of Assyria and Egypt, Persia and India, Scandinavia, Japan, the Philippines, Australia and the Americas. Even where representational art has been rejected,

tree symbolism often survives, as in the Jewish menora and the Islamic tree-of-life pattern.[5]

The emphasis on oaks in Celtic primal religion has probably been exaggerated. Certainly in Ireland the oak was only one of a number of species which could be regarded as sacred. Yew, ash and hazel also have frequent saintly, angelic or Otherworld associations in the medieval texts. One twentieth-century survey of sacred trees in the folk tradition, found that more than half of them were whitethorns – i.e. hawthorns. The author of the survey also noted the survival of the word *bile* – the principal term for a sacred tree – in more than twenty place-names from all over Ireland, including Billy, Billa, Aghavilla, Ballinvilla, Corravilla, Knockvilla, Drumaville, Gortavella, Lissavilla, and Moville.[6]

Some medieval writers believed that 'tree worship' was definitely a part of Irish primal religion. The Dagda was said to have given his hazelwood shield to Eitheor Mac Cuill 'because Eitheor worshipped the hazel', and in the *Book of Conquests / Lebor Gabála*, the three sons of Cermait are listed as 'Mac Cuill, the hazel his god; Mac Cecht – Tethor the ploughshare his god; Mac Greine – Cethor the sun his god'.[7] Mac Cuill means literally, 'son of hazel' or 'hazel man'. Other names formed in the same way include Mac Cairthin (rowan), Mac Ibair (yew) and Mac Cuilinn (holly). Statements about 'tree worship' may sound clear and straightforward, but they are best treated with caution. They may well contain a misleading mixture of knowledge and ignorance, like the allegation, heard recently on a television documentary, that Eastern Orthodox Christians worship icons. The focus of an act of worship is not always what it appears to be.

TREES AND KINGSHIP

Trees had a particular association with sacral kingship. In the following extract from the *Dindshenchas* of Loch Garmun, a young man dreams of a beautiful woman in multicoloured clothes. She is the daughter of a 'hundreded-hospitaller', that is, a landholder whose duty it was to provide food and lodging for travellers and the king's household. The woman is pregnant and gives birth to a boy-child who is stronger than she is and immediately overcomes her. Behind them is a high hill, and on it a shining tree. The leaves of the tree are full of melodies, and the ground around it is speckled with fruit. The young man, whose name is Catháir, calls his druid who offers him the following interpretation:

> This is the young woman, the river which is called Slaney. These are the colours of her raiment, artists of every kind ... This is the

hundreded-hospitaller who was her father, the Earth, through which come a hundred of every kind. This is the son ... the lake which will be born of the river Slaney, and in your time it will come forth ... This is the great hill above their heads, your power over all. This is the tree with colour of gold and with its fruits, you [king] over Banba with its sovereignty. This is the music that was in the tops of the tree, you eloquence in guarding and correcting the judgements of the Gaels. This is the wind that would tumble the fruit, you liberality in dispensing jewels and treasures.[8]

The masculinity of the Earth is unusual here, as is the precise allegorical interpretation, but there are familiar elements in Catháir's vision as well. It is interesting to compare the young woman with Boand who was also a river and a source of inspiration to artists. Banba is one of the names of Ireland, and a form of the 'sovereignty goddess'. But our main focus here is the tree, which is identified with Catháir himself, and the hill which is probably a reference to his inauguration place. The upshot of the vision is of course, that Catháir is destined to be king.

Sacred trees often grew on raths and forts, some of which were traditional inauguration sites. These were the trees under which the king was ritually married to the goddess, in a ceremony which persisted even in christian times. The Maguire kings were traditionally inaugurated on a hill known as *Lisnaskeagh* – the 'whitethorn` fort' – in Co. Fermanagh. The place-name continues to this day. The Dál gCais tribe had their inauguration tree at Magh Adhair near Tulla in Co. Clare. *Craebh Tulcha* – 'tree of the mound' – near Glenavy, Co. Antrim, and *Ruadh-bheitheach* – 'red birch' – in Killeely, Co. Galway, were probably also inauguration trees. Some royal *bileda* (plural of *bile*) were protected by law, and compensation was payable if they were injured. One of the worst possible insults which an enemy could offer was to desecrate the inauguration tree of a neighbouring tribe.[9]

The link between kings and trees was of a particularly intimate kind. A 'marvellous tree' is said to have been born on the same night as Conn Cétchathach, along with various other wonders, and in later times the bardic poets frequently described their patrons as 'trees' or 'branches'. Tadhg Mac Ruairhri, for example, is described as 'a rugged branch of a kindly tree', referring to his royal ancestry; and another king is simply called *an bile*, the sacred tree.[10]

Trees were also associated with kingship in the Hebrew Bible. There is even an example of a Hebrew 'inauguration tree' in the story of Abimelek's coronation 'by the oak of the pillar at Shechem'. When he turns out to be a disastrous ruler, a parable is told in which he is satirised as a bramble bush.[11] Some of the most magnificent tree imagery is used of foreign rulers, to convey their power and over-weening pride, but the longed-for Messiah was also to be 'the scion of David', 'the man called Branch', 'the shoot from the stump of Jesse'.[12] Jesus's triumphal entry into Jerusalem is accompanied by the waving of branches.[13]

PATRICK'S CHURCH IN THE WOOD OF FOCHLOTH

The wood of Fochloth is first mentioned by Patrick himself in the *Confession*. One night in a dream, he hears people calling him from the wood of Fochloth, or Foclut, as he calls it. Many years later, he says, God granted their request.[14] Tírechán includes the wood of Fochloth in his account of Patrick's missionary journeys. He begins his narrative at the well of Loígles where Patrick has been baptising large numbers of people. He overhears two men talking behind him in the crowd, one of them introducing himself as Énde from the wood of Fochloth. Immediately Patrick is interested and wants to go there, but Énde has reservations:

> When Patrick heard the name of the wood of Fochloth, he felt great joy and said to Énde son of Amolngid: 'I shall go out with you, if I am alive, because the Lord told me to go there.' Énde said to him, 'You shall not go out with me, or we both may be killed.' The holy man said 'On the contrary, you shall not reach your region alive unless I come with you ...'
> Énde said to Patrick: 'Give baptism to my son, for he is of tender age, but I and my brothers cannot accept the faith from you until we have come to our people, for fear they should laugh at us.' Conall was then baptised, and Patrick bestowed a blessing on him and took him by the hand and gave him to bishop Cethiachus and Cethiachus brought him up and taught him, and so did Mucneus, brother of bishop Cethiachus, whose relics are in Patrick's great church in the Wood of Fochloth.[15]

'Patrick's great church in the wood of Fochloth' was obviously a historical place, known to Tírechán's listeners at the end of the seventh century. Since Ireland was much more thickly forested in those days than it is now, this must have been a wood of some significance if it was known by reputation at such a distance. We are told nothing directly about the source of its fame, but it is interesting that when Patrick arrives there a year later, he is met not by a king and his warriors, but by 'a very great number of druids.' No king appears throughout the entire episode. It seems possible therefore, that the wood of Fochloth was once a druidical grove, a pre-christian religious centre of some importance. The druids meet Patrick at the river Moy and there is a brief but decisive confrontation in which Patrick carefully identifies their leader and calls down curses upon him. The druid drops dead, his followers scatter and a large number of people are baptised. Tírechán, clearly a follower of the 'heroic approach' (59) with regard to druids, goes on to describe the provision which Patrick makes for the young community which clearly survived to Tírechán's own time:

> And he ordained holy Macneus ... and gave him the seven books of the Law which he bequeathed to Macc Erce son of Mac Dregin. And he founded a church in the Wood of Fochloth in which there are the holy bones of bishop Mucnoe, for God told him to abandon the study of the Scriptures and ordain bishops and priests and deacons in that region ... and behold two maidens came to Patrick and received the veil from his hand, and he blessed for them a place in the wood of Fochloth.[16]

The church in the wood of Fochloth is not an isolated example. The cathedral of Patrick at Armagh may also have been surrounded by trees. The *Annals of Ulster* for the year 996 record that several parts of the abbey were struck by lightning, including the *fidnemed* – possibly a sacred wood.[17] St Brigit's sixth-century monastery was founded at *Cill dara* (Kildare) which means 'church of the oak'. Its altar was described a century later as resting on a wooden beam or base which had miraculous healing properties and 'flourishes fresh and green to the present day'.[18] The hermitage of Óengus of the *Céli Dé* was said to be next to 'the *bile*' – not just any tree in the neighbourhood but obviously a well-known sacred tree – under which he chanted his psalms.[19] The annals also mention 'the great oak' at Clonmacnoise, a yew said to have been planted by Patrick at another monastery, the *bile* of Swords, and the great oak tree at Kells. There are also place-names like Killure, Killanure etc. which are probably derived from variants of *Cell iubhair* – church of the yew.[20] St Finnian built his church at *Magh Bhile* (Moville) on the 'plain of the *bile.*' Colum Cille may have studied there and later founded two of his own monasteries in oakwoods: *Daire Choluim Chille* (Derry) means literally, Colum Cille's oakwood (91), earlier known as *Daire Calcaig* after a previous inhabitant. The Columban abbey of Durrow was also surrounded by an oakwood and a churchyard yew appears in the following ninth-century poem, also from the Columban tradition:

> There is here above the host
> A tall bright glistening yew

> A sweet bell sends out a clear note
> In the church of Colum, descendent of Níall.[21]

ABRAHAM'S OAK

Towards the end of his seventh-century *Life of Patrick*, Muirchú tells the story of a young woman called Monesan, who arrived at her christian faith by questioning the world around her rather than through any kind of formal catechesis.[22] Muirchú attributes this to the action of the Holy Spirit and remarks that 'she searched for the maker of all creation through nature, following in this the example of Abraham the patriarch' (183). But when exactly, and where, did Abraham look for the maker of all creation through nature? Was Muirchú thinking of the covenant under the stars or the smoke and fire of Abraham's night-time visions?[23] He could have been, but the major theophany in Abraham's life happens in the heat of the day, as he sits at the door of his tent in the shade of the oak trees of Mamre:

> And he lifted up his eyes and looked, and behold three men stood in front of him. When he saw them, he ran from his tent door to meet them and bowed himself to the earth and said, 'My Lord ...'[24]

These oaks are sometimes translated as 'terebinths'. The Hebrew word denotes large trees without being very specific as to species. In the earliest texts, the tree is singular.[25] At least one Irish writer equated 'terebinth' with *bile*, referring to one of the trees at Glendalough as the king's terebinth on top of the hill.[26] The author was obviously aware of the biblical tradition of sacred trees and its parallels in Ireland. Adamnán's seventh-century 'travelogue', *De Locis Sanctis / On the Holy Places*, is a particularly early example of this awareness. Based on the experiences of a bishop from Gaul, Arculf, who had visited Iona shortly after returning from a pilgrimage to the Middle East, it shows that Adamnán not only knew about the judeo-christian tradition of sacred trees, but wanted others to know about it too. He begins by describing 'the hill of Mambre' near Hebron, where there was a large stone church:

> At the southern side of this, between the two walls of the great basilica, wonderful to relate, there stands rooted in the earth, the oak of Mambre, which is also called the oak of Abraham, because once upon a time he entertained angels under it. The holy Jerome tells elsewhere that it remained from the beginning of the world up to the reign of Constantine. It was for this reason perhaps that he did not say it had perished completely, because at that time, though the whole huge oak was no longer on view (as it was formerly) yet a

portion of it remained fixed in the site. Of this, as Arculf relates,
who saw it with his own eyes, there still remains a truncated spur
rooted in the earth. It is protected under the roof of the church, and
its measure is about the size of two men. Now this cropped spur is
hewn about on every side with axes, little splinters being carried
away to the divers provinces of the world, out of veneration and
remembrance for the oak, under which, as was mentioned above, the
famous and noteworthy meeting with the angels was once vouch-
safed to Abraham the patriarch.[27]

The distinction between Yahweh and his angels is often blurred in Hebrew tradition. Later editors, feeling that direct appearances of God
were unlikely or unseemly, gradually substituted angels instead.[28] Thus
Abraham is visited by 'three men' but the earlier tradition leaves its mark
in the direct conversation between Abraham and the Lord. Christians
would later find great significance in the threeness of these visitors, and
this would surely have struck a chord with Irish listeners whose own
enthusiasm for the Trinity was pre-dated by a primal tradition of triple
deities. Elsewhere, we are told that Abraham prayed under a tamarisk
tree, by the well at Beersheba.[29]Another oak connected with Abraham
was the oak of Moreh which grew in the ancient holy place at Shechem.
Beneath it was an altar said to have been built by Abraham after the Lord
appeared to him there.[30]

The sanctuaries of semitic primal religion were often adorned with
sacred trees. The *'asherah*, which seems to have been a goddess symbol,
could be either a wooden pole or a living tree. Its male counterpart was
the *massebah* or standing stone which often stood beside it.[31] Biblical
writers usually associate the *'asherah* with the worship of Baal, but altars and
standing stones dedicated to El (in Genesis, the Hebrew God) were often
accompanied by sacred trees, as at Mamre. Hebrews and Canaanites often
worshipped on the same sites using the same natural symbols. Mamre
was probably sacred to the Canaanites before the Hebrews arrived and
continued to be sacred to different religious groups for some consider-
able time. The historian Sozomenus, writing just two centuries before
Adamnán, mentions 'Abraham's oak' as the site of an annual fair where
Jews, Christians and 'pagans' would meet to do business and worship
God. This was obviously not the original oak of Mamre, but another
which had replaced it.

Trees remain places of theophany throughout the Hebrew Bible.
Gideon meets an angel, makes food-offerings, and builds an altar beneath the oak of Ophrah. An angel comes to Elijah under a broom tree,

and to Zechariah among the myrtles.[32] One of the most famous tree theophanies is the burning bush which Moses sees on the side of Mount Horeb. Its sacred character is reinforced by its location – on the side of 'the mountain of God' – and the instruction for Moses to take off his shoes was typical of early semitic sanctuaries, as it still is of mosques and sikh, hindu and buddhist temples today. At first, an angel appears in the midst of the flames, but the voice is clearly that of Yahweh himself. Moses hides his face and the theophany is confirmed, 'for he was afraid to look upon God.'[33] This story was familiar in medieval Ireland and Muirchú describes a similar event in which an angel speaks to Patrick out of a burning bush 'but it did not burn down, as had happened to Moses before.'[34]

FINN AND THE MAN IN THE TREE

Trees may once have been places of theophany in Ireland as well, but it is difficult to establish which deity was mediated and re-presented by the tree. If the sacral king was once understood literally as a God–man, then the tree on his inauguration mound or by the door of his house could once have been his own divine symbol, marking the place where the king was revealed to his people. It could also have been the symbol of his divine partner. No one figure in the sagas or mythological histories stands out as an erstwhile 'tree deity', though several Otherworld beings are associated with trees. One possible 'icon' of a tree deity appears in an early part of the Finn Cycle, in the story translated by Kuno Meyer as 'Finn and the Man in the Tree.' Here, Finn banishes Derg Corra, one of his servants, for assaulting a young woman. In fact, Derg Corra is innocent, but Finn does not know this. He is also jealous, having desired the young woman for himself. He gives the lad three days' grace, and he flees for his life:

> Then Derg Corra went into exile and made his home in a wood and used to go about on deer's legs (if it is true) for his lightness. One day as Finn was in the woods looking for him, he saw a man in the top of a tree, a blackbird on his right shoulder and in his left hand a white vessel of bronze, filled with water, in which was a skittish trout, and a stag at the foot of the tree. And this was the practice of the man, cracking nuts; and he would give half the kernel of a nut to the blackbird that was on his right shoulder, while he would himself eat the other half; and he would take an apple out of the bronze vessel that was in his left hand, divide it in two, throw one half to the stag that was at the foot of the tree, and then eat the other

half himself. And on it he would drink a sip of the water in the bronze vessel that was in his hand, so that he and the trout and the stag and the blackbird drank together (§3).

There is no way of knowing whether this passage is consciously based on pre-christian iconography or whether it is a new invention of the author, but this image of Derg Corra – the mysterious 'man in the tree' – certainly invites a religious interpretation. His pose is like that of a many-armed Hindu deity bearing the symbols of his identity, or like the figure known as 'Lord of the Animals' on the Gundestrup cauldron. This gilded silver bowl, which was almost certainly used for ritual purposes, was discovered in Denmark and has been dated to the first or second century BC. It shows scenes and figures, some of them in the Celtic 'La Tène' style. One of the figures sits cross-legged, holding a serpent and a torc. He wears antlers on his head and is accompanied by a large stag and several smaller animals.

Derg Corra does not appear in any other tales, as far as I know. If he is related to one of the better-known Celtic deities, this relationship is no longer obvious, but he is surrounded by a collection of highly-charged symbols – the vessel, water, fish, nuts, birds, the stag – all of which have Otherworld associations in early Irish literature. Some of them also appear on Celtic ritual objects.[35] The ritual sharing of food and drink is found in many religions, as is the idea of the 'heavenly banquet'. Here, Derg Corra is in communion with the creatures of three cosmic regions: the wilderness, the air and the waters. He also has connections with fire, another traditional sign of the Sacred.

Medb was occasionally associated with trees as well. In the *Táin* we are told that trees called 'Medb's tree' – *bile Medba* – sprang up wherever she planted her horsewhip. This may not be the original myth of Medb's trees, but the very need for an explanation, suggests that trees of this name existed at some time during the composition of the *Táin*. We are even told the precise district in which they were to be found. The *Táin* also provides a little cameo-portrait or 'icon' of Medb with a bird on one shoulder and a squirrel on the other.[36] Medb is usually classified as a 'sovereignty goddess,' so her cult was presumably conducted, at least some of the time, under an inauguration tree. Were 'Medb's trees' once the inauguration trees of kings? Or were they simply trees sacred to Medb, as the cypress was sacred to Astarte?

It would seem that woodland deities, whether male or female, were not completely forgotten in medieval Ireland. There is also the image of the mad king, Suibne or Sweeney (130), cursed by St Ronán and hiding in churchyard trees. Suibne may be inspired partly by pre-christian iconography, as may the architectural image of the 'green man'. Tree imagery was also sometimes transferred to christian figures. Mary, for example, is described in late-medieval bardic poetry as, 'a queen, a branch bearing royal hazel-nuts,' and 'our blooming hazel tree'. Similar metaphors are used of Jesus – 'a branch sprung from Mary'.[37] But deities are not always imagined in human form. In parts of the Irish tradition, the tree almost becomes a sacred being in its own right. The Yew of Ross, for example, had a 'litany' composed in its honour.

THE YEW OF ROSS AND THE FIVE SACRED TREES OF IRELAND

The 'litany' of the Yew of Ross (*Eó Rossa*) comes from the twelfth-century *Book of Leinster*. Like most items of place-lore, it is probably based on older material and the Lives of Molaise and Moling both recount stories of its downfall during the early part of the seventh century. The 'litany' is made up of thirty-three descriptive titles, known as 'kennings'. Many of them are extremely obscure and cast no light whatever on the subject in hand, so they are not reproduced here. The following is an abridged version:

1	Tree of Ross	11	The Trinity's mighty one …
	a king's wheel		Mary's son
	a prince's right …		a fruitful sea …
	best of creatures …		diadem of angels …
5	a firm strong god	15	might of victory
	door [?] of heaven		judicial doom …
	strength of a building		glory of Leinster
	good of a crew		vigour of life
	a word-pure man		spell of knowledge
10	full of great bounty	20	Tree of Ross[38]

The form of the 'litany' is strikingly similar to old Marian litanies like the litany of Loreto – 'seat of wisdom, tower of ivory, ark of the covenant, gate of heaven'. However, the 'litany' of the Yew of Ross is unlikely to be modelled on any of these. The tree itself probably fell during the seventh century, and though the present form of its litany is certainly later, it is hard to imagine why anyone would re-create such a primal-sounding litany using the latest christian forms. The influence may even be the other way round.[39]

Some of the titles of *Eó Rossa* refer to the practical value of wood for chariot-making, construction, and boat-building (lines 2, 7, 8). Others link it with fertility (10, 13, 18), kingship and territory (2, 3, 15, 17), wisdom and judgement (3, 9, 16, 19). But the Yew of Ross is also, quite explicitly, a symbol of divinity (5, 11, 12, 14), though in a rather mixed and curious way. Parts of it are recognisably christian (11, 12) and the total number of kennings may be significant, one for each year of the life of Jesus. But who is the 'firm strong god'? Is this Jesus or an older deity? 'Best of creatures' would be an unorthodox title for Christ, but in certain religious outlooks it could be applied to a lesser god, for example, the god of a sacred tree. Whether by design or by accident, there is something for everyone in the 'litany' of the Yew of Ross, kings, warriors, scholars, craftspeople, seafarers, food-gatherers and clerics. The whole tribe can gather beneath it to voice their praises and their needs.

The Yew of Ross probably stood near Leighlinbridge on the river Barrow. It is said to have fallen during the time of Molaise / Laserian of Leighlin, who had a monastery nearby. The *Life of St Moling* tells how Molaise distributed parts of it to 'the saints of Ireland' and how Moling went to ask for a share and was given 'the roofing of his oratory'. The oratory, apparently known to listeners, is eventually built for him by Gobán Saor, the 'wright' or master-builder (131), sacred wood to a sacred purpose.[40] There is of course discontinuity as well as continuity in this story, but there is no sign of aggression towards the tree as there is, for example, in the Lives of Martin and Boniface.[41] The text says simply that it fell, and it is interesting that the hagiographer does not take the opportunity to make the propagandist point which was certainly available to him.

The Yew of Ross was one of a group known as the five *bileda* of Ireland, though in fact they were all within the boundaries of Leinster and Meath. None of them survived to the time of the place-lore collections. *Eó* normally means a yew, but it can be used for other large trees as well. Thus *Eó Mugna* is said to have been an oak which grew near the present-day village of Moone in Co. Kildare. It is described as being so broad that it covered an entire plain, so fertile that it continually grew enormous quantities of acorns, apples and hazelnuts all at once, and so vigorous that it never shed its leaves. Its name was explained as meaning 'greatest of sister's sons' which can be understood as a cryptic reference to Jesus. Mary appears as 'our sister' and Jesus as a 'sister's son', in two eighth-century texts.[42] If this was indeed the 'sister's son' in question, *Eó Mugna* provides a second example of a sacred tree mediating an experience of Christ, the first being *Eó Rossa* the Son of Mary.

Bile Tortan is described as an enormous ash, under which all the men of Tortan could shelter from 'the pelting of the storms'.[43] Like the oak of Moreh in the Bible, it was a tribal assembly place as well as a religious centre. Patrick built a church beside it, according to Tírechán.[44] *Craeb Daithi* – 'Daithi's branch' – was associated with a group of people called *fir bile*, so it may have been an inauguration tree or a place of tribal assembly. *Bile Uisnig* stood on the hill of Uisnech which had once been a major centre of Irish primal religion, and was still sometimes described as the centre or 'navel' of Ireland. Comparative mythology might wish to claim *Bile Uisnig* as an example of the 'World Tree'. Eliade describes this as a form of the *axis mundi*, which can also be represented by mountains and pillars. In primal religions, and often in the iconography of subsequent religions, these were believed to link different levels of reality, on earth, in heaven and in the underworld (104).[45]

The numinous quality of trees may have been diminished by Christianity, but even this is questionable, and there is no evidence that Irish saints called for the widespread destruction of *bileda*. Stories like that of Molaise and the Yew of Ross are the exception rather than the rule, and the *Life of Moling* says simply that it fell, without any mention of fasting saints.[46] In the place-lore tradition, the destruction of that other sacred tree, *Eó Mugna*, is ascribed not to a saint, but to 'the poets' – or more specifically, to Ninine the Poet, after the king had refused one of his demands.[47] It would seem therefore, that it was not just Christianity which could contemplate the destruction of an inauguration tree. Disenchanted members of a king's household might also undertake the desecrating act, as might enemies from outside the clan. The Annals of the tenth to twelfth centuries record several instances of inauguration trees being repeatedly chopped down, burned or uprooted by hostile neighbours.[48]

THE WOODS OF DERRY

As we have seen, Colum Cille may have studied at a monastery named after a sacred tree, Moville, and later founded two of his own communities in oakwoods: at Derry and Durrow. Adamnán says little or nothing about Colum Cille and trees, possibly because they are so scarce in Iona, but the saint must have found them an appropriate context for monastic life, to say the least. By the twelfth century, his love of trees had become legendary, particularly the trees of Derry (137). By this stage, his followers took a serious interest in their welfare and their feelings seem to go beyond the respect due to a place where their patron had lived and founded a church. There are many traditions and poems about Derry, but few pay much attention to the church. It was the trees which captured their hearts. When sixty of the ancient oaks blew down in the gales of 1146, the event was recorded in the *Annals of Ulster* along with the obits of kings, battles and so on. The same happened in 1178, when a further 120 of them were blown down. It was not just that people enjoyed these ancient trees for their association with the founder. They had other dimensions as well. Two poems of the twelfth century describe Derry as the 'noble angel-haunted city' and 'full of white angels from one end to the other.'[49] The nearest we get to a description of the church, is the sixteenth-century tradition that Colum Cille built his oratory facing north-south instead of east-west, in order to minimise damage to the trees.[50]

It is difficult to reconcile Colum Cille's respect for the oakwood, with the story that he deliberately set fire to Derry before building on it. The story is told as a Preface to the hymn *Noli Pater* in the Old Irish *Liber Hymnorum*:

> Colum Cille made this hymn ... at the door of the hermitage of Daire Calcaig in the time of Aed mac Ainmerech; because Colum Cille came once to speak with the king at Derry and the place was offered to him ... Then the place is burnt with all that was in it.
>
> 'That is wasteful,' said the king, 'for if it had not been burnt there would be no want of garment or food in it till Doom.'
>
> 'But people shall be there from now on,' said he, 'and the person who stays in it will have no night of fasting.'
>
> Now the fire from its size threatened to burn the whole oakwood and to protect it, this hymn was composed.[51]

This is a strange story of destruction and regeneration, the cancelling of one blessing and the promise of another, but the intention seems to have been to burn the fort, rather than the oakwood. If this is an act of exorcism (as it clearly is in the sixteenth-century version) it is directed primarily against the building, not the trees.[52] It might also be a form of foundation ritual, similar to the story that the Cashel dynasty was founded by lighting a fire on a flagstone under a yew tree.[53]

The woods of Derry were also believed to be protected by a curse. The *Annals of Ulster* for 1188 record how a man who had been chopping wood in Derry died after cutting his own foot, 'in consequence of the curse of the *familia* of Colum Cille.' Similar taboos applied to the woods of St Coemgen in Glendalough, and the woods of St Forannan elsewhere. Giraldus Cambrensis reports that a group of Anglo-Norman archers were smitten with pestilence 'in retribution for their impiety' after they had cut down the yews and ash trees of the monastery at Finglas.[54]

The abbeys may have benefited materially from stories like these, if their neighbours were thereby discouraged from grazing their pigs or collecting firewood on monastery land. But it is unlikely that the taboos were simply invented for that purpose. In Derry, the monks themselves seem to have been cautious about using the trees for fuel and special rules applied even to those which fell of their own accord. Even the later Columban tradition rules that they should be left lying for nine days, then taken up and divided among 'all the folk of the place, good and bad': a third to the guesthouse, a tenth to the poor.[55] The religious nature of the tree-cutting taboo is underlined in the following poem:

> Though I am affrighted truly
> By death and by hell
> I am more affrighted frankly
> By the sound of the axe in Derry in the West.[56]

As for yews of Finglas, yews certainly provide good shelter, but it is difficult to think which other material benefits the monks could have been jealously guarding, though yew was once the wood of choice for longbows. In the folk tradition there are still taboos against damaging saints' trees and 'fairy thorns' even when it would make economic sense to do so.[57]

TREES OF LIFE AND KNOWLEDGE

We have already mentioned the oak of Moreh which was claimed by the Hebrews as a place of theophany. God was said to have appeared to Abraham there, and the tree remained a distinguishing feature of the sanctuary at Shechem. Moreh means 'of the teacher' or 'of the sooth-sayer' and the idea that sacred knowledge might be imparted under a tree was quite familiar to the Hebrews. There would have been practical reasons for this as well, but if teaching and prophecy are seen as the out-workings of a theophany – as mediated forms of revelation – then where better to teach, than in the place of theophany, under the sacred tree? Joshua is said to have read the covenant to the people under the oak of Moreh, a story which may hark back to regular assemblies at Shechem for the teaching and renewal of the Law.[58] Elsewhere, Deborah gives judgement under a palm tree, and there are brief mentions of a 'diviner's oak' and an oak tree which is the seat of an anonymous man of God.[59]

Solomon's temple, 'the House of the Forest of Lebanon', was lined entirely with wood – 'no stone was seen' – and was decorated with carvings of cherubim and palm trees.[60] The idea of worshipping God indoors, in a special house, had previously been a feature of canaanite religion.[61] Here it enters the judeo-christian tradition, possibly for the first time, bringing with it the memory of the old outdoor sanctuaries in symbolic form. Flowers, gourds and pomegranates – images of beauty and fertility – were carved in other parts of the temple, while its great pillars can be seen as stylised trees.

The Tree of Life and the Tree of the Knowledge of Good and Evil are perhaps the most famous trees in the Bible. Commentators have often found it difficult to distinguish between these two, and at least one scholar has suggested that they were originally one and the same.[62] Knowledge and Life are closely related in the opening chapters of Genesis, where Adam 'knows' his wife and she conceives her first child. Trees were a feature of the earliest semitic sanctuaries, and continued to be a focus for the knowledge of God, in myths about theophanies or angelic appearances as well as in teaching, prophecy and judgement. But the God who gives insight and instruction is also celebrated, primarily, as the giver of life. The symbolism of trees reflects that reality, in the Bible as in parts of the Irish tradition.

OTHERWORLD TREES

Some of the sacred trees of Ireland were believed to have counterparts in the Otherworld. According to the tenth or eleventh-century tale *On the Settling of the Manor of Tara* / *Do Suidigud Tellaich Temra*, the five *bileda* of Ireland all grew from the berries of the same Otherworld tree.[63] These berries were distributed by a giant with a triadic or Trinitarian-sounding name, who appears in Tara on the first Good Friday carrying 'a golden many-coloured branch of Lebanon wood' with three types of fruit on it – nuts, apples and acorns – and a delicious perfume. After expounding the 'correct' division of Ireland into five provinces with Tara at the centre, he takes five berries from the branch and these eventually grow into the five *bileda* of Ireland. The idea that *Eó Mugna* was the 'son of the tree from Paradise' probably belongs to the same tradition.[64] In its present form, this myth seems designed to give divine authority to a set of contemporary political relationships, and is therefore of no great antiquity. But the image of the Otherworld tree or trees had already appeared in several earlier tales and was an enduring feature of Irish descriptions of the Otherworld throughout the middle ages.

Otherworld trees are particularly common in tales of Otherworld journeys and voyages. One of the earliest examples is *The Voyage of Bran* / *Immram Brain* in which a mythical king called Bran is visited by a woman who appears mysteriously at an assembly in his house. Her opening words describe the marvellous branch which she carries and she goes on to describe her island home, Emne, where there is a great tree (*bile*) full of music and singing birds:

> An ancient tree there is in bloom
> On which birds call to the hours:
> In harmony of song they all are wont
> To chant together every hour ...
>
> Unknown is wailing or treachery
> In the homely well-tilled land:
> There is nothing rough or harsh
> But sweet music striking the ear.
>
> Without grief, without gloom, without death
> Without any sickness or debility –
> That is the sign of Evin
> Uncommon is the like of such a marvel.[65]

The word for 'hours' in the first verse is the same as that used for the canonical hours, so the birds of this deathless paradise are imagined chanting psalms or canticles. Bran accepts the invitation to visit the woman on her island, puts to sea, and after a strange encounter with the god Manannán, reaches 'The Land of Women'. He and his companions are taken into a large house where there is 'a bed for each couple' and where the food constantly renews itself on their plates. They return to Ireland only to say good-bye.[66]

An apple from the Otherworld tree also appears in *Conlae's Journey / Echtra Chonlae* which tells how a mysterious woman invited Conlae to join the immortals in *Magh Mell* – the 'Delightful Plain'. She gives him a miraculous apple which becomes his only food and which remains whole no matter how much he eats.[67] Eventually he sails away with her, never to be seen again. *The Wasting Sickness of Cú Chulainn / Serglige Con Culainn* also features marvellous trees. In it we hear how Cú Chulainn's charioteer, Lóeg, made a journey to Labraid's *síd* mound in *Magh Mell* – which, in this story, is on an island in the middle of a lake. The trees are described afterwards as Lóeg recounts his experiences to Cú Chulainn. First he mentions 'The Tree of Victories' – *An Bile Búada* (132) – which he passed on his way to the Otherworld. No explanation is offered for this interesting-sounding tree, so presumably medieval listeners were already familiar with its significance. There must also have been a tree which bore golden apples, since Lóeg sees one of them tying back the hair of the Otherworld king. Finally, there are the trees around the palace itself:

> At the doorway to the east
> Three trees of brilliant crystal

Whence a gentle flock of birds calls
To the children in the royal fort.

A tree at the doorway to the court
Fair its harmony
A tree of silver before the setting sun
Its brightness like that of gold.

Three score trees there
Whose crowns are meetings that do not meet
Each tree bears ripe fruit
For three hundred men.[68]

These can be seen as idealised versions of the *bileda* which stood beside
the ring-forts of early Irish kings. Three of them face the rising sun, one
makes music at an inner door, one faces the setting sun, and a wood
provides food and shelter for the fairy host.

Monks could also visit the Otherworld and see the marvellous trees
there. In the late eighth or ninth-century *Navigatio Sancti Brendani /
Voyage of St Brendan*, the saint and his companions visit an island called
'The Paradise of Birds' where birds sing the hours in an enormous tree,
as they do in *The Voyage of Bran*. They also visit a thickly-wooded island
where all the trees bear grapes the size of apples and the perfume of the
trees is so sweet that it quite takes the edge off their fasting.[69] In the
eleventh-century version of the *Voyage of Snedgus and MacRiagla*, two
monks of Iona see a great tree on their voyage round various islands. Its
trunk and leaves never decay and its branches are full of beautiful birds
'singing Psalms and canticles and praising God, for they were the birds
of the Plain of Heaven'. Before they set off on their return voyage to
Iona, they are given a leaf from the tree to take back to Colum Cille.[70]

There are also significant trees and woods in *The Journey of Teigue son
of Cian / Echtra Thaidhg mheic Céin*. This is a late-medieval sequel to
Conlae's Journey and it tells how Teigue and his companions arrive at a
thickly-wooded island where the trees are so exquisitely perfumed that
the travellers are able to satisfy their hunger simply by inhaling. After
passing through an orchard full of apples, oak trees, hazels, and bril-
liantly-coloured singing birds, they meet a young couple who turn out to
be none other than Conlae and his woman visitor. They live in a silver
fort next to a miraculous 'wine-producing apple tree' which bears the
fruit of immortality – enough to satisfy everyone who will ever live in the
house. They also meet Clídna Cheinnfionn, one of the *Tuatha Dé
Danann*, who eats from the same tree.[71]

It should be clear by now that the Otherworld tree or wood is an extremely common image in early Irish literature. One could also cite the golden tree by Lug's house in *The Phantom's Frenzy / Baile in Scáil* (33), or the hazelgrove by the Otherworld well in the *Dindshenchas* of Sinann (68) and again in *Cormac's Adventure / Echtra Cormaic* (38) which opens with a young man carrying a musical silver branch with three golden apples on it. It is Cormac's desire for this branch which sets the whole sequence of events in motion.

Some commentators have suggested purely literary reasons for this proliferation of Otherworld trees. James Carney, for example, argues that the image of the tree with the singing bird was adopted into *The Voyage of Bran* from one of two christian poems on the Phoenix – one in Latin, the other in Anglo-Saxon – and that it became a sort of literary cliché thereafter.[72] There is no doubt but that later tales often build on earlier ones and that external influences have contributed to the tradition in various ways. The synthesis of native and christian paradises is an on-going project in the voyage and journey traditions. In the past, there was sometimes a tendency to overlook or simply to ignore the large number of christian references in these tales. But such references are undoubt-edly present, and the great trees of the Otherworld may sometimes represent enculturated versions of the Tree of Knowledge or the Tree of Life. It is more difficult to find obvious biblical parallels for gold and silver trees, crystal trees, musical trees, fragrant trees which suffice for food, trees full of blossom and singing birds, or trees bearing golden apples. Perhaps we should look for the native Otherworld tree among these, but we should also be aware of parallels in other literary and religious traditions.

The Norse myth of Yggdrasil could also have been known in Ireland after Viking raids, Yggdrasil being an enormous ash tree at the centre of the world.[73] The apples of the Hesperides might also have been familiar from classical mythology. These were believed to grow in a garden on an island in the extreme west, near the 'Isles of the Blessed', and they were guarded by nymphs, the Hesperides themselves. One of the labours of Hercules was to steal these apples which were the apples of immortality. Jason also visits the Garden of the Hesperides after a long voyage which takes him, interestingly, through the territory of the Celts, and past an island inhabited entirely by women. In the third-century *Passion of Perpetua and Felicity*, Perpetua has a vision of a man carrying a green branch with golden apples on it. This branch, which Perpetua under-stands to be a prize for her coming martyrdom, may also be derived from the apples of the Hesperides and from prizes awarded at the Pythian games. As for trees made of precious metals, a golden branch features famously in Virgil's *Aeneid*, where it guarantees safe passage to the Underworld and back.[74]

Irish monks and scholars were undoubtedly familiar with christian literature from abroad, as well as with Virgil and other classical authors. They might also have come in contact with the Norse myth of Yggdrasil. The search for external sources is fascinating and potentially endless, but parallels can also occur independently and spontaneously. This is particularly true of images from the primal imagination, since it deals primarily with basic experiences which are common to peoples throughout the world. The shamanistic lore of Central Asia, for example, can have had no direct connection with early Christian Ireland, and yet the initiatory dreams of Siberian shamans often involved a mystical journey to the cosmic tree which was sometimes located on a visionary island.[75]

The Otherworld trees of medieval Irish literature probably have many sources but given the importance of trees in inauguration places and other sacred sites in Ireland, it seems unlikely that the country was without a tree mythology of its own, and unlikely that the trees of *Magh Mell* and the paradise islands are completely unrelated to it, when so many other influences were admitted. It is difficult to know how its outline could ever be discerned today, but what we do know, and can say with confidence, is that the Christians of medieval Ireland loved to think about the Otherworld tree and the woods of Paradise, and were constantly finding new ways to describe them. They could scarcely imagine Paradise without fragrant fruitful woods or trees full of singing birds. Sometimes, they deliberately merged this imagery with images from scripture, as in the Irish Adam and Eve story – *Saltair na Rann* – which adds to the biblical tradition a flock of glorious birds singing 'perfect lively music' under the tree (*bile*) of paradise.[76]

THE BRANCH OF PEACE AND THE STAFF OF JESUS

A rod or branch seems to have been part of the insignia of Irish kings and poets. Some later references to inauguration ceremonies show that kings were traditionally handed 'the rod of kingship' by a person of spiritual authority who accompanied him to the inauguration mound. In some cases, this person was a poet (poets still had a quasi-religious role in medieval Ireland) in other cases it was a representative of a leading monastery. The involvement of clergy seems to have been a more recent development. The second Irish Life of Maedóc of Ferns insists that whenever a king of Bréifne is inaugurated, his 'wand' should be cut from the hazel tree at the site of St Maedóc's hermitage.[77] Here, the ecclesias-

tical and the traditional are combined – a christian holy place providing
the king with a native symbol of the divine wisdom which should char-
acterise his reign.

The silver branches desired by Bran and Cormac can be seen as
mythical counterparts of the rod of kingship, which appears in the
eighth-century tale *Bricriu's Feast / Fled Bricrenn* as a silver sceptre in
the hand of Conchobar, king of Ulster. He is described striking it against
the bronze pillar of his couch in order to restore order among the Ulaid,
who are fighting amongst themselves.[78] This rod or sceptre appears again
in a slightly later tale, where it is included in a description of the royal
house. Notice the golden apples:

> A rod of silver was above Conchobar, with three golden apples on
> it for instructing the host, and when it shook, or the sound of his
> voice arose, the host was silent, and though a needle should fall on
> the floor of the house, it would not be heard, owing to the silence
> in which they were from respect for him.[79]

Sencha, the chief poet of the Ulaid, wields a staff to similar effect in at
least three tales from the Ulster Cycle: in *Bricriu's Feast*, in the ninth-
century *Intoxication of the Ulaid / Mesca Ulaid* (where it is called a
'peacemaking branch' and seems to be made of bronze) and finally in the
twelfth-century *Violent Deaths of Goll and Garb*. Here again it is used to
stop a fight. Cú Chulainn has arrived late for a feast at Emain Macha and
been refused entry. He forces his way in and immediately the trouble
begins:

> The hosts arise. There was wrath hither and wrath thither in that
> place, storm and tempest. The thunderous wound-noise of the hosts
> was heard afar. Then Sencha rose up and shook the Branch of Peace
> (*Cráeb Sída*) over the hosts, so that they became peaceful like the
> children of one father and mother. Their shields were placed in
> order on their pegs, their swords on their cushions, and their spears
> on their racks. Every one came to his drinking place. Cú Chulainn
> placed his sword into its sheath. He took a wand of white silver and
> therewith gave a blow on the crown of Conchobar's head from the
> root of his long hair to his poll. 'If I liked,' says Cú Chulainn, 'It
> is the sword I would have given you, and you have not hosts enough
> to protect you – were you not my fosterer and my mother's brother.'[80]

The first branch in this passage is Sencha's 'Branch of Peace' which
effectively stops the fighting. Its name, *Cráeb Sída*, deserves some comment in that *cráeb* is sometimes used as a synonym for *bile* – a sacred tree

– and *sída* – 'of peace' – may also evoke connections with the fairy-mound. Sencha's branch can therefore be understood as having Otherworld connections, like Conchobar's rod whose golden apples remind us of the apple trees of *Magh Mell*. The second 'branch' is the 'wand of white silver' which Cú Chulainn uses to hit Conchobar about the head. The most famous silver wand in Emain Macha was Conchobar's 'rod of kingship'. If this is the rod in question, then the meaning of the gesture is plain. With his usual breath-taking audacity, Cú Chulainn is warning the king that he could take his kingship from him at any moment, but chooses not to.

The 'Staff of Jesus' (*Bachall Ísu*), mentioned several times in the *Annals of Ulster*, can perhaps be seen as the ecclesiastical equivalent of the 'Branch of Peace'. The entry for 1015 records that in that year the king of Bréifne was 'wickedly slain' by the king of Connacht despite being under the protection of the 'Staff of Jesus'. A similar outrage occurred in 1073, and in 1113 a protracted war was brought to a close when 'Cellach, successor of Patrick, with the Staff of Jesus made a year's peace' between the two sides.[81] The *Bachall Ísu* was said to be Patrick's crosier, given to him at the start of his mission to Ireland by Jesus himself. The story, as told in the *Tripartite Life of Patrick*, includes a visit to a mysterious island where some of the inhabitants seem to be immortal:

> Then Patrick went to sea with a company of nine. And it is then that he came to the island, and he saw a new house and the young married couple inside, and he saw the withered old woman in front of the house on her hands and knees.
>
> 'Who is this old woman?' says Patrick, 'Great is her feebleness.'
>
> The young man replied, 'She is a grand-daughter of mine ... If you could see the mother of that girl, she is feebler still.'
>
> 'How did this come about?' says Patrick.
>
> 'Not hard to say,' says the young man. 'We are here since the time of Christ, who came to us when he lived among us here, and we made a feast for him. He blessed our house and blessed ourselves, and that blessing came not upon our children, and we shall remain without age, without decay, here until the Judgement. And it is long since your coming was foretold to us,' says the young man. 'And God left with us that you would come to preach to the Gael, and he left a token with us, to wit, his staff, to be given to you.'
>
> 'I will not take it,' says Patrick, 'till he himself gives me his staff.'
>
> Patrick stayed three days and three nights with them, and went after that to Mount Hermon in the neighbourhood of the island. And there the Lord appeared to him and told him to go and preach

to the Gael, and gave him the staff of Jesus, and said that it would be a helper to him in every danger and in every unequal conflict in which he should be.'[82]

The 'Staff of Jesus', the hazel wand of the kings of Bréifne, the mythical silver branch, Conchobar's silver rod and Sencha's 'Branch of Peace' are all signs of the bearer's special relationship with the Otherworld powers or with God. Some of them were probably seen as symbolic or even actual branches of an Otherworld tree. They create an imaginary link between the world of mortals and the divine world, bringing some of its peace and wisdom to bear on human society. The fact that kings, poets and ecclesiastics were all associated with rods and branches of peace, underlines the traditionally religious nature of all three vocations in medieval Ireland.

THE CROSS AND THE PARADISE TREE

Trees figure in a late-medieval poem known as 'The Harrowing of Hell' from the *Book of Fermoy*. This belongs to the tradition of Irish apocryphal writings and is based on a Latin text known as *Christ's Descent into Hell*, which was probably known in Ireland as early as the eighth century.[83] The poem opens with Satan's cry of alarm on the morning of the resurrection as he sees Jesus approaching the gates of Hell to liberate some or all of its people. He shouts to his demons not to let him escape a second time, then introduces himself to the audience:

It was I who tempted Eve, out of her white-tipped hands and out of her eye so soft and grey, beneath the apple tree of transgression.

Then I sprang up in the form of one of my serpents and beguiled Eve, the tall and gentle lady, after we had gone aside beneath the cover of the wood.

I said to her – a false saying – 'Take this apple, Eve. They are the sweetest apples that grow, of the fragrance of Adam's isle.'[84]

Listeners would have recognised the island paradise with its fragrant apple trees from the voyage and journey traditions (94–6). In case there was any doubt about it, the synthesis with Genesis is made explicit in 'Adam's isle' and the 'the apple-tree of transgression'. Hell becomes a fair plain as Jesus approaches, and Adam cries out that the prophecy is being fulfilled. He goes on to explain which prophecy:

'One day,' said Adam the noble scion, 'I sent my son to Paradise of the fair-topped bright-stemmed apple trees which no man finds.

He saw at a distance the withered tree at which I and my great seed fell: there he saw a child, comely, graceful, soft-eyed.

Because of the child that bare tree had become covered with branches, leafy and bushy; his shapely fingers were shaking the apple tree, so that it became fresh.

'My son Seth came to the plain where I was waiting for him, tidings of the tree and of the Child he brought, and told with sweet gladness.'

'That young child,' said Adam, 'was He whom we see coming towards you. It will take trembling and pain from men – the Child's course upon the bare tree.'[85]

Adam's prophecy concerns the tree of the cross, which is identified here with one of the trees of Paradise. We hear how the tree withered when Adam and Eve sinned, and revived when the Christ-child shook it back into life by his 'course' or crucifixion on the dead tree. The cosmology of this poem is very interesting. The historical events of the crucifixion seem to be mirrored in a parallel universe, where Eden is a present reality and Jesus is still a miraculous child. It is unclear whether the tree in question is the Tree of Life or the Tree of Knowledge, if indeed these two can be distinguished. The apples suggest the Tree of Knowledge, though apples are not mentioned, of course, in the Genesis tradition – but the poem also includes powerful themes of life out of death: the revival of the dead tree, the death and resurrection of Jesus, and the freeing of death's prisoners.

Earlier prose versions of 'The Harrowing of Hell' describe how Adam sent Seth to the gates of Paradise to ask God for 'the oil of the Tree of Mercy' so that he could be 'anointed in his illness'. In response, God sends the Archangel Michael to explain that there will be no more of this oil till Jesus comes, but that he will bring the oil of mercy to all believers.[86] This sounds like a reference to the Sacrament of the Sick, as if at one time the oil used to anoint people in danger of death was thought to come ultimately from one of the trees of Paradise. Since Adam and his companions receive eternal life as a result of the Descent into Hell, we should probably identify the Tree of Mercy with the Tree of Life, and the Tree of Life with the Cross.

THE MYSTICAL TREE

Learned tradition tells of a wonderful tree, with its upper part above the firmament, its lower part in the earth, and every melody in its midst. Another of its marvellous features was that it grew downward from above, while every other tree grows upward. It grew downward from a single root, with innumerable roots coming from it below. There were nine branches, every branch more beautiful than that above. There were pure white birds on the forks of the branches, listening to their many melodies throughout the ages.

The tree is Jesus Christ, the acme of all God's creatures, above them by reason of his divinity, who came forth from the earth, assuming humanity from the Virgin Mary. All the melody in the tree's midst represents the perfection of bliss in the mystic depths of the divinity. It grew from the above, that is, from the Heavenly Father. Its single root from above is the one Godhead of his divinity. The roots below are the twelve apostles, the disciples, and the saints. The nine branches are the nine heavenly orders, with each order more noble than that before it. The white birds among the branches are the shining souls of the just among the heavenly orders.

Those of us who dwell together here implore the mercy of God that we may dwell among the branches of that tree, that is, among the heavenly orders.[87]

This passage from the *Yellow Book of Lecan* describes an upside-down tree growing from heaven to earth. The image is rare, if not unique, in early Irish literature, so it may well have come from an external source. Parallels have been noted elsewhere: in the *Upanishads*, in the Kabbalah, in Dante, and in Norse religion where Yggdrasil the ash tree at the centre of the world is sometimes described as having its roots in the sky.[88] Whatever the inspiration behind 'The Mystical Tree', it clearly belongs to the tradition of the 'World Tree' which occurs in many religions and cultures.

The author of this passage was also writing against a background in which musical trees and marvellous birds were instantly recognisable as having potential religious significance. The birds' identity as 'souls of the just' occurs in other contexts as well (113) and the 'key' to the image is particularly interesting when compared with the 'key' to Cáthair's dream in the *Dindshenchas* of Lough Garmun (82). Here the tree is Christ: there it is Cáthair's kingship. Here, the music is bliss in the 'mystic depths of the divinity': there it is Cáthair's eloquence while delivering true judgements. The image of the musical tree is common to both texts, but one uses it to extol traditional tribal values, while the other is a theological meditation, borrowing and transforming the familiar language of the sacred tree.

The image of Christ as a great tree growing from heaven to earth is probably not one which has instant appeal today. We are not used to picturing him in any form other than human, though most Christians would in fact be familiar with descriptions of the messiah as 'the scion of David' and 'the man called branch' and would recognise the famous verse about the suffering servant: 'he grew up before him like a young plant'.[89] Jesus is also 'the true vine' in John's Gospel, but if he lays claim to the tree image anywhere else it is through the parable of the Kingdom of God which grows from a tiny mustard seed to a great tree in which 'all the birds of the air' find shelter.[90] The present passage probably draws on a combination of these and other ideas which it would take too long to unravel. Basically, it is an image of universal integration and communion. Like Eliade's 'world tree' Christ is present throughout the cosmos, binding together different worlds or different levels of reality. Above he is rooted in God, while below he has a second set of earthly / aerial roots in his disciples and followers. He is completely one with them – as in the parable of the true vine – and also with the nine orders of angels and the souls of the just (113). The whole image can be understood as a graphic if rather complicated and 'top-down' illustration of the New Testament idea of 'being in Christ'.[91] Indeed, it could almost be a restatement, using arboreal imagery, of the famous hymn in Colossians in which the whole of creation is held together and reconciled in the mystical body of Christ 'in whom all things are created' and in whom 'all the fullness of God is pleased to dwell.'[92]

Chapter 6

Birds

Trees with birds are a favourite image in early Irish literature as we have seen, but birds had sacred associations of their own as well.[1] Even today they are one of nature's riddles with much of their activity unexplained: their sudden arrivals and departures, their secretiveness, their strange flockings and dispersals, their sensitivity to things beyond the normal range of human perception so that they do in fact have access to a kind of knowledge which human beings are not party to. Then there is the expressiveness of their songs and alarm-cries, from a different world of meaning but clearly intended to communicate. The idea that the birds are speaking a secret language occurs in many cultures, together with the belief that certain people, often religious leaders, can understand what they are saying and interpret it. An angel interprets the lament of the birds for St Molua in the *Félire Óengusso / Martyrology of Óengus,* and a late Columban tradition claims that Colum Cille also 'had the language of the birds'.[2] The present chapter examines some of the ways in which birds were understood in medieval Ireland and Iona, with a brief excursus into biblical tradition as well.

FALLEN ANGELS

The birds in the Otherworld tree rarely behave like ordinary birds. So who or what are they? The author of the Latin *Navigatio Sancti Brendan / Voyage of St Brendan* deliberately set out to provide an answer. Estimates for the date of the *Navigatio* range from late-eighth to early-tenth century, with recent scholars tending towards a later date. It was written by an expatriate Irish monk, but as we shall see, he must have been familiar with the earlier *Voyage of Bran* (95) and with other insular traditions about Otherworld birds. The *Navigatio* tells how Brendan and his companions spent several years at sea, looking for the 'Land of Promise of the Saints'. Each year they celebrate Easter on an island known as 'The Paradise of Birds'. They land at the mouth of a little

river, and pull their curragh upstream till they reach the spring or well
at its source:

> Beyond the spring, on higher ground, there was an exceptionally tall
> tree growing, with a trunk of colossal girth. This tree was full of
> pure white birds; so thickly had they settled on it that there was
> hardly a branch, or even a leaf, to be seen. Brendan wondered why
> so vast a number of birds should have flocked together. So keenly
> did he long to unravel the mystery that he threw himself on his knees
> and prayed silently: 'O God to whom nothing is unknown and who
> can bring to light every hidden fact, you see how anxious I am. I
> beseech your infinite majesty to deign to make known to me, a
> sinner, this secret design of yours which I see before me. I presume
> to ask, not because of any merit or dignity of my own, but solely
> on account of your boundless clemency.'
>
> He sat down in the boat and one of the birds flew down from
> the tree towards him. The flapping of its wings sounded like a bell.
> It settled on the prow, spread out its wings as a sign of joy, and
> looked placidly at Brendan. He realised at once that God had paid
> heed to his prayer. 'If you are God's messenger,' he said to the bird,
> 'tell me where these birds come from and why they are gathered
> together.'
>
> 'We are fallen angels,' the bird replied, 'part of the host which
> was banished from heaven through the sin of man's ancient foe. Our
> sin lay in approving the sin of Lucifer; when he and his band fell,
> we fell with them. Our God is faithful and just and, by His great
> justice, we were placed here. Thanks to his mercy, we suffer no
> torment: our only punishment is to have no part in the vision of his
> glory which those who stand before his throne in Heaven enjoy. Like
> the other messengers of God, we wander through the air, over the
> bowl of heaven, and upon earth, but on Sundays and holy days, we
> take on this physical form and tarry here to sing the praises of our
> Creator.'[3]

The bird then prophesies the success of Brendan's voyage and how long
it will take, before flying off to rejoin the flock. Like the unidentified
birds in *The Voyage of Bran*, these birds or fallen angels sing psalms and
canticles at all the canonical hours. We are told exactly which lines they
sing, and how Brendan and his companions found their song 'as sweet
and moving as a plaintive song of lament'. The author is careful to
distance these fallen angels from the inner circle of Lucifer and his band.
There is no hint of the demonic in them. On the contrary, they are still

regarded as messengers of God even though they no longer enjoy the beatific vision. The island is a sort of lesser paradise for them, where on Sundays and holy days they take on bird-form and live a monastic life. The fallen angels were a matter of particular interest in Irish and Hebridean Christianity. Some commentators took the view that the *Tuatha Dé Danann* were fallen angels, and the same explanation was commonly offered for the 'fairies' – *Síde* – of the folk tradition.[4] This can be seen as a way of coming to terms with the older spirit-world of deities and ancestors which could not easily be dismissed from people's minds. Some theorists presented the *Tuatha Dé* as demons or as ordinary mortals, but others turned to the myth of the fallen angels which provided a way of acknowledging their spiritual power, while locating them firmly within biblical 'history' as created beings under the authority of the Creator. Some writers combined this with the argument that they were demons. One of the editors of the *Book of Conquests,* for example, made the following contribution to the debate. It is a very different view from that taken in the *Navigatio:*

> Others say that the *Tuatha Dé* were demons of a different order, and that it is they who came from heaven along with the expulsion by which Lucifer and his demons came from heaven ... So those people go in currents of wind. They go under seas, they go in wolf shapes and they go to fools and they go to the powerful. Thence comes it that this is the nature of all of them, to be followers of the devil.[5]

The earlier author of *Navigatio* envisaged an order of angels who had been sympathetic to Lucifer, but had taken no active part in his rebellion. As a result, God had mercy on them and instead of sending them to hell, exiled them only from his immediate presence. Since then, they wander through the earth and the air, like the other angels. They still praise God, prophesy and act as divine messengers. And on Sundays and holy days they live a perfect monastic life-style on an island paradise, as befits their status as exiled members of the heavenly host.

As we shall see in the next section, it is not unusual in other parts of the tradition for birds to be Otherworld beings in disguise. The *Navigatio* seems to provide a cosmology which could accommodate such beings, though the author does not mention any of them by name. There is every chance, however, that he or she would have been familiar with bird-transformations like those of Óengus and Caer, Mider and Étaín, who all take the form of swans.[6]

OTHERWORLD BEINGS

Conaire was raised as a son of the king of Tara, but in fact his father was an Otherworld being who took the form of a bird and flew in through the skylight of his mother's house, leaving his feather-hood on the floor (34). Afterwards, he tells her that she will have a son whose name will be Conaire, and he is not to kill birds. Some years later, the king of Tara dies and a divination rite known as 'the bull feast' is held to find his successor. Conaire, meanwhile, is driving towards Dublin in his chariot:

> There he saw huge white-speckled birds, unusual as to size and colour. He turned and followed them until his horses grew tired, and the birds always preceded him by no more that the length of a spear cast. Then he took his sling and stepped from his chariot and followed the birds until he reached the ocean. The birds went on the waves, but he overtook them. The birds left their feather-hoods then, and turned on him with spears and swords; one bird protected him, however, saying 'I am Nemglan, king of your father's bird troop. You are forbidden to cast at birds, for by reason of birth, every bird here is natural to you.'
>
> 'Until tonight I did not know this,' said Conaire.
>
> 'Go to Tara tonight, for that will be more fitting,' Nemglan said. 'There is a bull feast there, and it will make you king.'[7]

Conaire's father is never named, but his Otherworld status is perfectly clear. He is also a shape-shifter, changing at will from bird form to human form and back again. His kindred have the appearance of birds as well, but at least one of them, Nemglan, is also a shape-shifter, later described as 'the man on the waves'. Nemglan prophesies that Conaire's reign will be distinguished, but he also lays on him a number of taboos which will be the conditions of the Otherworld's continuing support. The way in which Conaire hunts the strange bird-flock, travelling further and further from home, reminds us of later sovereignty tales in which Níall, Conn and Lugaid all find their destiny by travelling into the wilderness.[8] Conaire even begins a rudimentary 'voyage', as he pursues the mysterious bird-flock out to sea.

POETS, DRUIDS AND SHAMANS?

There also seems to have been a link between birds and the traditional Irish poets or *filid*. In *Cormac's Glossary* for example, we hear how a group of poets once set out by boat for a poetry competition, their leader wearing his *tuigen* – a word which the *Glossary* explains as meaning 'thatch of feathers.' The etymologies in *Cormac's Glossary* are often fanciful, but the bird-poet association is quickly reinforced by a metaphor in which the poets compare themselves to a flock of particularly fine birds. When a young fellow of loathsome appearance tries to join them in the boat, they cry out indignantly that he is 'not a bird fit for their flock'.[9]

In a later story from the *Book of Lismore*, Mogh Ruith, the blind druid of Munster, puts on his feathered head-dress in order to perform what looks very like a shamanistic feat. The armies of Tara, led by Cormac and his chief druid, Cithruadh, are contending against the armies of Munster. Both sides have lit druidical fires and watch anxiously to see which way the flames will turn. They pursue each other in circles, consuming all of the woods and forests of central Munster. They show no sign of abating:

> Then they brought Mogh Ruith his hide of a brown hornless bull and his speckled bird hood with its winged flight [?] and his other druidical gear, and he rose up into the air and into the sky along with the flames, and began to beat them so as to turn them towards the North, while singing the rhetoric 'I make the druid's arrows' etc. Then he began to beat the flames to turn them towards the North. And Cithruadh began to beat them in the same way towards the South. In spite of his efforts, Mogh Ruith turned the flames to the North, and they went away, over Cormac's camp and he gave them no chance to flare up again after he had managed to beat them down.[10]

Was there an Irish form of shamanism? This is certainly one of the texts which causes people to think there might have been.[11] Eliade describes shamanism as a spiritual technique in which adepts are believed to be able to leave their bodies and travel to other worlds. The purpose of these 'flights' or ecstacies is to communicate with the spirit-world, typically, with nature spirits, with spirits in bird or animal form, or with the souls of the dead. Shamans are employed as healers and to accompany the dead on their journey to the Otherworld. Their costumes are usually made of animal skins decorated with feathers and animal symbols. These ornaments are intended to give the shaman a 'body' similar in form to the spirits which he or she expects to encounter. They are also believed to have special mastery over fire, and their bodies are often said to give off heat. Shamanism is not a religion in itself, but exists alongside the normal religious life of the community. In some cultures, shamans are also poets or priests.[12]

Mogh Ruith, with his feathers, his animal skin, his 'flight' and his mastery over fire has many of the typical characteristics of a shaman. His story is set in the distant past, but it is intriguing to find such an exact description in the work of a twelfth-century christian author. Unfortunately, there is no way of knowing whether the figure of Mogh Ruith was based on a live or a dead tradition, or whether he sprang fully-fledged as it were, from the primal imagination of the author.

COLUM CILLE: DOVE OF THE CHURCH, CRANE CLERIC

Colum Cille's association with birds begins with his name, 'dove of the church', which seems perfectly poised between Christianity and native culture. It was traditional for religious leaders and guardians of knowledge and sacred lore to be associated in some way with birds (109–10) but it is hard to think of a single poet, druid or Otherworld being who is associated in any way with doves. The image was new and traditional at the same time, providing him with the bird symbolism of a scholar or religious leader, but through a bird whose sacred associations were entirely christian, calling to mind the Holy Spirit, and perhaps also Noah's dove setting out over the waters into the unknown.

There is however, a puzzling and ambiguous association between Colum Cille and cranes, or possibly herons. In a famous episode from Adamnán's *Life*, the saint makes provision for an exhausted crane which has been blown off course from Ireland and needs to be fed and sheltered till it can resume its journey.[13] Adamnán cites this as an example of Colum Cille's prophetic powers, since the saint had predicted its arrival. The story may also be intended to illustrate his compassion for all God's creatures.

The vernacular traditions about Colum Cille and cranes are rather different however. Soon after his death in 597, an *Amra* or eulogy was composed in his honour by an eminent Irish poet.[14] This is one of the earliest pieces of Irish vernacular writing in existence. It is heavily glossed and difficult to decipher, with a Preface which was added around the beginning of the eleventh century. This is where we find the other crane traditions of Colum Cille. The setting is the Convention of Druim Cett, part of whose business, according to the Preface, was to decide the succession to the kingship. Colum Cille, we are told, returned to Ireland for the convention and played a decisive role in the appointment of the future king. At a certain point in the proceedings, the queen whose son had been passed over in the succession refers to Colum Cille contemptuously as the 'crane cleric' (*corr-chlérig*), a phrase whose exact meaning is obscure, but which is clearly intended as an insult. The saint responds by turning her into a crane (*corr*). Stokes translates *corr-chlérig* as 'tricky cleric' and suggests that when she accuses Colum Cille of *corrgainecht*, she is referring to the one-legged (crane-like) posture which the *filid* traditionally adopted when cursing a king. A similar posture of standing on one leg with one eye closed is associated elsewhere with sorcery.[15] It is sometimes suggested that Colum Cille was in fact a poet – a *fili* – himself. This would certainly be in keeping with his bird associations, but there is no evidence that the abbot of Iona was ever a *fili* in the traditional sense. More likely, he was recognised as being like a *fili* in many respects: poets were traditionally respected as scholars and seers; Colum Cille was famous both for his scholarship and for his prophetic powers; he was also known for his hymn-writing and his remarkable voice, and the *filid* were also associated with music, many of their compositions being sung rather than simply recited. Later writers sometimes headed their work *Colum Cille cecinit*, as these were the kind of songs he might have written. He may well have been sympathetic towards the *filid*, defending their right to royal patronage and receiving the famous eulogy in return. But the Preface also pictures him undermining their position, displacing the chief poet from his traditional role as king-maker by naming the future king.[16]

The Columban tradition is curiously complicated about birds. On the one hand there is the 'dove of the church' with his compassion for all God's creatures, even those with eerie reputations.[17] On the other, there is the crane-cleric and the crane-woman with her abusive tongue, accusing him of trickery, possibly even sorcery. The discrepancy between these two should probably be sought in the very different ages and types of literature in which they are found: Adamnán's seventh-century Latin hagiography and the eleventh-century vernacular of the Preface. It might also reflect differences of opinion within the Columban tradition as to how far native beliefs about birds could be accommodated.

VICTOR AND MICHAEL

Angels are sometimes presented as birds in later writings. When Muirchú and Tírechán refer to the angel Victor they say nothing about wings or feathers, but by the time we get to the *Notes on Fíacc's Hymn*, he appears without apology or explanation, 'in a bird's shape' as the saint is tending pigs in a valley near Slemish.[18] Presented like this, Victor is virtually indistinguishable from Conaire's mentor, Nemglan (109), and other bird-personages of native mythology.

The archangel Michael had received similar treatment in the slightly earlier *Life* of St Brendan or Brénainn:

> One day when I was in this church, seven years ago to this very day, after preaching here and after Mass, the priests went to the refectory;

I was left alone here and a great longing for my Lord seized me,
when I had gone up to the Body of Christ. As I was there, trembling
and terror came upon me; I saw a shining bird at the window, and it
sat on the altar. I was unable to look at it because of the rays which
surrounded it, like those of the sun. 'A blessing upon you, and do
you bless me, priest,' it said. 'May God bless you,' said Brénainn.
'Who are you?' said Brénainn. 'The angel Michael,' it said, 'come
to speak with you.' 'I give thanks to God for speaking with you,'
said Brénainn, 'and why have you come?' 'To bless you and to make
music for you from your Lord,' said the bird. 'You are welcome to
me' said Brénainn. 'The bird then set its beak on the side of its wing,
and I was listening to it from that hour to the same hour the next
day; and then it bade me farewell.' Brénainn scraped his stylus
across the neck of the harp. 'Do you think this sweet, student?' he
said; 'I give my word before God,' said Brénainn, 'that after that
music, no music of the world seems any sweeter to me than does
this stylus across the neck.'[19]

The speaker is Brendan himself and the unfortunate student has just
been playing him some of his best tunes on the harp. He wanted to know
why the saint kept stuffing balls of wax in his ears.

SOULS OF THE JUST, THE DEAD AND THE UNBORN

We have already noted the 'souls of the just' in the branches of the
Mystical Tree, and the author's prayer that we may join them one day
(103). The *Life of Brendan* from the *Book of Lismore* uses the very similar
image of the souls of the righteous in the Tree of Life. Written after the
Navigatio, the Lismore *Life* tells how Brendan completed his voyage and
arrived in the Land of Promise where he and his companions received
spiritual instruction from a saintly old man:

Now thus was that holy old man: without any human raiment, but
all his body was full of bright white feathers like a dove or sea-mew,
and it was almost the speech of an angel that he had. After the striking
of the bell, they celebrate tierce. They sing thanks to God with their
mind fixed on him. They dare not ask anything, and they receive
spiritual instruction of him at the uplifting of the gospel.

This old man can be linked with the tradition of bird-like saints and
angels, but his identity is slightly unclear. In a similar passage in the
Navigatio, he is a hermit from the monastery of Armagh. In the Lismore
Life, he seems to be Elijah:

This then is the preaching which Elijah is wont to make to the souls of the righteous under the Tree of Life in Paradise. Now when Elijah opens the book for the preaching, then come the souls of the righteous in the shapes of bright white birds to him from every point. Then he first declares to them the rewards of the righteous, the happiness and delights of the kingdom of heaven, and at that time they are exceedingly joyful. Then he declares to them the pains and punishments of hell and the banes of Doomsday ... The birds then make an exceedingly great wailing, and beat their wings against their bodies ...[20]

The 'souls of the righteous' are of course the dead, or some of them at least. We have already noted a link between the dead and the fairy hills (44–5), but there was also a tradition that the dead gathered on certain islands, for example on *Tech Duinn* – Donn's House – off the coast of Kerry. Islands were in fact used for burials in other parts of Ireland and Scotland. Iona is a prominent example, where the path to the graveyard of the kings is known as 'the path of the dead'. As for Donn, he is often described by modern commentators as the pre-christian god of death, though his identity may well be more complex and subtle than that.[21] Some scholars distinguish between *Tech Duinn* and the happy Otherworld islands, as if *Tech Duinn* were a kind of Hades in contrast to their Elysium, but the distinction between a gloomy and a blissful Otherworld is really quite untypical of early Irish literature and should probably not be made.[22] Most native Otherworld locations are either wholly blissful, or contain both blissful and frightening elements together. In the Lismore *Life of Brendan*, the island paradise and the home of the dead are clearly one and the same and it may be that other birds in similar contexts also represent the dead, the ancestors or the souls of the just.

In later Croagh Patrick legends, the birds who were merely 'troublesome' in Tírechán's version have become friendly and unfriendly spiritual beings (48–50). Patrick is made to encounter, variously, black demon-birds and white angel-birds, a visiting bird-flock from the Land of Promise, and a bird-flock composed of all the saints of Ireland, past, present and to come.[23] This last example is particularly interesting since it suggests a belief that the saints of the future already exist in some way before they are born. The idea of birds as souls of the unborn is comparatively rare in early Irish literature, though some hagiographers describe moments of 'ensoulment' when future saints enter their mothers' wombs in other forms – though not as birds – and similar moments are described in some of the sagas.[24]

The idea of pre-existent souls is known in other cultures, of course. In parts of Siberia there is a tradition that the souls of unborn children perch like little birds in the branches of the Cosmic Tree.[25] Pre-existence is also found occasionally in the Hebrew Bible: 'Your eyes beheld my unformed substance', 'before I formed you in the womb, I knew you.' Verses like these may well have contributed to the Johannine view of Jesus, as the pre-existent Logos or Word of God.[26]

IN THE SHADOW OF YOUR WINGS

In the Book of Deuteronomy, birds are among the creatures which the Hebrews are forbidden to depict in 'graven images' and St Paul reproves the newly-converted Romans for having once exchanged the glory of the Creator for images of birds and animals.[27] In both cases, the fear is of idolatry. There was clearly an awareness that in some religions, gods and supernatural beings were depicted in bird-form and that this could be misleading if it were taken too literally. There are signs, however, that at one time the Hebrews did use bird-imagery for God and also for members of the heavenly host. This practice survives mostly in metaphors. One of the prophecies of Isaiah, for example, promises that the Lord of hosts will protect Jerusalem 'like birds hovering', and the phrase 'in the shadow of your wings' is particularly common in the psalms where it is used to evoke God's shelter and protection.[28] In Exodus, Yahweh reminds Moses how he bore Israel up 'on eagles' wings' to save the people from their enemies, and the same image is found in Deuteronomy.[29] In the New Testament, Jesus sets aside the grandeur and the predatory nature of the eagle to describe himself as a mother hen, longing to gather her chicks under her wings. This daringly domestic image seems appropriate somehow, for a leader who apparently chose a donkey rather than a horse for his moment of public triumph. Finally, the dove, an image of gentleness and a term of endearment in the Song of Songs, becomes in the New Testament one of the principal signs of the Holy Spirit.[30]

Despite the prohibition on 'graven images', sculptures of winged-creatures are described in relation to the ark of the covenant and the inner sanctuary of the first temple. According to Exodus, the ark was built according to a pattern laid down by God, and included a 'mercy seat' with two gold cherubim spreading their wings above it. These appear again in descriptions of Solomon's temple, where they stand in the inner sanctuary, their wings touching either wall and apparently covering the ceiling.[31] These are not birds, strictly-speaking, but angels, messengers of God. In an Irish context, we might well call them 'Otherworld beings in bird-form'. Their relatives, the seraphim of Isaiah's vision, have six wings, and in Ezekiel's vision the throne of God is surrounded by all kinds of extraordinary winged creatures.[32] One interpretation of the winged nature of gods and divine messengers is that the wings symbolise their ability to travel between worlds or between different levels of reality. It is as well to be wary of global explanations for religious symbols, but this one seems to make sense in many different contexts.

Birds were routinely used for sacrifices and ritual healings in Hebrew religion. The offering for the cleansing of a leper, for example, began with the sacrifice of a bird in an earthen vessel over running water. A second bird was then dipped alive into the blood of the first, together with a piece of cedar wood, a scarlet thread, and a bunch of hyssop. These were used to sprinkle the blood over the leper and the bird was then set free. The patient was to remain in quarantine for a set period before returning with an offering of lambs, oil and cereals; or if he could not afford these, pigeons and turtle-doves. These were still the poor-woman's offering after child-birth in the time of Jesus.[33]

Some birds were taboo and were not to be eaten. The unclean birds include eagles, vultures, ospreys, buzzards, kites, ravens, ostriches, 'nighthawks', sea gulls, hawks, owls, 'water hens', pelicans, cormorants, storks, herons and hoopoes. Peter was apparently still observing these dietary laws when he had his rooftop vision instructing him to set them aside.[34] The fact that the eagle could be an image of God as well as an 'unclean' bird, suggests that not all of these prohibitions were based simply on disgust, but that other factors might also have been involved, such as awe and dread. Many are predators and water birds with unusual habits or appearances. Others eat carrion and probably were regarded with distaste. Both Ezekiel and the author of Revelation envisage the fall of the wicked as a gruesome feast for the birds. The birds are not blamed however, indeed the prophet is instructed to invite them.[35]

Birds in the Bible have more religious associations than we tend to be aware of nowadays. Most of them come from the Hebrew Bible and from older parts of the tradition, though bird imagery continues in the New Testament, sometimes to powerful effect. In places, it is possible to sense some common ground with the Irish tradition, particularly where spiritual beings are concerned. No doubt some of this exists at a primal level, and some through continental imagery of angels. Ordinary birds however, do not seem to have attracted quite so many strange or supernatural associations in Israel. Indeed, their very ordinariness is often seen affectionately as a sign of God's care even for the least of creatures, so that swallows and sparrows nest in the Temple, birds roost in the great tree of the Kingdom, and every sparrow that falls is seen by God.[36] If there was bird prognostication we hear little about it, nor do we find people changing into birds, birds which speak or sing praises to God, or shamans or bird-souls, or poets in feather-costumes. These are from a different world.

POWER WITHOUT ILL

One of the interesting things about the story of Colum Cille and the exhausted crane, above, is that it remains a bird, nothing more, nothing less. This could be a simple story with no hidden meaning whatsoever, but there is just a chance that Adamnán is quietly making another point as well. There is some evidence from later texts and from the folk tradition, that cranes were generally disliked and regarded as birds of ill-omen. For example, three cranes from a certain *síd* mound were said to be a presage of disaster if seen by a warrior on his way into battle.[37] Crane meat was once loathsome to the Irish, according to Giraldus Cambrensis, and similar beliefs have been noted in the Scottish folk tradition. One of the prayers in *Carmina Gadelica* invokes protection against the malevolence of cranes and the spleen and envy of women, through the intercession, interestingly, of Colum Cille.[38] If traditions like these were current in the seventh century, then Adamnán might well be demonstrating how Colum Cille treated the bird kindly in spite of its sinister associations and came to no harm. The saint's reputation would thereby be enhanced, while at the same time releasing people from their fears and the bird from persecution.

A more direct condemnation of bird-lore is found in a protection prayer attributed to Colum Cille from the *Yellow Book of Lecan*:

> I adore not the voices of birds, nor sneezing nor lots in this world, nor a son, nor omens, nor women. My druid is Christ the Son of God.[39]

The objection here is probably not to birdsong, but to the ancient belief that it is possible to tell the future from the cries of birds. This is mentioned widely in the work of classical authors and in continental christian writings from the early medieval period.[40] Isidore of Seville is only one of those who condemn it, but the very fact that he does so indicates its persistence. The attribution of the saying to Colum Cille might indicate that parts of the Columban tradition had a particular antipathy towards this aspect of traditional bird-lore. Bird prognostication did not die out in medieval Ireland any more than it did in Spain: two texts in middle-Irish carefully instruct readers how to tell the future from the cries of ravens and wrens.[41]

Some poets write about birds with obvious delight (127–9), among
them the anonymous scribe who wrote the following bird poem in the
margin of the *Martyrology of Tallaght* in the early ninth century. He
begins none the less by reassuring his readers, and possibly himself, that
there is nothing at all sinister about birds. He is still susceptible to their
mystery, comparing them to a hidden army singing in the dark among
the trees. It is unclear whether he is thinking of a human army or the
'fairy host', but in either case he sees their influence as benign. He
imagines them singing the hours as in a well-ordered monastery, their
call and response like antiphonal singing. By welcoming the sun in the
depths of winter, the birds also celebrate the renewal of the source of life
and light, with all the religious overtones of that image and occasion:

> The birds of the world, power without ill
> [Come] to welcome the sun
> On January's nones, at the different hours
> The cry of the host from the dark wood.

The poem goes on to mark the passing of the seasons by describing the
activities of particular birds – swallows, cuckoos, wild geese. Somebody
at Tallaght was obviously a keen observer of nature and a lover of birds
and measured the year by their comings and goings, just as the body of
the *Martyrology* measures it by the feast-days of saints. The poem closes
with a scene from the end-time, in which birds sing like choirs of angels
around God's throne:

> Melodious music the birds perform
> To the king of heaven of the clouds
> Praising the radiant king
> Hark from afar the choir of the birds.[42]

Once again the distinction between angels and birds has become blurred,
and the bird-flocks of the Land of Promise find a place in christian
apocalyptic.

Chapter 7

Poetry of the Woods and Seasons

Early Irish nature poetry is one of the most accessible parts of the Celtic tradition, in the sense that it is still possible to read it without feeling too far removed from the cultural and historical landscape from which it sprang. It is also a form which is still vigorously alive today, unlike the sagas and the Lives of saints. Nature continues to be a source of inspiration for many modern Irish poets, the occasion or the mirror of powerful human experiences. Of course, poetry and religion have both changed enormously since medieval times. Nuala Ní Dhomnaill's view of nature is fiercely and deliberately post-christian. Seamus Heaney shows an ambivalence towards both nature and Christianity, but returns to them again and again.[1] Patrick Kavanagh's farmers in 'The Great Hunger' are perhaps the closest to the world of the primal imagination with their sudden moments of illumination. In the midst of a harsh unromantic existence, they nevertheless see, in certain kinds of light, God the Father in a tree, the Holy Spirit in the rising sap, and 'Christ will be the green leaves that will come, at Easter from the sealed and guarded tomb.'[2]

The focus is just as sharp, but the experience more elusive in John O'Donohue's 'After the Sea':

> As it leaves
> the sea inscribes
> the sand
> with a zen riddle
> written in Japanese
> characters of seaweed.
>
> Above the white selves
> of seagulls
> mesh in repetitions
> of desire.

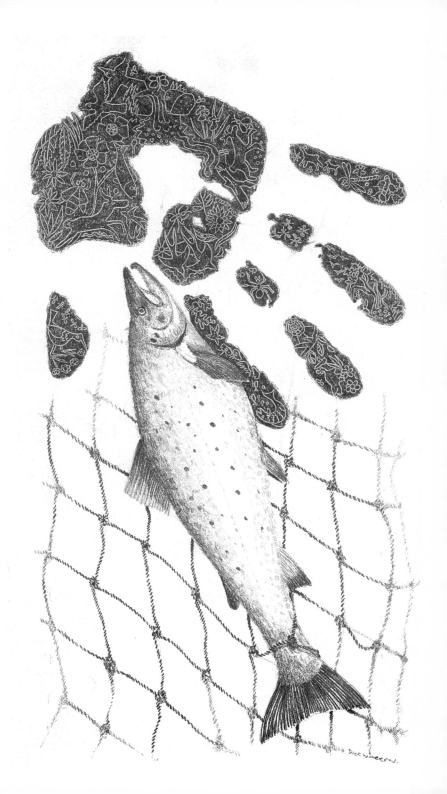

Here nature has become unreadable, its meaning hidden, while the birds of appetite criss-cross the infinity of the sky, which in the inner landscape is also the surface of the mind. Fittingly, the observer remains undisclosed. Where once there might have been angels, there are now scavengers. No easy theophany here. Only a vulnerable landscape and the irregular breaking of waves. This is none the less a religious poem, a sequel perhaps to Matthew Arnold's 'On Dover Beach' and a step beyond it as well. It is a poem for the end of the twentieth century, but one which inherits, in its pared-down simplicity, something of the asceticism of the Celtic monastic spirit, while its clarity and imagery also link it with the nature poetry of earlier times.

Early Irish nature poetry is usually anonymous and often survives only in fragments. Some of the authors would have been *filid* or professional poets. Others would have been in religious orders, but it would be a mistake to assume that these two groups were entirely separate from each other or that the work of the *filid* was always 'secular', while the work of the monks was 'religious'. Distinctions like these are questionable even now, but they are particularly questionable in medieval Ireland where the *filid* traditionally saw themselves as guardians of wisdom and knowledge, including sacred knowledge and knowledge of Otherworld traditions. Poetry was closely related to prophecy and many poets were also reputed to be seers. In some circumstances, their words were thought to have efficacious power, the belief that the satire of a poet could be fatal persisting into late medieval times.[3]

We know very little about how either the *filid* or the monastic poets prepared for work, but the author of *Cormac's Glossary* describes three of the traditional rituals of *filidecht* – the poetic art. They are all divination rituals. The first two involved non-christian sacrifices and were banned by Patrick, according to the *Glossary*. This certainly indicates clerical disapproval, but it is interesting that the ninth-century author describes them in the present tense – 'this is how it is done' – as if they were still being practised. The third ritual, known as *díchetal do chennaib* or 'extempore incantation', was apparently permitted because it did not involve 'offerings to demons.' The author accepts its efficacy as a matter of course: 'there is a revelation at once from the ends of the poet's fingers'.[4]

One late-medieval bard complained about a younger colleague who took to composing out-of-doors 'without a dark hut, without hardship' as if an earlier generation of poets had regarded these as somehow traditional and essential.[5] Some of the divination rituals had also involved periods of darkness and isolation. Even from these few glimpses, it is easy to see the traditional relationship between religion and *filidecht* in

medieval Ireland. One of its master practitioners was Finn, the mythical
poet, warrior and seer.

Summer time, season supreme
Splendid is colour then.
Blackbirds sing a full lay
If there be a slender shaft of day.

The dust-coloured cuckoo calls aloud:
Welcome splendid summer!
The bitterness of bad weather is past,
The boughs of the wood are a thicket.

Panic startles the heart of the deer,
The smooth sea runs apace –
Season when ocean sinks asleep,
Blossom covers the world.

Bees with puny strength carry
A goodly burden, the harvest of blossoms;
Up the mountain-side, kine take with them mud
The ant makes a rich meal.

The harp of the forest sounds music,
The sail gathers – perfect peace;
Colour has settled on every height,
Haze on every lake of full waters.

The corncrake, a strenuous bard, discourses,
The lofty cold waterfall sings
A welcome to the warm pool –
The talk of the rushes has come.

Light swallows dart aloft,
Loud melody encircles the hill,
The soft rich mast buds,
The stuttering quagmire prattles.

The peat bog is as the raven's coat
The loud cuckoo bids welcome,
The speckled fish leaps –
Strong is the bond of the swift warrior.

Man flourishes, the maiden buds

In her fair strong pride.
Perfect each forest from top to ground
Perfect each great stately plain.

Delightful is the season's splendour,
Rough winter has gone:
Every fruitful wood shines white,
A joyous peace is summer.

A flock of birds settles
In the midst of meadows,
The green field rustles
Wherein is a brawling white stream.

A wild longing is on you to race horses,
The ranked host is ranged around:
A bright shaft has been shot into the land,
So that the water-flag is gold beneath it.

A timorous, tiny, persistent little fellow
Sings at the top of his voice,
The lark sings clear tidings:
Surpassing summer-time of delicate hues.[6]

These are presented as the first words which Finn uttered after eating
the salmon of wisdom from Féc's pool on the river Boyne (69). To be
strictly accurate, he does not eat the fish, but only licks his fingers. His
master, a teacher of poetry, who had caught it, meant to eat it himself.
He sets Finn to guard it while it is roasting, but the boy touches it and
puts his fingers in his mouth. As a result, he receives the prodigious gifts
of poetry and prophetic insight for which he was to become famous. In
later stories, he uses a similar gesture, sticking his thumb under his
'knowledge tooth' in order to gain knowledge and insight about particular things.

In fact this poem, known in Irish as *Cétamon* – 'Mayday' – is much older
than the surrounding story and must have come originally from a different context. Scholars used to think that its archaic flavour was contrived
by the poet to make it seem like a genuine utterance of Finn, but James
Carney later identified it as a genuinely ancient metrical form, dating it to
around the year 600.[7] This would make it one of the oldest pieces of
vernacular poetry in Ireland. Carney concluded from this, and from the
lack of religious references in the poem, that early Irish nature poetry did
not originate in the monasteries as some people had thought, but was
already present in the repertoire of the professional poets.

To Carney, *Cétamon* is a praise-poem in the form of an extended riddle. He sees it as an allegorical anthem in honour of a visiting chief, while the birds represent various court poets singing his praises and receiving their rewards.[8] This is an ingenious interpretation, full of wit and humour, particularly in the characterisation of the bird-poets. The poem is treated independently of the surrounding story, and since there are no explicit references to Christianity, Carney concludes that it is not a 'religious' poem. He does not discuss the attitude of the poet to his or her work or the possibility that 'summer' might represent a divine figure rather than a human one.

Another commentator, Maria Tymoczko, sees the poem as the work of a poet-seer contemplating with his supernatural vision all the happenings of an eternal summer.[9] Like Finn, she suggests, the poet is using his mantic or divinatory skills to reveal the essential nature of summer to the assembled company. In some ways this is fair enough, but I wonder whether we really need to use such esoteric language when there is so much undiscovered depth in the everyday faculties of memory and imagination. Simply by naming, skilfully, the sights, sounds and emotions of a May morning, the poet acknowledges them and celebrates them, for anyone who will listen, divine or human. The fact that there are no pious fingerprints on *Cétamon* need not mean that it is an entirely 'secular' poem.

There are in fact a number of religious loose-ends in this poem. Firstly, there is the association with Finn – not original perhaps, but certainly considered appropriate by whoever placed the poem in its present context. Then there is the salmon of wisdom and the pool on the river Boyne, both of which contribute to an understanding of the poem as a miracle of Otherworld eloquence, a gift from a sacred source. There is also the fact that the poem is a celebration of Mayday, or Belteine. This was one of the old Celtic quarter days and was probably a religious festival in origin. There are also the Otherworld associations of birds, and the tradition of sacred landscape – trees, water, mountains, all of which are presented here in many forms. None of this adds up to a coherent religious explanation, but it does make it difficult to dismiss *Finn's poem on Mayday* as a purely secular poem.

SUMMER IS GONE

My tidings for you: the stag bells,
Winter snows, summer is gone.

Wind high and cold, low the sun,
Short his course, sea running high.

> Deep-red the bracken, its shape all gone –
> The wild goose has raised his wonted cry.
>
> Cold has caught the wings of the birds;
> Season of ice – these are my tidings.[10]

The end of summer and the onset of winter are announced in this mournful ninth-century poem which occurs as a gloss in the *Amra* or Eulogy of Colum Cille. Irish seasonal poetry could be just an attractive way of talking about the weather or of presenting a sequence of 'gnomes' or maxims on the same subject. Nature gnomes are common in Welsh and Anglo-Saxon poetry, according to Kenneth Jackson, who thought it possible that *My tidings for you* might have been influenced in some way by the gnomic tradition, but he also observed that Irish gnomes are usually in prose and rarely about nature. Some other explanation seemed called for.[11]

Jackson suggested tentatively that spring and autumn poems like this one, and like *Cétamon* above, might be derived ultimately from pre-christian seasonal carols. He noted a theory that continental poetry of this type might have its roots in pre-christian seasonal ceremonies. In parts of the continental folk tradition, ritual 'contests of summer and winter' mark the beginning of spring or the end of summer, and the suggestion is that these are survivals of the ceremonies at which the carols were sung. This is only a theory, and Jackson is rightly cautious about transferring it to Ireland, but he does draw attention to a tantalising reference to seasonal singing in the *Wasting Sickness of Cú Chulainn / Serglige Con Chulainn.*

The tale begins with a description of the Samain festival in Cú Chulainn's day: for three days before and after Samain, and on Samain day itself, there was 'nothing but meetings and games and amusements and entertainments and eating and feasting'. At this point, a glossator has added the words 'And from this are the laments of Samain throughout Ireland'. No one now knows for certain what these laments were, but the glossator, writing some time after the completion of the twelfth-century manuscript, takes it for granted that his or her contemporaries will understand. Jackson thought they might well be laments to bewail the passing of summer.[12]

Samain was associated with other deaths as well, including the death of Mongfinn, the 'fairy woman' or woman of supernatural power. 'Women and the common people' were still offering their prayers to this Otherworld woman in the eleventh century or later (31, 43). The festival of Lughnasad at the beginning of harvest, was also associated with meetings and games, and with the deaths of Otherworld women like Macha, Tailtiu and Carmun (27–31). It is possible that what we are seeing here are the remnants of a number of local cults, in which the deity dies in the autumn and is born again in spring. Cults like these, for male and female deities, were once widespread in the Middle-East, in Graeco-Roman religion, in northern Europe and beyond.[13] Some customs from the folk traditions of Scotland and Ireland may reflect similar beliefs. For example, the last sheaf of the harvest was often known as the 'granny' or 'hag' (*cailleach*) and this same word was used in the medieval tradition for all kinds of old and frightening Otherworld women, including the 'sovereignty' goddess in her loathsome aspect (32–3). Then at the beginning of February, at the festival of Bride or Brigit, it was the custom in the Hebrides to take a sheaf from the previous year's harvest, form it into a female figure, and carry it from house to house. This effigy was known as the Bride or little Bride. In some places, the older women of the townland would make her a cradle. There were similar customs in Ireland.[14]

There may of course be no connection between Otherworld women who die in the autumn and the folk-figure of Bride who is born in spring. Brigit was a pan-Celtic deity, worshipped throughout the Celtic-speaking areas of Europe. The Otherworld women who die in the autumn are much more local in character. Without the tantalising glimpse, from the Hebrides, of an old wheatsheaf transformed into a 'little Bride', we would have no grounds for connecting them at all. In fact the link could be due to a creative synthesis, by the folk tradition, of two quite separate myths. For the moment then, the question of seasonal deities remains unresolved, but Jackson's proposal that *My tidings for you* might have been derived from songs sung at seasonal ceremonies, remains a possibility.

He has another suggestion as well, namely that Irish seasonal poetry could have been an offshoot of the prophetic tradition. There was once, he suggests, an Old Irish genre of prophecy in which predictions about the weather were given in chant metre, and he invites us to compare *My tidings for you* with the *Prophecy of Néde* from the tenth-century *Colloquy of the Two Sages*:

> Good tidings
> Sea fruitful
> Strand overrun
> Woods smile
> Wooden blades flee
> Fruit-trees flourish
> Cornfields grow

> Bee-swarms are many
> A radiant world
> Happy peace
> Kindly summer ...
> Tidings good.[15]

The sequence of short images and phrases is indeed reminiscent of the winter poem from the *Amra*, as is the introductory reference to 'tidings'. Jackson suggests that the phrase 'My tidings for you' – *Scél lem duib* – is a conventional opening phrase for a prophetic poem, noting that a prophecy in *The battle of Magh Léana* opens with a similar phrase. *Finn's Poem on Mayday* and the *Prophecy of Néde* also have a phrase in common. *Síd subach sam* (joyous peace is summer) in *Cétamon*, becomes *síd subach, sam sogar* (joyous peace, kindly summer) in Jackson's translation of the *Prophecy of Néde*. Jackson concludes that even if the seasonal poems are not prophecies in themselves, they may have been strongly influenced by the tradition of prophetic chanting.[16] Of course, the Finn poem is considerably older than either the *Prophecy of Néde* or *My tidings for you*, so these cannot be examples of the actual prophecies which inspired the innovation. For seasonal poetry to be an outgrowth from the prophetic tradition, it would have to spring from an older generation of prophetic poetry, now lost.

While it is true that seasonal poems like *Cétamon* and *My tidings for you* contain no obvious 'religious' language or imagery, they do show a primal sense of kinship with nature and an awareness that the universe is governed by a power or powers on whom human beings depend for their happiness and survival (19). The growth and decay of vegetation, the strength or weakness of the sun, the presence or absence of natural produce, the friendliness or hostility of the elements, were all minutely observed and acknowledged.

THE SCRIBE IN THE WOODS

> A hedge of trees surrounds me
> A blackbird's lay sings to me
> Praise I will not hide.
> Above my lined booklet
> The trilling of the birds sings to me.
>
> In a grey mantle the cuckoo's beautiful chant
> Sings to me from the tops of the bushes
> Truly, may the Lord protect me –
> I write well under the green wood.[17]

This poem, known in English as *The Scribe in the Woods*, survives as a piece of marginalia in a Latin grammar book. It was probably written in Leinster some time during the ninth century, but found its way soon afterwards to the library of the Benedictines of St Gallen in what is now Switzerland. St Gallen traces its origins to St Gall (c. 550–645), an Irish monk who accompanied Columbanus on his missionary journeys.

The author of this poem has been much-mocked recently, accused of egocentricity and a scandalous lack of humility about his or her work. Presuming that this is a personal poem, there are indeed an unusual number of first-person references in it; scarcely a line passes without one; but unless the poem also had a strong sense of external reality, it would lose its rhythmic balance, and would in fact have nothing to say. The trees, the blackbird, the birdsong and the cuckoo have at least as much presence here as the personal pronouns. The poet experiences them as part of a harmonious reality, sheltering him or her on all sides and producing a feeling of personal well-being. Since the traditional Irish paradise was also imagined as a place of woods and birdsong then, imaginatively speaking, the poet is in heaven. No wonder he or she feels inspired.

THREE SHORT BIRD POEMS

The religious dimension of these poems is less obvious, but birds have so many sacred associations in early Irish literature that they deserve more than just a passing glance:

> The little bird has given a whistle from the tip of its clear yellow beak. He calls out over Loch Loígh, a blackbird from a yellow-heaped branch.[18]

Loch Loígh is also known as Belfast Loch, and some scholars have linked this poem to the monastery of Bangor nearby. There is no evidence either for or against this, or for Robin Flower's idea that the author was a hermit. In fact, the poem is completely anonymous and could equally well have been written by a lay person. It ended up, cut off from its original context, in an eleventh-century poetry manual whose purpose was to familiarise apprentice poets with different poetic metres. Kenneth Jackson dates it to the eighth or ninth century, but there seems to be some doubt about this.[19]

As for the subject-matter, the bird, the branch, the water's edge and the singing, all have mythological resonances in Irish literature. We are not told what kind of branch the bird is sitting on. Some translations call it 'yellow-tufted' which might describe a whin bush, if indeed birds sing among such dense thorns. Most willows could be described as yellow in the spring, as could the poets' sacred tree, the hazel with its mass of yellow catkins.

Many of the same elements are present in the poem known in English as *The Blackbird on the Willow*. This also served as a text-book example for apprentice poets and is without context or author. It probably dates from the ninth century:

> The bird which calls from the willow: beautiful its little beak with its clear note: musical yellow bill of a jet-black hardy bird: lively the tune that is played, the blackbird's call.[20]

Here again we have the bird, the music and an unidentified tree. No water is mentioned, but willows love to grow beside lakes and streams.

A third blackbird poem, this time from the twelfth or thirteenth century, appears in the margin of the manuscript known as the *Lebor Brecc*, literally, the 'Speckled Book':

> Ah blackbird, you are satisfied, where your nest is in the bush. Hermit that rings no bell, sweet, soft, peaceful is your note.[21]

The comparison between the blackbird and the hermit is probably based on their common woodland habitat, rather than any shared musical talent. Bells in early Christian Ireland were struck rather than rung, and may have been intended to ward off evil spirits. This is part of their traditional function in many religions, and we can identify at least one Irish example in 'Brigit's gapling', the bell which Patrick uses against the demonic black birds in the *Tripartite Life* version of the Croagh Patrick story.[22] The present poet finds nothing sinister about birds, even black ones, and clearly enjoys the idea of a hermit without a bell. The blackbird's song seems to represent a deliberate contrast – sweet, soft, and peaceful.

This blackbird is at ease with the world in a way which the hermit is not. In particular, it is at ease with the woods and the wild places which were the hermit's *díseart*, not in the sense of a refuge from the world's cares, but as a spiritual battle-ground, like the desert hermitages of Egypt. There is no reason to think that this poem was written by a hermit. In subject matter as well as in date, it is closer to the Finn Cycle, with its enthusiasm for the outdoor life, and to traditions about Suibne the 'wild man' with his clear ambivalence towards all things ecclesiastical. In a very similar passage from *The Frenzy of Suibne / Buile Suibne*, the 'wild man' reflects that he prefers to hear the cuckoos singing on the banks of the Bann than the 'grig-graige' of the monastery bell.[23]

There is nothing overtly religious about these blackbird poems. The birds may simply be blackbirds, in and for themselves, but the poems have an immediacy and a particularity (and a metrical discipline) which anticipates the later tradition of Japanese nature poetry. Nature and the seasons are essential ingredients in haiku-writing, as well as in Japanese religion. One of the greatest haiku writers, Matsuo Basho, is known to have practised Zen meditation. As for the Irish poems, it would be impossible to prove that their authors were similarly motivated, that they practised some kind of 'spiritual exercises' in preparation for their work, or that they were deliberately evoking the mystical connotations of birds and birdsong. Their poems can certainly be read as examples of what would later be called 'the sacrament of the present moment', but whether this is in the text, or in the mind of the reader, is an open question.

THE IVIED TREE-TOP

My little hut in Tuaim Inbhir, a mansion would not be more delightful, with its stars in due order, with its sun, with its moon.

It was Gobán that made it (that its tale may be told you); my beloved God of heaven, was the thatcher who has thatched it.

A house in which rain does not fall, a place in which spear-points are not feared, as open as if in a garden without a fence around it.[24]

Various explanations have been offered for this riddling poem. What sort of place is this? Is it a hermit's cell? Murphy suggests 'oratory' instead of 'hut' in the first line. It would certainly seem to be some sort of little room, but it appears to be open to the sky – to the stars, the sun and the moon. Is it perhaps a tree-house, thatched with a canopy of leaves? The 'little hut' reminds us of the huts of Manchán and Marbhán and of the wooden church which Gobán is said to have built for Moling with wood from the Yew of Ross (90, 132–5). But why is it 'thatched' by God and open to the sky?

A closer look at the manuscript provides a clue. The poem was probably written during the ninth century, but at some stage a glossator has added the headings 'Suibne Geilt' and 'The ivied tree-top', as if he recognised it as part of Suibne tradition. Suibne (later known as Suibhne or Sweeney) is the main character in *The Frenzy of Suibne*. This was written several centuries after *The ivied tree-top*, but is known to be based on earlier traditions.[25] Suibne enters the tale as king of the small north-eastern kingdom of Dál nAraide. The year is 637, and he hears that St Ronán, uninvited, is marking out a church in his territory. Enraged, he rushes to attack him, throws his psalter into the water and generally abuses him. Ronán responds by cursing his assailant, and soon after, during the battle of Magh Rath, Suibne loses his mind and panics, rising up into the air like a bird, and fleeing. He even grows feathers. He spends several years like this, hiding in trees and glens and on lonely mountain-sides, pursued by his family and by supernatural terrors, till he comes at last to the well by Moling's church. Moling befriends him there, and finds that the 'wild man' has become a 'saintly madman', sharp-witted and pro-phetic, but no submissive penitent. The man who preferred birdsong to church bells still prefers real leaves to the leaves of psalters, and would rather be leaping through the woods than going to mass.[26]

Throughout *The Frenzy of Suibne*, ivy-covered trees are among Suibne's favourite hide-outs:

A proud ivy bush which grows through a twisted tree
If I were right on its summit, I would fear to come out.

A little later, we find the place-name Tuath Inbhir, similar in sound, if not in meaning, to Tuaim Inbhir.[27] It is easy to see why the glossator assigned *The ivied tree-top* to the Suibne tradition. Trees are often Suibne's equivalent of the hermit's hut or oratory, and I would guess that the poem describes a tree or a tree-house rather than any kind of ecclesiastical building.

One complicating factor is the reference to Gobán. Gobán Saor – Gobán the wright – was a legendary builder of churches. He may also have been a christianised version of Gobniu, the divine smith or crafts-man of the *Tuatha Dé Danann*. His presence in this poem has been explained in various ways. The most convincing is perhaps James Carney's suggestion that in this context *gobán* is not a proper noun at all, but means simply an artisan, a master craftsman. He can then be under-stood either as an anonymous builder or, as Carney suggests, as the divine craftsman who also made the roof and the tree itself.[28] The Gobán reference could also be the result of genuine confusion between Suibne and Moling since their two traditions are closely related.

If the 'oratory' is a tree, it is also a place of safety, giving shelter from the rain and concealment from enemies. It functions as a sort of sanctu-ary, in rather the same way as a medieval church. We lack the evidence to know whether this was in fact a traditional function of sacred trees in Ireland, but Suibne hides in trees all over the country and feels safe nowhere else. This could be for purely practical reasons, were it not for the fact that they are so often designated as sacred trees – *bileda*. In a different part of the Suibne tradition, a crowd of spectators watch the battle from the top of a tree. Again, this is not just any tree but *an bile buada* – the tree of victories – which is mentioned elsewhere as a tree on the way to the Land of Promise (95). Here it is on the edge of the battle-field, and seems to be regarded as in some way neutral territory. Suibne makes for it immediately during his first panic attack, but the people scream at him and push him back into the fray, as if the tree were no place for a combatant. Outside the Suibne tradition, Derg Corra climbs a tree to escape from Finn (87), who makes no attempt to injure him when he finds him there.

For whatever reason, the tree-sanctuary at Tuaim Inbhir is 'a place where rain does not fall, where spear-points are not feared.' There is a sense of relief here: no more exposure to the elements, no more fear of violence. While other nature poems concentrate exclusively on the delights of the summer woods *The ivied tree-top* hints at a history of terror. This gives added poignancy to the expressions of delight and tenderness – 'my little hut', 'my beloved God of heaven' – and to the celebration of a sense of cosmic order – 'with its stars as ordained, with its sun, with its moon'. As for the openness of the garden, Suibne experiences imprisonment of mind and body in the later epic, and could well be imagined enjoying a lack of fences if he were in the tree-top looking out. But we can also imagine him at a distance from the tree, looking towards it. Now the lack of fences becomes even more welcome. The tree is seen as a refuge without conditions, a sanctuary without an enclosure. Anyone can find shelter in it, even someone as marginalised as Suibne. With its tree and its garden, Tuaim Inbhir is a paradise regained.

MANCHÁN'S WISH

Little is known about the historical St Manchán who died in the mid-seventh century. The remains of his monastery at Lemanaghan can still be visited, some fifteen miles east of the more extensive and prestigious ruins of the abbey of Clonmacnoise. At Lemanaghan there is a tiny oratory, a holy well, and a rock associated with a female figure called Mella. St Mella is said to have been Manchán's mother.

As for the poem, it is not by Manchán himself, but by an anonymous tenth-century poet imagining the sort of ideal monastic community for which Manchán might have prayed. Nature encloses the monastery, but it is not peripheral to it, in the sense of incidental or merely decorative. It is an essential part of Manchán's wish, occupying nearly half the poem. The monastic buildings are unpretentious, the ecclesiastical fur-nishings simple. For the rest, the poet focuses almost entirely on nature, beginning with the lark at the door of Manchán's hut:

I wish, O Son of the living God, O ancient eternal King, for a hidden hut in the wilderness, that it may be my dwelling.

An all-grey lithe little lark to be by its side, a clear pool to wash away sins through the grace of the Holy Spirit.

Quite near, a beautiful wood around it on every side, to nurse many-voiced birds, hiding it with its shelter.

A southern aspect for warmth, a little brook across the floor, a choice land with many gracious gifts such as be good for every plant.

A few men of sense – we will tell their number – humble and obedient to pray to the King: –

Four times three, three times four, fit for every need, twice six in the church, both north and south.

Six pairs besides myself, praying for ever to the King who makes the sun shine.

A pleasant church and with the linen altar-cloth, a dwelling for God from heaven; then, a shining candle above the pure white Scriptures.

One house for all to go to for the care of the body, without ribaldry, without boasting [?] without thought of evil.

This is the husbandry I would take, I would choose and will not hide it: fragrant leek, hens, salmon, trout, bees.

Raiment and food enough for me from the King of fair fame, and I to be sitting for a while praying to God in every place.[29]

The church with its linen, its candles and its 'holy white scriptures' does not occupy a particularly prominent position in the poem or receive any special emphasis. Its uncluttered interior, without gold or silver, vestments or reliquaries would have appeal for those who like their spirituality simple, then as now. It takes its place quietly in the midst of the woods, without rivalry or fuss. It is a place of prayer, but only one among many in the surrounding area. Meanwhile, the 'King of fair fame' provides for body and soul through nature, which is sometimes explicitly sacramental, the clear pool, for example. It will be remembered that in other contexts the wilderness is often a mysterious place, where people find their destiny in encounters with Otherworld beings. *Manchán's Wish* probably owes something to the christian tradition of 'Desert spirituality' and the hermit life, but it is also like a primal *temenos* or sacred space.

MARBHÁN'S HERMITAGE

We turn now to the famous dialogue of Marbhán and Guaire, in which Marbhán the hermit explains to his brother Guaire, king of Connacht, why he has chosen to live in the woods rather than at court, where Guaire thinks he would be more comfortable. Like *Manchán's Wish* this poem was written during the tenth century, but set in the seventh. Guaire's part is minimal. He appears only to ask a question at the beginning and to comment on Marbhán's answer at the end. The rest of the poem is Marbhán's eulogy on the hermit life:

> I have a shieling in the wood, none knows it but my God. An ash tree on the hither side, a hazel bush beyond, a huge old tree encompasses it.
>
> Two heath-clad doorposts for support and a lintel of honeysuckle. The forest around its narrowness sheds its mast upon fat swine.
>
> The size of my shieling tiny, but not too tiny, many are its familiar paths. From its gable a sweet strain sings, a she-bird in her cloak of the ousel's hue.
>
> The stags of Oakridge leap into the river of clear banks. Thence red Roiny can be seen, glorious Muckraw and Moinmoy.
>
> A hiding mane of grey-barked yew supports the sky. Beautiful spot! The large green of an oak, fronting the storm.
>
> A tree of apples – great its bounty! Like a hostel, vast! A pretty bush, thick as a fist, of tiny hazel nuts. A green mass of branches.
>
> A choice pure spring and princely water to drink. There spring watercresses, yew berries, ivy bushes thick as a man.
>
> Around it, tame swine lie down. Goats, pigs, wild swine, grazing deer, a badger's brood.
>
> A peaceful troop, a heavy host of denizens of the soil, a-trysting at my house. To meet them foxes come. How delightful!
>
> Fairest princes come to my house, a ready gathering. Pure water, perennial bushes, salmon, trout.
>
> A bush of rowan, black sloes, dusky blackthorns, plenty of food, acorns, pure berries, bare flags.
>
> A clutch of eggs, honey, delicious mast, God has sent it. Sweet apples, red whortleberries and blaeberries.

Ale with herbs, a dish of strawberries of good taste and colour, haws, berries of the juniper, sloes, nuts.

A cup with mead of hazelnut, bluebells, quick-growing rushes, dun oaklets, manes of briar, goodly sweet tangle.

When brilliant summer-time spreads its coloured mantle, sweet-tasting fragrance, pignuts, wild marjoram, green leeks, verdant pureness.

The music of the bright red-breasted men, a lovely movement. The strain of the thrush, familiar cuckoos above my house.

Swarms of bees and chafers, the little musicians of the world, a gentle chorus. Wild geese and ducks, shortly before summer's end. The music of the dark torrent.

An active songster, a lively wren, from the hazel bough. Beautiful hooded birds, woodpeckers, a vast multitude.

Fair white birds come, herons, seagulls, the cuckoo sings between – no mournful music. Dun heathpoults out of the russet heather.

The lowing of heifers in summer, brightest of seasons. Not bitter, toilsome over the fertile plain, delightful, smooth.

The voice of the wind against the branchy wood, upon the deep-blue sky. Falls of the river, the note of the swan, delicious music.

The bravest band make cheer to me, who have not been hired. In the eyes of Christ the ever-young, I am no worse off than you are.

Though you rejoice in your own pleasures, greater than any wealth, I am grateful for what is given me from my good Christ.

Without an hour of fighting, without the din of strife in my house, grateful to the prince who gives every good to me in my shieling.[30]

The main aim of this long exuberant poem seems to be to show the abundance, indeed the luxury of nature, provided freely by God to those who serve him. There are all kinds of wild foods – apples, cresses, salmon, trout, eggs, honey, strawberries, sloes, nuts, wild marjoram, leeks. The hermitage is surrounded by trees, many of which have sacred or Otherworld associations – ash, hazel, yew, oak, apple (§§1, 5, 6, 7). Like many religious foundations, Marbhán's hermitage is protected by a *bile* – 'a huge old tree' (§1) – which was also the traditional sign of a king's house; and the royal comparison continues with the wild creatures being presented as if they were an entourage of warriors and princes (§8–10). Marbhán also has musicians: birds, insects, lowing cattle, tumbling water, the wind in the trees (§16–21). While Guaire must pay for his music, the hermit gets it for free (§22). Marbhán's life is presented as supremely blessed. He lives in what amounts to an earthly paradise and enjoys all the benefits which were traditionally associated with good kingship – peace, harmony, fruitfulness. These were traditional signs of a good relationship with the Otherworld, at one time through the 'sovereignty goddess'. Here, the equivalent relationship is with the christian God (§§1, 12) and with Christ the generous prince (§§22–24) who indulges his people with an amazing cornucopia of delights. This is not a deity who has to be begged and bullied into bestowing favours or one who rejoices in tears and austerities.[31] Marbhán's God is an intensely creative ingenious God, a God of fertility as well as salvation. As a member of Christ's court, the hermit feels at least as well-off as Guaire the king – for less effort, less expense, and no military duties. In the end, his brother envies him:

> I would give my glorious kingship with the share of my father's heritage – to the hour of my death I would forfeit it, to be in your company, my Marbhán.

Somewhere in the background to this poem are various biblical invitations to live as simply as possible, trusting in the providence of God. In the sermon on the mount for example, Jesus tells his disciples to consider God's care for the birds and the wild flowers and to live as they do, taking no thought for the morrow. This verse is quoted by St Athanasius in his fourth-century *Life of Anthony*, a text which the author may have known.[32] He or she would certainly have heard the saying of Jesus that it is easier for a camel to pass through the eye of a needle than for a rich man to enter the kingdom of God, and that anyone who leaves home and family for the sake of the kingdom of God, will receive at least as much companionship in the present time, and in the age to come, eternal life.[33]

Marbhán could have been intended to illustrate the fulfilment of this promise; but he also relates to Irish traditions about the sacramentality of nature. The culture of the court distances Guaire from God, but Marbhán's hermitage is almost a return to Eden. The poem has been described as 'disconcertingly unrealistic' and, of course, it is.[34] There is no mud, no rain, no winter winds. But it is possible that Marbhán's hermitage is not intended to be realistic, any more than say, first-Isaiah's vision of paradise, where the wolf dwells with the lamb and the leopard lies down with the kid.[35] There may even be an echo of this passage in the 'peaceful troop' (§9) described in Jackson's translation as 'the grave host of the countryside', who assemble at Marbhán's door. In some ways, the hermitage can be seen as a rural equivalent of the New Jerusalem. The image of heaven as a great city would have been almost meaningless in medieval Ireland, with its small settlements separated by expanses of countryside. The paradise grove has a similar symbolic value.

It might be observed that Marbhán's grove is a private paradise. He has no human companions at all. Individual hopes and experiences have already been the subject of other poems in this chapter, but the individualism of Marbhán's hermitage is intense – particularly in his personal access to the horn of plenty which gives the poem an almost epicurean feel. I would guess that this poem was conceived of first and foremost as a celebration of nature's bounties. The prodigality of the Creator is also an important theme, as is the argument that the religious life is preferable to the life of kings. But this is not a serious treatise on the hermit life, though the author was familiar with its basic principles.

ANGELS ON EVERY LEAF

The oakwoods of Derry seem to have been particularly important to the later Columban tradition (91). Sometimes they are presented as meeting places of heaven and earth where one might almost hear the beating of angels' wings overhead:

> ... It is for this I love Derry
> For its smoothness, for its purity,
> And for its crowd of white angels
> From one end to another.

> It is for this I love Derry
> For its smoothness, for its purity,
> All full of angels
> Is every leaf on the oaks of Derry.

> My Derry, my little oak grove
> My dwelling and my little cell,
> O living God who is in heaven above
> Woe to him who violates it.[36]

This poem was placed in the mouth of Colum Cille himself, by an anonymous poet of the twelfth century. It has many variants, all based on the same idea, which obviously had a strong appeal. There is a similar poem about a yew:

This is the yew of the saints
Where they used to come with me together
Ten hundred angels were there
Above our heads, side close to side.[37]

This one comes from the sixteenth-century *Life of Colum Cille*, a text which contains many earlier traditions. It is quite in keeping with earlier Columban tree poems, notably with the one in which the assembly gathers outside Colum's church, by a 'tall bright glistening yew' (84–5).

Chapter 8

Fire and the Sun

Some five thousand years ago, a group of immigrant farmers settled in the Boyne valley. They are known today simply as the passage-grave builders after the distinctive houses which they made for their dead. The best known of these are at Knowth, Dowth and Newgrange near the present-day village of Slane. Newgrange has one narrow entrance to the south-east. Behind the kerb-stone decorated with spiral patterns, a narrow passage leads to the inner chamber and to three small anterooms containing the basins in which the ashes of the dead were placed. For fifty-one weeks of the year the chamber is in total darkness, but on the morning of the winter solstice the first rays of the rising sun travel slowly up the passage illuminating the place of the dead.[1]

It is an event to stir the imagination, a carefully-staged drama whose meaning can only be guessed at. Was it seen as a divine visitation to the spirits of the ancestors? In ancient Egypt, the sun-god was believed to conduct the souls of the élite to the other world.[2] Was Newgrange designed for a similar purpose? Was it a weather-dependent oracle for the year ahead? The phenomenon varies from year to year depending on the amount of cloud-cover and this could have been taken as a sign of divine favour or disfavour. Was it a piece of cosmic match-making for the begetting of new life in the belly of the earth? The timing of the event must surely be significant: just as the sun seems poised for extinction, it halts and draws back, so that the solstice can be seen as a moment of salvation, a victory of light and life and warmth over darkness and death. When the sun rose again on that dark morning at the turn of the year, did the dead also rise? Newgrange is a particularly ancient example of the link between nature and religion in Ireland. It shows beyond doubt that the sun – and fires for the cremation of the dead – had a place in Irish primal religion from earliest times. It also bears witness to the continuing power of the primal imagination. Present-day visitors still fall quiet in the darkness of the chamber and catch their breath as the light approaches,

even if what most of them see is only a reconstruction.

There are obvious differences between the small fire in the hearth and the great fire in the heavens, but sun and fire are treated together in this chapter, simply because it is so difficult to keep them apart. This is particularly clear when it comes to imagery and descriptive language. Words like 'bright', 'radiant', 'shining', 'flaming', 'sparkling', are common to both. It follows that when a person or object is described in terms like these (and such descriptions are common) it is difficult to know whether the imagery is of fire or the sun or both.

In general, the present work avoids a detailed discussion of secondary sources, but 'sun worship' in early Irish religion has given rise to a substantial body of literature whose influence is still very much with us. It has proved difficult to illustrate the various points of view from the medieval sources. My solution has been to be to describe two of the main theories briefly, leaving aside arguments which can only be debated by experts in Indo-European mythology, etymology and folklore, but with close reference to what can and can not be discovered from the medieval texts. This results in a necessarily limited view of the work of some major Celtic scholars, but it also raises some interesting questions. The quest for Celtic solar deities continues today, wisely or unwisely, and the texts in this chapter can only be a small part of the evidence. Their most obvious value however, is the way in which they demonstrate the continuing importance of fire and the sun in the faith experience of early Irish Christians.

PATRICK'S SUN EXPERIENCE

As a young man, Patrick seems to have had a mystical experience in which the sun mediated a sense of salvation for him. He describes a terrifying dream in which Satan fell on him like a huge rock, pinning him to the ground:

> It came to me, into my mind, that I should call out 'Helias'. And at that moment, I saw the sun rise in the heavens; and while I was crying out 'Helias' with all my might, behold the splendour of the sun fell on me, and at once removed the weight from me. And I believe I was aided by Christ my Lord, and his Spirit was then crying out for me.[3]

One of the difficulties with this passage is how to interpret the word 'Helias'. One reading is that Patrick is calling on Elias (Elijah), though exactly why he should be doing this is unclear. Perhaps he looked on the prophet as a kind of protector or patron saint. Perhaps he identified with his experience of God on the mountain, or with his sense of being alone among unbelievers.[4] It is interesting that one of the favourite stories about Patrick in later times would be one which presents him contending with the druids of Tara in a way which is reminiscent of Elijah's contest with the prophets of Baal (146).

Elijah has a number of associations with fire. Fire falls from heaven during his contest with the prophets, and at the end of his life he is taken up to heaven in a fiery chariot, like the chariot of Ezekiel's vision, or indeed the chariot of the sun.[5] Patrick could be telling us that in his half-waking half-dreaming state, he saw the rising sun as the chariot of Elijah, coming to rescue him. Elijah was also the traditional forerunner of the Messiah, and there could be a hint here that Patrick was prepared to see the sun as the forerunner of Christ and 'sun worship' as the forerunner of the Gospel, but if so, this did not prevent him from condemning 'sun worship' in the strongest possible terms only a few paragraphs later.

An alternative suggestion is that Patrick is not calling on Elijah, but on the sun, under its Greek name, Helios. At first sight, this might seem perilously close to 'sun worship'. Certainly it would ascribe some kind of spiritual power to the sun. Also, the reference would have been completely lost on his Irish converts, few of whom would ever have encountered Greek, except perhaps in the Kyrie. This problem is lessened by the fact that the *Confession* does not seem to be addressed to them, but to certain 'brethren', perhaps his fellow-clergy abroad, whom Patrick clearly felt to be far more learned than himself.[6] It is also questionable how much Greek Patrick would have known. His Latin is limited, and he constantly apologises for his lack of education. From another point of view however, this actually enhances the miracle – that he should call for help in a language which he barely knew, but which would have been considered highly appropriate for the voice of the in-dwelling Holy Spirit.

But if it was unclear why Patrick should call for Elijah, it is even less clear why he should call for the sun. The word 'Helias' simply comes into his mind, and as the sunlight falls on him he has a profound experience of liberation. It is difficult to say whether he believes himself to have been saved by the inner voice of the Spirit crying out, or by 'the splendour of the sun'. Ultimately, he has no doubt that he was aided by Christ, but is Christ in the voice or in the sun? Patrick seems unable, or unwilling, to distinguish between the inner world of the voice, the outer world of the sun and the in-between world of the dream. For a moment, all three are connected. It seems that this experience has emerged, but only just, from an older Celtic experience of the sacramental universe (18–19). The young slave who found the presence of God in the woods and on the mountain seems to have found it in at least one memorable sunrise as well.[7]

He returns to the subject later in the *Confession*, in a passage on the resurrection which he also sees as a kind of sun-experience:

> Without any doubt, we shall rise in that day in the brightness of the sun, that is in the glory of Jesus Christ, our Redeemer, as 'sons of the living God,' and 'joint-heirs with Christ,' ... For that sun which we behold, at God's command, rises daily for us – but it shall never reign, nor shall its splendour continue; but all even that worship it, miserable beings, shall wretchedly come to punishment. But we who believe in the true sun, Jesus Christ, will never perish; neither shall he 'who does his will,' but 'shall continue for ever' – as Christ continues for ever...[8]

It seems that Patrick is uncomfortable here, picking his way awkwardly between theology, experience and the 'sun worship' which he clearly believed to be a contemporary reality. The passage is packed with biblical allusions, including no doubt a reference to the famous Easter hymn from Ephesians – 'Awake sleeper, rise from the dead and Christ will shine on you.' [9] He may also be drawing on his own experience of rising 'in the brightness of the sun'. But he moves immediately into a strong condemnation of 'sun worship', as if anxious not to be misunderstood. But in the opening lines, before he feels the need to explain himself, sun metaphors of Christ are still the ones which come naturally to his mind.

Preaching about Christ the true sun persisted down the centuries. One Old Irish litany begins with the words: 'O holy Jesus, O gentle friend, O morning star, O mid-day sun adorned, O brilliant flame of the righteous ... O Fountain ever-new.'[10] It quickly moves on to more theological epithets, but the sun and fire are there at the beginning, like part of the a-b-c of prayer. Centuries later, the *Life of Patrick* from the *Book of Lismore* begins with the famous prophecy of Isaiah – 'The people who walked in darkness have seen a great light'.[11] This prophecy has a historical context, says the author, but it is also an image for what happened among the gentiles, by which he means the pre-christian peoples of Ireland, when the true sun rose upon them, even Jesus, the Sun of righteousness – *Grian na firinne* – who is 'the splendour, the flame, the precious stone and the shining lamp.'

SOLOMON'S TEMPLE

When Solomon's Temple was built during the tenth century BC, it was constructed in such a way that on the morning of the spring and autumn equinoxes the first rays of the rising sun would enter through the east gate and cross through the various courtyards into the sanctuary itself. This was seen as a theophany, not of a 'sun god' but of Yahweh himself. In the autumn, this coincided with the festival of Sukkoth or 'Tabernacles' when people would assemble in the dark, before dawn, to witness the triumphal entry of their God and his enthronement as king of the nations.[12]

> Open to me the gates of righteousness
> That I may enter through them and give thanks to God.
> This is the gate of Yahweh,
> The righteous shall enter through it ...
> This is the day which Yahweh has made
> Let us rejoice and be glad in it ...
> Blessed be he who enters in the name of Yahweh.
> We bless you from the house of Yahweh ...
> El is Yahweh and he has given us light.
> Bind the festal procession with branches
> up to the horns of the altar.[13]

In post-exilic times, these lines were proper to the feast. The 'gates of righteousness' were probably the east gate, through which the royal procession would enter. The refrain of Psalm 24 – 'Lift up your heads, O you gates' – is traditionally connected with the same occasion.[14]

The sun symbolism of Yahweh was probably inherited or borrowed from semitic primal religion and from Israel's immediate neighbours. In pre-Davidic times, Jerusalem seems to have been a jebusite shrine, sacred to a deity called Elyon – 'the Most High' – who may well have been a solar deity.[15] The solar orientation of Solomon's Temple was probably copied from canaanite and phoenician architecture, the temple of Melcarth in Tyre being a likely model.[16] Even the jewish festival of Matzoth or 'unleavened bread' was originally a canaanite agricultural festival which took place around the time of the spring equinox. It celebrated the death and resurrection of the deity who gave life to the grain, the resurrection being symbolised by the first rays of the rising sun.[17]

From time to time, a religious leader would emerge who felt that the sun-symbolism of Yahweh had degenerated into idolatry or been transferred to other gods. King Josiah is said to have 'removed the horses that the kings of Judah had dedicated to the sun at the entrance to the house of the Lord', and 'burned the chariots of the sun with fire.'[18] From his exile in Babylon, Ezekiel has a vision in which he sees 'about twenty-five men with their backs to the temple of the Lord, worshipping the sun towards the east.'[19] After the exile, the east gate of the temple was permanently closed, presumably to remove the solar element from the spring and autumn festivals. The Mishna describes how, during the Sukkoth liturgy, the priests now deliberately faced west, into the sanctuary, away from the rising sun.[20]

But sun-fire imagery remained in people's minds, in visionary experience and in poetic language. Sun-worship may have been an abomination to Ezekiel, but like Patrick, his own religious experience was full of sun-fire imagery. As he sits by the river Chebar in Babylon, he has a vision of a storm cloud full of brightness, and within it four shining wheels above which stands a fiery figure, 'like bronze encased in fire.'[21] To Ezekiel, this is not a 'sun god' in his chariot, but 'the appearance of the likeness of the glory of the Lord' – in other words, the fire and the brightness are at several removes from the inner nature of God, who always remains invisible. For all that, his vision of the restoration draws heavily on the sun symbolism of the Sukkoth liturgy:

> Afterwards he brought me to the gate facing east. And behold the glory of the God of Israel came from the east; and the sound of his coming was like the sound of many waters; and the earth shone with his glory ... and I fell upon my face. As the glory of the Lord entered the temple by the gate facing east, the Spirit lifted me up, and brought me into the inner court; and behold the glory of the Lord filled the temple.[22]

Prayers for Yahweh to 'shine' upon his people are found frequently in the Psalms and again in the Aaronic blessing: 'The Lord bless you and keep you, the Lord make his face to shine upon you'.[23] 'The Lord God is a sun and a shield', says one of the psalmists, and the prophet Habakkuk evokes the power of God in the traditional imagery of sunrise over the holy mountain:

> God came from Teman, and the Holy One from Mount Paran. His glory covered the heavens ... his brightness was like the light, rays flashed from his hand.[24]

Solar imagery was sometimes transferred to the king, as in the 'last words of David':

> When one rules justly over the people, ruling in the fear of God, he dawns on them like the morning light, like the sun shining forth on a cloudless morning.[25]

Since the Davidic king was also 'the anointed one', the Messiah of the future was sometimes described in very similar terms,[26] and many New Testament writers draw on solar imagery when speaking about Jesus. Zechariah looks forward to him as 'the dawn from on high'.[27] Matthew's Gospel quotes the text from Isaiah 'the people who walked in darkness have seen a great light', and describes Jesus as the 'light of the world' whose face shines like the sun on the mountain of Transfiguration.[28] In John's Gospel he is the 'light of life', and in Acts the risen Christ appears to Paul as a blinding light from heaven.[29] Again, this is the language of poetry and visionary experience, but its message is plain: just as the sun was formerly the sign of God's life-giving presence in the temple, so now the divine radiance is present to the world in the risen Christ. As for fire, it is an enduring symbol of the Holy Spirit.

This brief review of biblical material illustrates two important points. Firstly, the sun can be a sacramental symbol for a deity who is no longer simply a 'sun god'. Secondly, sun symbolism can be concerned with other aspects of nature as well, for example, fertility (Sukkoth and the feast of unleavened bread were both harvest festivals) but it also has a non-material dimension. This is particularly clear in the book of Amos, where the prophet warns that the 'day of Yahweh' (the Sukkoth festival) will bring darkness and not light, because there is so much injustice and oppression in the land.[30]

It is sometimes assumed that the passage-grave builders worshipped the sun in itself, as part of an ancestral or fertility cult, but there is no reason to think that the Hebrews were the first ancient people to experience the sacramentality of the sun as part of a more integrated worldview. Similarly, with Patrick's non-christian contemporaries, we may assume that sun symbolism was part of their worship, but we have no independent way of judging their theology. Patrick clearly found it objectionable, but this could have been the result of his own doctrinal prejudices. On the other hand, his first-hand experience of Irish primal religion might have disturbed him for other reasons as well. There seem to have been no lack of willing converts.

PATRICK AND THE DRUIDS

After the *Confession*, we hear next to nothing about 'sun worship' from the Irish medieval tradition, but we do begin to hear a great deal about sacred fire. Muirchú, one of Patrick's first hagiographers, tells the story of a confrontation between Patrick and Loegaire, king of Tara. There are a large number of fire references, including a particularly early mention of the lighting of Paschal fires at the Easter vigil.[31] Patrick sets out to provoke Loegaire by celebrating Easter within sight of Tara. He and his companions leave their boat at the mouth of the Boyne and trek upstream as far as 'the graves of Fíacc's men', that is, the area of the tumuli around Slane including Newgrange. They pitch their tent and prepare for the Easter vigil. Meanwhile a 'feast of pagan worship' is being held at Tara.[32] Muirchú compares it to the biblical assembly of Nebuchadnezzar, at which Shadrach, Meshach and Abednego refuse to worship a golden image and are cast into the burning fiery furnace.[33] Muirchú omits this part of the story, but the allusion would not have been lost on his educated listeners. He goes on to describe the specific circumstances which gave rise to the confrontation:

> [The people of Tara] also had a custom which was announced to all publicly, that whosoever, in any district, whether far or near, should have lit a fire on that night before it was lit in the king's house, that is in the palace of Tara, would have forfeited his life. Holy Patrick then, celebrating Easter, kindled the divine fire with its bright light and blessed it, and it shone in the night and was seen by almost all the people who lived in the plain. Thus the fire from his tent happened to be seen at Tara, and as they saw it, they all gazed at it and wondered. And the king called together the elders and said to them: 'Who is the man who has dared to do such a wicked thing in my kingdom? He shall die.' They all replied that they did not know who had done it, but the druids answered: 'King may you live for ever! Unless the flame which we now see, and which has been lit on this night before the [fire] was lit in your house, is extinguished on this same night on which it has been lit, it will never be extinguished at all; it will even rise above all the fires of our customs, and he who has kindled it and the kingdom that has been brought upon us by him who has kindled it on this night will overpower us all and you, and will seduce all the people of your kingdom, and all kingdoms will yield to it, and it will spread over the whole country and will reign in all eternity' ...[34]

The king is greatly alarmed and sets out before dawn with thrice-nine chariots and two of his most powerful druids (149) to see who is threatening his kingdom in this way:

> ... towards the end of the night [they] went out from Tara to the burial place of the men of Fíacc; they turned the faces of the men and horses to the left, as was befitting them. As they went along, the druids said to the king: 'King, do not yourself go to the place where the fire is, lest perhaps you afterwards adore him who lit it,

but stay outside, and that man will be summoned to your presence that he may adore you and you be his lord' ... And they came to the above mentioned place and dismounted from their horses; and they did not enter the perimeter of the place that was illumined by the light, but sat down beside it.[35]

Patrick is then summoned and the druids begin to debate with him. One of them pours scorn on Patrick's faith, and he calls for divine retribution. His opponent is immediately caught up into the air, dropped, and dashed to pieces.[36] The king orders his warriors to attack, but Patrick calls for help in the words of Psalm 68. A thick darkness descends so that the warriors massacre each other in confusion. The king retreats, Patrick follows and the confrontation continues at Tara. This time he neutralises poison, dispels snow and fog summoned by the chief druid, whose name is Lucet Máel, and agrees to a trial by water, which Lucet Máel then refuses to take part in on the grounds that water is a god of Patrick's. He is also uneasy about a trial by fire, believing that Patrick worships fire and water in alternate years. Patrick denies this and Lucet Máel eventually agrees to the trial by fire.[37] He allows himself to be sealed into a wooden house with one of Patrick's companions. The house is constructed in two halves, one of green wood, the other of dry. It is set on fire, and the druid is burned in the green part of the house, while Patrick's companion is unharmed – 'the fire did not even touch him'. At this, Loegaire decides to become a Christian, more out of terror than conviction.

Patrick is presented here as a sort of super-druid outdoing the 'heathen' at their own game. The confrontation is played out as a contest over sacred fire – who may light it, whom it will empower, whose judgements it will endorse and so on. Both sides lay claim to fire as a sign of the Sacred, and Patrick uses it with enthusiasm. Not for him the token gesture. His Paschal fire is an enormous bonfire which can be seen at a distance of at least ten miles. Muirchú's narrative deliberately plays on the resemblance between this fire and the fires of Irish primal religion. Patrick's fire has all kinds of biblical associations, from the fire theophanies of the Hebrew Bible to the Pentecostal flames of the New Testament.[38] Today's Paschal fires are supposed to symbolise the Glory of the Lord, while the candles lit from it represent the light of Christ. Seventh-century listeners may have had a similar understanding, with the added dimension, perhaps, that Patrick's fire was also a king's fire – the fire of the King of Heaven.

Muirchú's narrative is not a historical document, but it strongly suggests that some kind of periodic fire ritual was used to legitimise the Tara kingship. Its importance is clear. The lighting of the king's fire takes precedence over all other fires. The penalty for offenders is death, and the Tara establishment is horrified at seeing Patrick's illegal fire in the distance. He has 'brought a kingdom upon them' they say, and unless his fire is put out immediately, 'all kingdoms will yield to it and ... it will reign to all eternity'. Lighting a rival fire was seen as a direct challenge to the kingship, and Loegaire is warned not to go near the fire 'lest you perhaps adore him who lit it.' In some way, lighting the fire has given Patrick supreme political and spiritual authority over Loegaire, who would otherwise have claimed the same over Patrick – 'that man will be summoned to your presence so that he may adore you and you be his lord'. There is an interesting parallel in the place-lore tradition where we are told that it was from the 'first fire' at Uisnech that all the fires in Ireland were kindled, and that the chief druid who tended it was entitled to receive tribute from every house in Ireland as a result.[39]

DESSEL – SUNWISE

As Loegaire and his druids ride out to see who has lit the illegal fire, Muirchú mentions, almost in passing, that 'they turned the faces of the men and horses to the left, as was befitting them'.[40] This seems to be an early reference to the custom, which is known from Ireland to Tibet, of keeping a sacred person, place or object always on one's right when passing or walking round it. This involves turning to the left and proceeding clockwise or *dessel,* which means literally to the 'right' or 'right-handwise'. It is often translated 'sunwise', since it is thought to derive from the observation that in the northern hemisphere the sun always appears to move from left to right. To go sunwise can be seen as a way of assenting to a cosmic pattern, taking one's place in the scheme of things. To go in the opposite direction – *tuaithbel* – would be a 'sinister' act, a violation of the natural order, likely to attract misfortune. To some this might seem like 'magic' or naked superstition, to others it is the body-language of prayer.

Boand walks *tuaithbel* round a forbidden well which rises up and drowns her, and in *Cormac's Glossary* a strange figure called 'the spirit of poetry' walks *dessel* round a leading poet, presumably to honour him.[41] These episodes involve figures from the pre-christian past, but the custom was not regarded as inveterately 'pagan'. Even Colum Cille, when the time comes for him to sail for Scotland, leaves the Black Church at Derry, goes down to Lough Foyle, washes his hands in a certain stream and makes a sunwise circuit:

> And he blessed a stone close by there and made a circuit around it sunwise and from that stone it was that he went into his boat. And

he said that whoever should make a circuit round it from that time, going on a journey or a pilgrimage, it would be likely that he would come home safe.[42]

This is a late piece of hagiography, explaining a custom which was probably still going on at the time, but it is not the only *Life* to speak approvingly of sunwise circuits. One hagiographer even explained that the reason why Cathbad, the famous druid of Ulster, performed all his prophecies and divinations sunwise, was because he believed in Christ.[43]

Examples from the folk tradition are numerous. In the Hebrides of the late-seventeenth and early-eighteenth centuries, people leaving or arriving at churches, fishermen leaving port, bird-hunters arriving at the Flannan Isles, islanders greeting a visiting clergyman, and pilgrims visiting holy wells, might all make *dessel* circuits around the sacred place or personage. The custom of carrying fire in *dessel* circuits around houses, corn and cattle had apparently ceased by this time, though the informant's unsympathetic attitude might have had something to do with this. Some of the older midwives still carried fire morning and evening around mothers and their newborn babies as a rite of protection between the birth and the christening, or in the woman's case, between childbirth and churching.[44] In Ireland, pilgrims still observe the custom of walking sunwise around holy wells and round the rocky 'beds' of saints in places like Lough Derg and Croagh Patrick.

LUG?

During the late nineteenth and early twentieth centuries, there was a sudden wave of interest in Indo-European solar mythology. This included the search for 'the Celtic sun god' who was presumed to have existed as part of the wider whole. Henri D'Arbois de Joubainville, John Rhyss, Alfred Nutt, Eleanor Hull, and Charles Plummer all wrote in their various ways about the Celtic 'sun god' and the 'solar hero', Lug and Cú Chulainn being the favoured candidates.[45] It is possible that the name 'Lug' is related to the Greek *leukos*, meaning 'white', and to the Latin *lux*, light. Unfortunately, there is no general agreement about this and the Irish common noun *lug* means 'warrior, hero, fighter', originally perhaps 'lynx'.[46] Lug's reputation as a solar deity seems to have been based mainly on an early-modern text called *The Fate of the Children of Tuirenn / Oidhe Chloinne Tuireann*. The story takes place in mythological time, before the arrival of the Milesians (25), at a time when the *Tuatha Dé Danann* were under the oppression of the Fomorians, a race from across the sea. These impose heavy taxes on them and treat them cruelly, till one day, during an assembly at the hill of Uisnech, the *Tuatha Dé Danann* look up and see their liberator approaching from the east:

> At this time the Fair Assembly was held by the King of Erinn on Balor's Hill, which is now called Uisnech. And the people had not been long assembled there before they saw the array of a goodly army coming over the plain from the east towards them; and one young man came in the front of that army, high in command over the rest; and like to the setting of the sun was the splendour of his countenance and his forehead; and they were not able to look in his face from the greatness of his splendour. And he was Lug Lamfada [Lug of the Long Arm] with his army from the fairy mounds and the Land of Promise, and his own foster brothers, the sons of Manannán. ...The [horse] Aenbharr of Manannán was under him and she was as fleet as the naked cold wind of spring, and sea and land were the same to her and her rider was never killed off her back; and he wore Manannán's breastplate upon the ridge of his breast and front, so that no weapon could pierce him; and he had a helmet upon his head to protect it, with a beautiful precious stone set behind it, and two of them in its front; and as bright as the sun on a dry summer's day was the complexion of his face and forehead when he took off his helmet.[47]

The *Tuatha Dé Danann* greet him, but immediately lapse into subservience when the Fomorians arrive to collect their tax. Lug kills most of them and sends the survivors home with the news. It takes some time for the subsequent war to develop, but one morning Bres, the Fomorian leader, looks up and sees a strange glow in the west:

> Then arose Bres son of Balor, and he said, 'It is a wonder to me' said he 'that the sun should rise in the west today and in the east every other day.'
> 'It is better that it were so,' said the druids.
> 'What else is it?' said he.
> 'The radiance of the face of Lug of the Long Arm,' said they.

There is so much sun-fire imagery in this text that, at first sight, Lug's reputation as a sun god seems assured. Later, when he puts on Manannán's helmet, his face has the radiance of the sun, and forests of flames rise from the battle-field from the weapons of both armies. The problem is with the date of the text. This version of *The Fate of the Children of Tiurenn* dates only from the sixteenth century, and while there are at least two earlier versions, sun-fire imagery is conspicuously absent from them both.[48] Since the earlier of the two – *The Battle of Moytura / Cath Maige Tuired* – describes the same battle as *The Fate of the Children of Tuirenn*, it would seem that Lug's fiery radiance is a late development. There is no sign of it in the *Táin* when he comes to heal Cú Chulainn of his wounds, and the gold furnishings in his house are most easily understood as signs of his kingly wealth.[49] All of this seriously undermines the case for his being originally a solar deity.

In other mythologies sun gods often ride in chariots, and Lug does in fact do this in *The Battle of Moytura*. But if this is an Irish version of the chariot of the sun, it is well disguised. There is plenty of scope for sun-fire references in the twenty-five names of his chariots, charioteers, and charioteers' goads, but the opportunity is never taken. He also has eleven horses, one of which is called Lasaid, which means 'burning' or 'blazing', but the rest have names like 'Poem', 'Fear', 'The Sea', 'A great Song' and so on.[50] Lug himself is known *Samildánach* – 'possessing all the arts at the same time' – because of his wide variety of skills,[51] and there is a parallel here with Apollo, the Greek god of light and the sun. Apollo also had many skills, being the patron of music, prophecy, medicine and the law, but whether this parallel is due to the fall-out from a distant Indo-European myth is an open question.

Some nineteenth-century scholars seem to have based their understanding of Lug almost entirely on *The Fate of the Children of Tuirenn*. D'Arbois de Joubainville, for example, used it to support his theory that Celtic religion was basically a dualism of light and darkness. He thought he could detect at the root of all 'Aryan' cultures the 'dualistic idea of the beneficent deities of Day, Sunshine and Life, warring against the malevolent powers of Death, Storm and Night', Lug being the leader of the former.[52] This works well enough for *The Fate of the Children of Tuirenn* with its sun-like Lug and its 'gloomy, grim-looking' Fomorians, but it makes no sense in relation to *The Battle of Moytura*. Indeed, one of the most brilliant, shining, gold-bedecked figures in the whole of early Irish literature is Elatha the Fomorian who makes love to Ériu at the beginning of the tale.[53]

The polarity of light and darkness simply does not occur in *The Battle of Moytura*. Instead, it expresses conflict in terms of justice and injustice, plenty and hunger, fertility and infertility. The main complaints against Fomorian rule are that Bres allows foreigners to impose crippling taxes, treats heroes dishonourably, gives miserly hospitality, neglects the arts, and fails to bring prosperity to the land. Lug's victory over him is a triumph of plenty over famine, and Bres is forced to reveal to him the auspicious days for sowing and reaping.[54] Significantly,

Lug's annual festival – Lughnasad (27–8, 30) – is also connected with agriculture and is celebrated at the beginning of August, rather than at the solstice or the equinox. There are of course Lughnasad bonfires, but these are not necessarily connected with Lug, since fires are also traditional at Belteine, Samain, St John's Eve and the Midwinter festival. As for the supposed dualism of Celtic religion, there is no absolute distinction between the warring gods in *The Battle of Moytura*. Lug is the son of Ethne of the Fomorians, while Bres is the son of Ériu of the *Tuatha Dé Danann*. This intermarriage of the two sides seems to be deliberate and suggests a more subtle theological outlook than the radical dualism proposed by Arbois.[55]

It has been suggested that Lug and Finn were different names for the same Otherworld being, and Finn does seem to have a number of early associations with fire.[56] This need not mean, however, that either of them was a sun god. Enter the solar hero.

SUN GOD AND SOLAR HERO

When T. F. O'Rahilly turned to solar mythology in key chapters of his *Early Irish History and Mythology*, he rejected the idea that Lug was 'the Celtic sun god', seeing him instead as an example of the solar hero. He did however identify a large number of Irish Otherworld beings, male and female, who were 'ultimately the sun god' or the 'sun goddess', many of whom can be linked with other aspects of nature as well. His argument can be summarised as follows: the Celts believed that lightning, thunder and fire, all had their source in the sun; the sun god was the god of lightning and thunder, the Lord of the Otherworld, and the ancestor or maker of humankind; he was conceived of as the eye of the heavens, a huge one-eyed being, who appears in the Irish texts under a variety of names including Balor, Goll, Aed Álainn, the Dagda, Aillill Áine and Nuadu while his consort, the sun goddess, appears as Áine, Grian and Ethne.[57] All of this derives, he suggests, from an ancient Indo-European sun myth, out of which grew the myth of the solar hero who kills the sun god with his own weapon; this weapon appears in Irish literature as a shining sword, spear, 'solar stone', thunderbolt, or as Cú Chulainn's famous weapon, the *Gaí Bulga,* which O'Rahilly translates as 'the lightning weapon'. He identifies Finn, Lug and Cú Chulainn as Irish developments of the solar Hero.

O'Rahilly's erudition is impressive, but it is difficult to share his conviction that 'the ancient Indo-European sun myth' can unlock quite so many of the secrets of medieval Irish literature. Firstly, the sun myth is itself a reconstruction, and secondly, there are so many other less

remote influences at work: Christianity and dynastic politics, forgetful-
ness and creativity. It is also difficult to feel entirely confident about the
weight which he places on what primitive versions of the texts would have
said had they survived. Only a scholar with O'Rahilly's breadth of
knowledge could examine all of his arguments in detail, but take the
example of Balor the Fomorian.

Balor, one of the most famous one-eyed characters in early Irish
literature and therefore a favourite candidate for the 'the eye of the
heavens', appears in *The Battle of Moytura* as one of the Fomorian
champions. He has an 'evil eye' which fatally weakens anyone who looks
at it. When Lug blinds him with a shot from his sling, O'Rahilly interprets this as an example of the hero killing the sun god with a solar stone.
A parallel is available in the story of David and Goliath – which is of
course a semitic rather than an Indo-European tale – but O'Rahilly does
not discuss this. Balor's eye is described in *The Battle of Moytura* as
poisonous rather than dazzling or burning, and the author does not make
clear whether it is Balor's only eye, or a sort of third eye, which is open
only in battle.[58]   The fiery eye certainly appears in the folk tradition
where we hear that if his tenants fell behind with their rent, Balor would
uncover his eye little by little, scorching the grass, the trees and finally
burning up the whole countryside. Elsewhere there was a tradition that
the black tips on rushes, the blackness of bog oak, and the darkness of the
hillsides were all due to Balor's burning eye.[59] The problem here is
similar to that of Lug, whose sun-like features are plentiful in the modern period, but conspicuously absent from the medieval tradition.

Why should this be so? Does Balor appear in the earlier tradition
under another name? Have early references to his fiery eye and Lug's
sun-like radiance simply been lost? Or were they suppressed by the
medieval church, surviving only in remote districts through the oral
tradition? The folk tradition does sometimes preserve stories and world-
views which have long since vanished from the world of the educated
élite, but there is no way of knowing whether that is what happened in
this case. Another possibility is that the sun-fire imagery of a number of
pre-christian deities was transferred wholesale to the christian saints; an
impressive number of these do in fact show a remarkable affinity with
fire and the sun, as we shall see, but if the transfer was mainly from Lug
and/or Balor, it was accomplished with remarkable thoroughness. This
could be interpreted simply as a sign of the church's determination, but
a fourth possibility has yet to be excluded: namely, that neither Lug nor
Balor had any fiery characteristics in the medieval period; that they
acquired their solar features late in the day from another source or

sources. This is not, at present, the favoured solution, but it has simplicity on its side. As for other deities of sun and fire, perhaps we should look again at the Dagda, Aed Álainn, Ogma 'sun face' and others.[60] Their early associations with sun and/or fire certainly mark them out as possible candidates, though the evidence is widely scattered and perhaps too tenuous for reassembly. In the meantime, a number of female figures also deserve consideration.

THE SUN OF WOMEN – GRIAN

We have already encountered Grian at the end of the story of Macha wife of Crund (27). She is mentioned almost as an aside, in this tiny fragment:

> And men say that she was Grian Banchure, 'the Sun of Womanfolk', daughter of Mider of Brí Léith.

However, the editor of the place-lore clearly knew – and expected the listeners to know – of an Otherworld woman whose name means unequivocally, Sun – *Grian*. As far as I know, this is Grian Banchure's only appearance in the literature, but we do hear of other women called Grian who may be related to her. A hill, formerly known as Cnoc Gréne, in County Limerick was traditionally the burial place of Grian, daughter of Fer I, son of Eógabal, also known as *Grene gruadhsoluis* – bright-cheeked Grian.[61] Another Grian, daughter of Finn, is mentioned in a different part of the place-lore tradition.[62]

Macha wife of Crund is of course the Macha who runs faster than the king's horses, and there is an association in comparative mythology between horses and solar deities. Chariots of the sun once stood outside Solomon's Temple where twice a year the faithful gathered before dawn to witness the Glory of the Lord (143). In the Greek tradition, Helios and his sister Eos (Dawn) both ride in horse-drawn chariots, as do Surya (Sun) and the goddess of Dawn in the Rig Veda. In Ireland, we find a horse called Grian and a woman called Láir Derg – Red Mare.[63] Macha Mong-ruad (Red-haired Macha) is the daughter of Aed, which means 'fire', and Étaín, beloved of Mider, is described as *Echraide* – horse-riding Étaín – and spends part of her life in a crystal *grianán* or 'sun house'.[64] Horses and horse-sacrifices seem to have played a role in the inauguration of kings, which was also the time of their traditional marriage to the 'sovereignty goddess'.[65] This is all very tantalising, but difficult to form into any kind of system.

Áine may also have been associated with the sun, but it was not her exclusive sphere of influence. We have already met her in connection with wells, a lough and a little river. In one ninth-century tale, an Áine daughter of Eogabal emerges from a *síd* mound on the night of Samain to be wooed roughly and unsuccessfully by Ailill, king of Munster.[66] This looks very like a sovereignty motif; a Munster earl claimed her as his 'wife' during the fifteenth century, and she was still linked with a local family as late as 1896.[67] Her association with light and fire comes mainly from her name which, according to O'Rahilly, denotes brightness, radiance and also speed.[68] Cnoc Áine, a hill by the village of Knockainy in County Limerick, is named after her and in folk tradition fires were lit there on St John's Eve – the eve of the summer solstice – as they were in many parts of Ireland. The hill would be crowded that night, as people prepared to carry bundles of flaming straw or hay in procession into the fields and among the cattle in order to bless them. A story from this period tells how, as the night wore on, Áine appeared to a group of girls and revealed to them a host of invisible fairy folk, the *síd* people, mingling with the crowd, and waiting to have the hill to themselves.[69]

THE SUN OF WOMEN – MARY

Let me have from you my three petitions, beautiful Mary, little bright-necked one; get them, sun of women, from your son who has them in his power,

That I be in the world till old with the Lord who rules starry heaven, and that thereafter there be a welcome for me into the eternal ever-enduring kingdom.[70]

This seventh-century protection prayer was to be said night and morning or on Fridays, fasting with heart-felt tears. Its author, the seventh-century monk Blathmac, wrote it as part of a larger poem lamenting the death of Jesus, but our main interest is in his affectionate address to Mary as 'sun of women' – *Grian na mba(n)*. Elsewhere, he addresses her as 'bright Mary' and 'Sun of our race'.[71]

The woman clothed with the sun in Revelation 12 is often understood as a reference to Mary. The early Christians of Ireland probably enjoyed this image and set about making it their own. Just as on the continent, Mary inherited some of the attributes of Mediterranean goddesses, so in Ireland the title 'sun of women' may well have been influenced by pre-christian sources.

This sort of imagery seems to have been particularly popular in the later medieval period. For one poet, she is 'a red Easter sun', for another 'our great candle-light ... our flaming torch', 'the sun setting red after its circuit'. A third calls her 'summer sun of the skies' and 'early sunrise ripening corn', also declaring that 'the round gold circle of her face makes the virgin as a dazzling sun.'[72] Mary is compared with other aspects of nature as well: sheaves of corn, a calm rainless sky, sea-wealth cast on the shore, an unfenced fruit tree, a brimming lake-well.[73] The sun is certainly not the only metaphor for her and it is perhaps misleading to quote so many of them together, when in reality they are widely scattered throughout the bardic collections. But as the 'sun of women' and the 'sun-bright graceful maid' she has an enduring appeal which is at once primal and christian.

BRIGIT

Giraldus Cambrensis (Gerald of Wales), visiting Ireland during the twelfth century, describes how 'Brigit's fire' burned perpetually in a special enclosure at St Brigit's Abbey in Kildare:

> It is not that it is strictly speaking inextinguishable, but that the nuns and holy women have so carefully and diligently kept and fed it with enough material, that through all the years from the time of the virgin saint until now it has never been extinguished ... Although in the time of Brigit there were twenty servants of the Lord here, Brigit herself being the twentieth, only nineteen have ever been here after her death ... They all however take their turns, one each night, in guarding the fire. When the twentieth night comes, the nineteenth nun puts the logs beside the fire and says, 'Brigit, guard your fire. This is your night.' And in this way the fire is left there, and in the morning the wood, as usual, has been burnt and the fire is still alight.
>
> This fire is surrounded by a hedge which is circular and made of withies, and which no male may cross. And if by any chance any one does dare enter – and some rash people have at times tried it – he does not escape the divine vengeance. Only women are allowed to blow the fire, and then not with the breath of their mouths, but only with bellows or winnowing forks. Moreover because of a curse of the saint, goats never have young here. There are also very fine plains hereabouts which are called 'Brigit's Pastures' but no one has dared to put a plough into them. It is regarded as miraculous that these pastures, even though all the animals of the whole province have eaten the grass down to the ground, nevertheless when morning comes, have just as much grass as ever.[74]

This was certainly not the only perpetual fire in medieval Ireland. We hear of at least one other, in St Molaise's church on the island of

Inishmurray.[75] Other monasteries were not so lucky, or maybe just not so careful: a Latin *Life* of St Cíarán of Saigir tells how he decreed that the fire in his monastery should not be put out during the year. It is put out however, leaving the community entirely without heat or cooking facilities. Cíarán tells them that unless God sends them fire as a gift, they will be without it till the following Easter. It begins to snow. But Cíarán prays and immediately, a ball of fire falls into his lap.[76] The providence of God, the reputation of the saint and the sacred origins of fire are all illustrated here, but we also get a glimpse of a situation in which the Paschal fire was kept burning from one Easter to another, for practical as well as liturgical reasons.

If Brigit's fire had been simply a Paschal fire, Gerald would probably not have remarked on it. It seems to have been a fire of a different sort, with its circular enclosure and its hedge of withies. There was also a taboo against male intruders, special directions for tending the fire and reports of a recurring miracle whereby Brigit herself looked after it every twentieth night.[77] Parts of Gerald's account are reminiscent of the cult of Vesta or Hestia, the Roman hearth goddess. It has even been suggested, that the 'nuns and holy women' of Kildare might have been the christian descendants of a college of women who were once attendants at the shrine of Brigit the goddess.[78] This can neither be proved nor disproved, but it is certainly an interesting idea.

Brigit the saint inherits a great deal from Brigit the goddess, as most scholars would agree. Brigit the goddess is not a single figure, however. There seem to have been several different Brigits, many of whom have an association with fire. Three Brigits, daughters of the Dagda, are described in *Cormac's Glossary* as the goddesses of poetry, leechcraft, and smithcraft.[79] The work of the smith, often a semi-religious activity in the ancient world, clearly involves fire, in the fashioning of metal objects and in the smelting of ores. Fire would also have been used in the preparation of medicines, brews and potions – hence, perhaps, a fire association for the 'woman of leechcraft'.[80] Sunlight also has curative properties and can help to heal wounds, skin conditions and seasonal depression. In summer it brings out the essential oils in medicinal herbs. The leeches of medieval Ireland may have been aware of some of these factors at least.

As for the Brigit of poetry, poetic inspiration is sometimes described in terms of light and fire. *Cormac's Glossary* describes a prophetic technique known as *imbas forosnai* which can be translated as 'great knowledge which illumines / kindles'.[81] And the author of the Old Irish text known as the *Cauldron of Poesy* imagines poetry as a sort of inner light or fire when he says that everyone has poetry within them, but 'in every

second one it does not shine forth'. The image is of an inward illumination rather than an outward physical one, but in the same text the inner
and the outer worlds come together in a gloss on the word *imbas* (literally
'great knowledge') which reads: 'a bubble which the sun causes on the
plants, i.e. on the hazels of Segais, and whoever consumes them will have
an art'. For this commentator at least, the outward physical sun contributed mysteriously to the 'enlightening' or 'kindling' of the soul.

If the name Bríg is interchangeable with Brigit, as Kim McCone
suggests, there may well have been more than three Brigits in pre-
christian times. He mentions several, but of particular interest here is
Bríg the hospitaller who appears briefly in the law tracts and may have
provided some of the inspiration for St Brigit's famous generosity and
her miracles of food and drink.[82] Given the hospitaller's function of
providing food and drink for large numbers of people, she may also have
been connected with cooking and the hearth. In parts of the Hebridean
folk tradition, the protection of St Bride was invoked along with that of
Mary, at the lighting and smooring of the fire.[83]

Doubts are often raised about whether St Brigit ever existed. The
Brigit who appears in the hagiographies could well be a christianised
goddess and nothing more, but it is difficult to be certain that there is
not a mortal woman hidden somewhere in the depths of the Brigit myth.
For practical purposes, it was the Brigit of faith who mattered to her
christian followers. To them, she was a friend in high places, a power to
be reckoned with, and a saint who was at least as interested in farming
and domestic matters as she was effective in prayer and leadership.
There is sun-fire symbolism in all the various *Lives* of Brigit. In
Cogitosus's seventh-century *Life*, the main emphasis is on her miracles
of food and drink, her generosity, her healing powers, her skill with
animals, and her dealings with powerful men, but there are also a small
number of sun-fire miracles involving the preservation from fire of domestic implements – a loom and a quernstone – and a curious little story
in which Brigit is caught in a downpour while out tending sheep. She
takes off her wet cloak and hangs it on a sunbeam to dry. It is difficult
to know whether this is intentionally humorous or not, but it certainly
shows her on excellent terms with the sun, which is here either her
servant or her gracious friend.[84]

Fire plays an important part in the opening sections of the early
ninth-century *Life* of Brigit – *Bethu Brigte*. The hut in which the infant
Brigit is sleeping catches fire, but she survives unscathed. Her christian
uncle and a friendly druid see a fiery column rising from her hut during
the night and agree that she must be a holy girl. When she grows up and

prepares to take the veil, a fiery column rises from her head as the bishop reads the words of consecration over her. At the same time, she touches the wooden beam supporting the altar and it subsequently survives three fires.[85] In the folk tradition, the St Brigit's Cross, a four-armed cross made of rushes, was believed to protect buildings against fire. Every year on St Brigit's Day, the old Celtic festival of Imbolc, a new cross was added to the collection.

In the *Life of Brigit* from the *Book of Lismore*, a druid prophesies that she will be 'a daughter conspicuous and radiant, who will shine like the sun among the stars of heaven'. She is born at sunrise, as her mother steps over the threshold with a bowl of milk. The women of the house wash her with milk, as befits 'the brightness and sheen of her chastity', and with her first prayers, a column of flame is seen rising from the house. The people who run to her rescue find her completely unharmed and 'full of the grace of the Holy Spirit'. Educated listeners would certainly have recognised in this a reference to the fires of Pentecost.[86] The same *Life* also refers to a thoroughly non-biblical miracle involving cow-dung – 'the cow dung which lay before the girl they beheld ablaze'. The onlookers stretch out their hands towards it, but the flames disappear.[87]

Fire and the sun were only part of what interested the hagiographers about Brigit, but she is persistently associated with them from the seventh century onwards. It is from this earliest part of the tradition that we get the beautiful Old Irish hymn to Brigit with its famous opening lines:

> Brigit ever-excellent woman
> Golden sparkling flame
> Lead us to the eternal kingdom
> The dazzling resplendent sun.[88]

Here, the sun seems to represent the heavenly kingdom, or perhaps Christ himself, while Brigit is able to act as our guide because with her sparkling nature she is kin to God, as a flame is kin to the sun.

COLUM CILLE

Adamnán describes so many miracles of Colum Cille that we may not immediately notice the pillars of fire and the heavenly lights:

> On that night when St Columba, by a happy and blessed death passed from earth to heaven, while I and others with me were engaged in fishing in the valley of the river Find – which abounds in fish – we saw the whole vault of heaven become suddenly illuminated. Struck by the suddenness of the miracle, we raised our

eyes and looked towards the east, when lo, there appeared something like an immense pillar of fire, which seemed to illuminate the whole earth like the summer sun at noon; and after that column penetrated the heavens, darkness followed, as if the sun had just set. And not only did we, who were together in the same place, observe with intense surprise the brightness of this remarkable luminous pillar, but many other fishermen also, who were engaged in fishing here and there in the different deep pools along the same river, were greatly terrified as they afterwards related to us, by an appearance of the same kind.[89]

Night fishing, the deep pools, the awesome sunset – it is easy to see why a young fisherman might remember it all his life. Adamnán tells us that he got this story from an old monk who was living in Ireland at the time, in what is now Donegal. A few chapters earlier, he recounts how St Brendan saw a ball of fire 'like a comet burning very brightly' on the head of Colum Cille while he was celebrating the sacred mysteries, and that it remained there, rising upwards like a column, throughout the mass. Fiery pillars are common in the *Lives* of Irish saints, but Adamnán's must be one of the earliest. The tradition that Brendan also saw a fiery pillar preceding Colum Cille on a journey seems to be modelled to some extent on the fire theophany in Exodus, though the image of fire rising from the head is also reminiscent of the 'hero–halo' which rises from the top of Cú Chulainn's head during his battle frenzy.[90] Adamnán does not explain what the ball of fire might mean, but it seems to be a sign of energy and spiritual power and, in an age when monks were taught to see themselves as soldiers of Christ, it could represent a Celtic vision of the spiritual warrior.[91] As for the pillar of fire, the circumstances in which it often appears – during births and deaths, at the moment of consecration, while saints are at prayer, above holy places – suggests that in addition to its biblical resonances, it marks a point of contact between heaven and earth and acts like a sort of pathway between the two.

Towards the end of his book, Adamnán devotes five consecutive chapters to miracles of light and fire. A young monk, praying in a side-chamber on a winter's night, sees Colum Cille enter the oratory accompanied by a brilliant light. Two other brothers have similar experiences. These lesser mortals are frightened by the strange lights, but the saint seems to be in his element:

At another time, when the saint was living in the Hinba island, the grace of the Holy Ghost was communicated to him abundantly and unspeakably, and dwelt with him so that for three whole days and as many nights without either eating or drinking, he allowed no one to approach him and remained confined in a house which was filled with heavenly brightness. Yet out of that house, through the chinks of the doors and keyholes, rays of surpassing brilliancy were seen to issue through the night. Certain spiritual songs also, which had never been heard before, he was heard to sing. He came to see, as he allowed in the presence of a very few afterwards, many secrets hidden from men since the beginning of the world fully revealed; certain very obscure and difficult parts of sacred scripture also were made quite plain, and clearer than the light of the eye of his pure heart.[92]

Hinba island seems to have been a place of retreat for Colum Cille. There was a hermitage on Hinba, a tiny church and a small monastic community with its own prior and a number of penitents. Its exact location has never been established.[93] The image of a house filled with brightness is reminiscent of the 'king's fire' which escapes through all the outlets of Da Derga's hostel. Poets practising *imbas forosnai* – 'great knowledge which illumines' – might also once have spent the night alone in a secluded hut.[94] Traditions like these could be at work here, contributing to the reputation of a noble and learned saint. But Adamnán makes it quite clear that the light comes from the grace of the Holy Spirit, who in John's Gospel is the great teacher, the Spirit of truth.[95] The heavenly brightness in Colum Cille's oratory seems to be the external manifestation of an inner light, which enlightens the mind and inspires music and singing. Colum Cille has a special relationship with other aspects of nature as well, but like the author of the Old Irish hymn to Brigit, Adamnán chooses the imagery of light and fire to show the extraordinary kinship which exists between the saint and his God.

OTHER SUN-FIRE SAINTS

Sun-fire miracles and solar imagery proliferate in the *Lives* of saints after the seventh century, so much so that it would almost be easier to count Irish saints who have no connection with the sun or fire. Phenomena of light and fire attend their births.[96] They survive in burning houses.[97] Pillars of fire rise from their heads.[98] They have bright or dazzling faces.[99] Their bodies melt snow or heat cold liquids.[100] Their cells and oratories blaze with light.[101] They handle burning objects and make it possible for their disciples to do the same.[102] They provide miraculous fires in cold weather.[103] They are able to prolong daylight or make the sun come out.[104] They ride in fiery chariots.[105] Their fingers burst into flames.[106] Fiery spheres fall into their laps or hover over their houses.[107]

Some of these stories are clearly inspired from the Bible: we find direct references to the shining faces of Moses and the transfigured Christ, to Elijah, and to the light which blinds Paul on the road to Damascus.[108] Stories of prolonged daylight may owe something to Joshua 10, and Shadrach, Mesach and Abednego also survive in the midst of flames.[109] The text from Habakkuk – 'His brightness was like the light, rays flashed from his hand' – may have encouraged stories of saints whose fingers burst into flames, though the desert fathers had a similar tradition.[110]

Another possible source might be the various Apocrypha and Pseud-epigrapha which were highly regarded in Ireland, but some miracles have no obvious connection with any christian text. Finan is conceived as his mother dreams of something like a reddish-gold fish, flying towards her from the rising sun and entering her womb; a divine light appears on the hill of Bangor for three days and three nights at the time of Comgal's ordination and the bishop sees 'the flaming hair of his head' and angels flying around him.[111] Saints who stand in freezing water as an ascetical exercise have their counterparts in the Eastern Church, but those who warm cold water and other liquids with the heat of their bodies are more easily compared to Cú Chulainn, who has to be plunged in several changes of cold water to cool his warrior ardour.[112] Other miracles relating to cold and darkness seem to be very much the product of their environment.

If Eliade's description of shamanism is applicable to Ireland (110) then some stories of the mastery of fire may be intended to show that the saint could excel in the same feats as shamans or indeed, druids. In mainland Europe, people continued to resort to traditional healers, diviners and wonder-workers throughout the middle ages, and one of the tasks of hagiography was to show that christian saints could either defeat or outshine these non-ecclesiastical rivals.[113]

A number of saints may even be descended, mythologically speaking, from pre-christian sun or fire deities. Several of them have fiery names: Buite means 'heat'; Lasair/Molaise and Daig[114] are all variations on 'flame.' Maedoc may be a diminutive of Aed – 'fire' – which is a saint's name as well as a common name for kings and Otherworld beings. Sun-fire imagery in the *Lives* of Lugaid, Molua and Finan could be due to a possible relationship with Lug and Finn,[115] but it could equally well be inherited from the *Lives* of other saints. Whatever its source, there can be no doubt as to the importance and popularity of the theme. The enthusiasm with which Patrick and, later, the seventh-century hagio-graphers set out to claim these potent signs of the Sacred for Christian-ity, strongly suggests the existence of a rival cult or cults. But the names and natures of these rival gods are still a matter of debate.

Chapter 9

God of the Elements

In most of the chapters so far, we have looked at aspects of nature singly, but the medieval texts also speak about 'the elements' collectively, often as 'the elements of God'. There seems to have been no fixed membership of this group. Sun and moon, sea and stars, earth, wind, fire, the sun – all appear in various combinations, acting together. It is this joint activity of the elements that we shall be looking at in the present chapter. Stories about the weather, particularly stormy weather, might be included under the same heading, as might feats of endurance by exposure to the elements. We shall touch on some of these as well.

In one of his studies of the canaanite myths, John Gibson remarks on the terror felt by the ancient peoples in the face of the ambivalent forces of nature.[1] And they are very ambivalent. The waters of peace are also the waters of the Flood. The psalmists were constantly invoking Yahweh's protection against their enemies and other gods, but it was his power over the frightening forces of nature which inspired some of their most lasting and universally accessible poetry. Still today, the elements can display their power even over the technological defences of the rich countries, while people who make their living on the land or at sea still contend with them on a daily basis. Biblical writers were keenly aware of this, seeing Yahweh as one who could send or withhold rain, and Jesus as one whom even the winds and the sea obey. Celtic Christians lived in the same kind of world, holding the elements in enormous respect while seeking to make sense of their wild and sometimes unpredictable nature. They also sought to influence them in various ways through prayer and ritual.

WEATHER-WORKERS

The island of Inishmurray off the Sligo coast is uninhabited today, but when John O'Donovan visited it in 1836, people still lived there, despite its exposed situation on the edge of the Atlantic. Sometimes they would be storm-bound for weeks on end, especially during the spring and

winter months. At times like these they sought spiritual and practical assistance through the waters of a certain well:

> On the northern coast of this island is a well called *Tobernacoragh*, i.e. the well of aid or assistance. When the inhabitants of the opposite coasts are too long detained on the island by tempestuous weather, they drain this well into the sea, and repeat certain prayers by which the storm will immediately subside through the miracles of God and St Molaise, who blessed this well to such a degree of sanctity that its waters might allay the anger of old ocean.[2]

And a little later he says:

> I was not able to learn from the islanders the precise time when the well had last been drained. It is probably some years since a rite so very pagan in character was practised and an offering poured forth that would seem originally intended to propitiate some old sea-god of Celtic mythology.[3]

Whatever the origins of this ritual, the people who performed it were clearly Christians. The saint they appealed to was Molaise of Devenish (157–8) whose ruined monastery is still an important feature of Inish-murray today. Clearly they believed that God would listen to him and perform a miracle for them, through the friendly waters of the holy well. They knew from experience that the rite was not infallible, but they performed it anyway. It was their kind of Christianity, whatever outsiders might think of it.

Weather-working saints like Molaise are common in Celtic Christianity, in its medieval literature as well as its folk tradition. Patrick's contest with the druids (146) involves weather-working, though he limits himself to clearing up bad weather created by the chief druid. Colum Cille also influences the weather, again in competition with a druid, who has called up unfavourable winds to prevent him from putting to sea.[4] If early traditions like these show pre-christian weather-workers in a poor light, later texts sometimes take a more positive view. In the *Lebor Gabála / Book of Conquests*, Amairgen, chief poet of the Milesians, chants a poem to dispel an off-shore wind which is preventing his people from landing.[5] There is no sense of embarrassment here on the part of the christian editor. On the contrary, the mood is buoyant and several other Amairgen poems are cited at the same time.

THE ROUGH HEALING OF WIND AND WAVES

At times the elements seem to have been part of the judicial process. We do not know whether trial by fire, mentioned in the story of Patrick and the druids, was once a traditional practice, but trial by casting adrift is mentioned in several texts. In *Adamnán's Law* (169) it is the sentence for a woman murderer, and in Muirchú's *Life of Patrick* it is given as a penance for attempted murder.[6] The penitent is a king called Macuil Maccugreccae who used to kill passing strangers in a particularly savage and brutal way. One day he attempts to do this to Patrick, but is so changed by the encounter that he asks for baptism instead. Then he asks what his penance should be:

> And Patrick said: I cannot judge, but God will judge. But as for you, go away unarmed to the sea and cross quickly from this land of Ireland taking nothing of your possessions with you except some poor little garment with which to cover your body, and tasting nothing and eating nothing of the produce of this island, and with the mark of your sin on your head; and when you reach the sea, shackle your feet together with iron fetters and throw the key into the sea, and put yourself into a boat made of one skin, without rudder and without oar, and be ready to go wherever wind and sea may take you; and whatever land Divine Providence may bring you to, to dwell in it and carry out God's command. And Macuil said: 'I shall do as you say' ... And Macuil journeyed from there as quickly as he could to the sea to the south of Magh Inis, in the unshakeable confidence of faith; he shackled himself on the shore, throwing the key into the sea as he had been instructed, and put out to sea in a boat. And the north wind blew on him and carried him to southwards and cast him up on an island called Evonia – The Isle of Man.

In a later tale, the people of Ross receive a similar penance from Colum Cille for killing their tyrannical king. They had been sentenced to be burned alive in a house, but the king's brother seeks advice from Colum Cille, his soul-friend – who sends two monks, Snedgus and MacRiagla (96) from Iona with the message that a certain number of them should be cast adrift and left to the judgement of God. They are later discovered living on a distant island, in the company of Enoch and Elijah, completely purged of their sin.[7] Patrick's penitent, Macuil, also undergoes a spiritual transformation. On the Isle of Man he meets two holy bishops and lives with them for the rest of their lives, training himself 'body and soul in accordance with their rule'. When they die, he succeeds them as bishop of Man.

If these penances sound harsh today, it is because the Irish Penitentials are harsh by our standards – and certainly not the sort of medicine to be prescribed indiscriminately, century after century. It is also worth noting that in the case of the people of Ross, the penance is less harsh than the original sentence. There is a clear similarity between these penances and the practice of 'white martyrdom' or *peregrinatio* recommended by Columbanus and others.[8] Adamnán describes Colum Cille's exile to Iona as a pilgrimage for the sake of Christ, though it was later presented as a penance for his role in the battle of Cúl Drebene; a later *Life* compares him to Abraham and other biblical figures who went on pilgrimage for the sake of the Lord of the Elements.[9] The voyage literature seems to take some of its inspiration from practices like these. *The Voyage of the Úi Chorra* (8) is undertaken by three brigand-bothers turned monks who have just completed a series of penances. Snedgus and MacRiagla prescribe the penance of casting adrift to the people of Ross, and then decide to undergo a voluntary experience of it themselves. They make a turn sunwise, ship their oars and drift out into the ocean at the mercy of the wind. The elements play an important role in all of these penances and spiritual exercises, and also in many accounts of austerities practised out of doors. These are mentioned in the Penitentials, and in Lives of saints and Martyrologies, where people deliberately seek out challenging encounters with the elements, for the good of their own or other people's souls: on mountainsides, or standing in water, or buried in the earth.

THE ELEMENTS IN ADAMNÁN'S LAW

Adamnán's Law / *Cáin Adamnáin*, passed by the synod of Birr in 697, laid down a system of fines for acts of violence against church property, clerics, women and children. It may well have been framed by Adamnán himself though surviving versions of it date only from the ninth century, as does the lengthy preface. This presents the law's main purpose as being to release women from military service. It paints a horrific picture of the degradation and violence suffered by women in the time before *Adamnán's Law*, including a sickening description of a battlefield in the aftermath of a battle. We are told how Adamnán was crossing the battlefield carrying Ronnat, his mother, on his back. Appalled by what she sees, she orders him to bring such massacres to an end. He accepts the task, fasting against God and undergoing a series of extreme austerities, standing in water and burying himself in the earth, till an angel appears from heaven with the new law.

The author's outrage is spoiled slightly at the end of the Preface, where he itemises exactly what each class of women owes to the successors of Adamnán for bringing them out of bondage: a horse every quarter from queens, a tunic with a black border from nuns, a scruple of gold from chieftains' wives and so on, down to seven cakes, a lamb and a wether from every flock from the lowliest class of women. It seems that a law originally designed to protect clergy, clerical students, women and children (in that order) was subsequently used to tax women. Our main interest however, is in guarantors of *Adamnán's Law*. It has two guarantor lists, that is, lists of persons responsible for unholding the law and bringing offenders to justice. The first comprises a long list of Adamnán's contemporaries. The second might be called the spiritual guarantor list, since it invokes guardians from another realm altogether:

> These are the securities: sun and moon and all the other elements of God; Peter, Paul, Andrew and the other apostles; Gregory, the two Patricks, the two Cíaráns, the four Fintans ... [list of twenty-five names] ... Those guarantors gave three shouts of malediction on every male who would kill a woman with his right hand or left, by a kick, or by his tongue, so that his heirs are elder and nettle and corncrake. The same guarantors gave three shouts of blessing on every female who would do something for the community of Adamnán however often his reliquaries would come ...[10]

Notice how the elements are invoked here, side by side with the saints – in fact, before the saints, before Pope Gregory, and before the apostles. The image of them shouting their 'three shouts of malediction' recalls the tradition, mentioned later in the *Colloquy of the Ancients*, that the *lia fáil* or 'stone of destiny' at Tara could tell if a person were lying or speaking the truth. Similarly, if the rightful king stepped on it, it would cry out, while the 'three great waves' of Ireland – the wave of Cleena, the wave of Ballintoy and the wave of Lough Rury – boomed in reply.

The elements could have been included in the guarantor list of *Adamnán's Law* simply as a convention or as a way of influencing traditionally-minded rulers, but if that was the only reason, why do they also appear in christian prayers? The famous eighth-century hymn known as 'St Patrick's breastplate' (17) invokes the power of the elements alongside the Trinity, the angels, patriarchs, apostles and so on, to protect the singer by means of the sun's light, the moon's radiance, fire's splendour, the sea's depth, the wind's swiftness, the earth's stability and much more. At least two other christian prayers make similar invocations.[11] Are these purely decorative, or could it be that many Celtic Christians at this period still saw the elements as personal spiritual powers? If this sounds strange and unlikely, it is worth remembering that St Paul also believed in the *stoicheia* – the 'elemental spirits of the universe' – though he considered them 'weak' and 'poor' and was exasperated by the Galatians' inability to ignore them.[12] Only gradually would the complexities of cross-cultural evangelism come to be realised. Perhaps, like the Galatians, many Irish and Hebridean Christians found themselves unable to ignore the 'elemental spirits' but found a way of accommodating them for a while, by placing them under the authority of the Creator as 'the elements of God'.

THE ELEMENTS AT THE CRUCIFIXION

Blathmac son of Cú Brettan was an eighth-century monk. We know very little about him apart from his poetry, but this reveals an educated man with a good knowledge of scripture and a desire to tell the story of salvation, powerfully and emotionally, to a popular audience. He takes the custom of keening for the dead, something everyone would have been familiar with, and shapes his poem along the lines of a keen or lament. He invites Mary to keen with him and imagines himself beating his hands in the traditional way, while praising her son, his life and his achievements.

Blathmac's account of the Crucifixion is only a small part of this lengthy poem. He bases it partly on the New Testament where the elements are already present in the form of darkness and an earthquake.[13] These details were important enough to find their way into the Gospels of Matthew and Luke, but neither evangelist places any great emphasis on them. Blathmac's version is different. As Jesus utters his cry of dereliction – 'Why have you abandoned me, Living God?' – nature is thrown into turmoil:

> The sun hid its own light; it mourned its Lord; a sudden darkness went over the blue heavens, the wild and furious sea roared.

> The whole world was dark; the land lay under gloomy trembling; at the death of noble Jesus great rocks burst asunder.

> Jerusalem swiftly released the dead from ancient burial; when Christ suffered slaying the veil of the temple was rent.

> A stream of blood gushed forth – severe excess – so that the bark of every tree was red; there was blood on the breasts of the world, in the tree-tops of every great forest.

> It would have been fitting for God's elements, the beautiful sea, the blue heaven, the present earth, that they should change their aspect when keening their hero.

> The body of Christ pierced by points warranted severe lamentation; – it would be fitting – that they should keen in a stronger manner the man by whom they were created.

The king was patient at the crucifixion of his only-begotten, for had his good elements known, they would have keened sweetly.

That the sky did not fall on them, that the great fire did not burn them, that the ocean did not drown them! Their reproaches [i.e. that of the elements] would not have been light.

That the heavy earth did not swallow them, the miserable pack who committed a great crime! That the hasty people led by Annas and Caiphas should not have been turned to ashes!

That there were not [predatory] birds in the stead nor wild beasts on Pilate's land, because without great fear, he beat Christ with the scourge.[14]

The elements are intensely involved here. The sun grows dark and the earth shakes, as in the biblical accounts, but Blathmac also introduces a wild and furious sea and all the forests of the world. It is not entirely clear why these should be covered with blood. They could be shedding blood in sympathy with Jesus or in reparation for the role of the cross or 'tree' on which he died.[15] Or are they stained with blood from the injured body, like the cross itself, or like Deirdre and Emer who in the poetry of a later age embrace their dead and even drink their blood as they keen for them?[16] Blathmac compares these changes in nature to the changes which come over people in moments of intense grief. The normal aspects (literally 'faces') of the sea, heaven and earth are changed as they keen for Jesus. But he also seems to imply that the elements were not in full possession of the facts. This part of the poem presents problems of translation, but the meaning seems to be that God deliberately concealed from the elements the reasons for Jesus's death.[17] 'Had his good elements known, they would have keened sweetly' may be an ironic reference to the satisfaction they would have felt at avenging him. Blathmac invites his listeners to be amazed that the miscreants went unpunished: the sky did not fall on them, the fire burn them or the earth swallow them up. He attributes this to God's extraordinary patience which suspended, temporarily, the 'natural justice' of the elements.[18]

The image of the elements as people keening over their beloved hero might be simply a poet's conceit. But Blathmac could also be appealing to a contemporary view that the elements were not just inanimate energies, but personal powers and upholders of cosmic order. He may even have shared this view himself. Interestingly, Blathmac rarely uses the elements as raw material for metaphors of Christ or the saints. He integrates the old cosmology with the new in a different way, by allowing the

elements to become part of the household of heaven.[19] True, he calls
Mary 'sun of women' and Christ a 'victorious flame', but normally the
elements retain their own identity. Blathmac is careful to emphasise that
they are part of the created order: sun and moon, earth and sea – all
plants and animals belong Christ, who has power over the seasons, raises
the waves and calms the screech of the storm.[20] He also states that they
are not eternal: the 'the forms of the elements' will perish as the day of
judgement approaches. This is paralleled in 2 Peter 3:10–11, where they
are replaced by new heavens and a new earth, but Blathmac is not
interested in this at the moment. As he moves into his description of the
end-time, with Christ avenging the blood of the martyrs, those old
avengers, the elements, simply drop out of the picture.[21]

THE BENEDICITE

'It is the duty of all the elements to render thanks unto God and to bless
him, as it is said: *Benedicite* etc.' [22] The anonymous preacher who wrote
this in his homily some time during the Old Irish period, took it for
granted that his listeners would know what he meant by '*Benedicite* etc.'
The canticle *Benedicite* was probably better known in the medieval
church than it is today. Since it occurs only in the Septuagint version of
the book of Daniel, it was not included in the canon of the Reformed
Churches though it did find its way into the Book of Common Prayer. It
has always been part of the Catholic and Orthodox canons and was
widely used in medieval liturgies. Said to be the song of Shadrach,
Mesach and Abednego in the burning fiery furnace, it begins like this:

O all you works of the Lord, O bless the Lord
To him be highest glory and praise for ever.

And you angels of the Lord, O bless the Lord
To him be highest glory and praise for ever.

And you, the heavens of the Lord, O bless the Lord
And you clouds of the sky, O bless the Lord
And you, all armies of the Lord, O bless the Lord
To him be highest glory and praise for ever.

And you, sun and moon, O bless the Lord
And you, the stars of the heavens, O bless the Lord
And you, showers and rain, O bless the Lord
To him be highest glory and praise for ever.

And you, all breezes and winds, O bless the Lord

And you, fire and heat, O bless the Lord.
And you, cold and heat, O bless the Lord.
To him be highest glory and praise for ever ...[23]

The song continues for nearly forty stanzas, calling on frost and snow, day and night, lightning, the earth, mountains and hills, springs, rivers and seas, plants and animals – to praise God together with the angels and the spirits and souls of the just.

There is no complete record of where and when this canticle was used in Ireland. It occupies a prominent position in the mass in the seventh-century *Antiphonary of Bangor*, and the *Céli Dé* community at Tallaght sang it every day between the evening meal and vespers.[24] It may even have been used in pre-monastic times, making it one of the first canticles to be introduced into Ireland.[25] Coming to it as they did from a culture in which the elements were still in some sense spiritual powers, the people who sang this hymn during those early centuries may well have understood it rather more literally than we do today. They may also have been closer to the world-view from which it originally sprang.

THE ONE AND THE MANY

There is no denying the beauty of the *Benedicite*. A theologian from the Orthodox tradition describes it as 'the secret aspiration of the whole creation, its song of glory to the creator.'[26] This mystical interpretation is very important and almost certainly has more value for us today than a cold analysis of its historical context. For present purposes however, it is useful to be aware that part of its original dynamic may have been to call on foreign deities and their followers to join with Israel in praising the universality of Israel's God. This is certainly the message of the surrounding story in the Book of Daniel where Nebuchadnezzar is astonished that Shadrach, Meshach and Abednego can defy the gods of Babylon and still be defended by their own God.

Many primal religions see the elements as governed by individual deities. One thinks of Agni, Vayu, Surya and the Maruts in the Rig Veda, while in canaanite mythology, Baal was the god of the wind, lightning and rain, Yam of water and the sea, and Shapash the sun goddess. The biblical monsters Rahab and Leviathan are probably also remnants of ancient gods. It would be a mistake to think that the Hebrews suddenly became monotheists overnight. Other gods are mentioned frequently and openly in many parts of the Hebrew Bible, sometimes as judges:

> God has taken his place in the divine council;
> in the midst of the gods he holds judgement:

'How long will you judge unjustly
and show partiality to the wicked?'[27]

'Holy ones' and 'heavenly beings' – literally 'sons of god' or 'sons of gods'
– were probably also deities, though under this name they are almost
indistinguishable from angels.[28]

The Psalmist's declaration, 'For I know that the Lord is great, and that
our Lord is above all gods', is typical of the way in which some Hebrew
authors deliberately drew attention to other gods, in order to exalt the
greatness of Yahweh by contrast.[29] Descriptions of his power over nature
invite us to contemplate a divine architect whose influence is universal,
not a departmental deity with a particular sphere of influence in the sky,
or in water or earth, but a deity of a different kind and on a different
scale altogether:

Who has measured the waters in the hollow of his hand
and marked off the heavens with a span,
enclosed the dust of the earth in a measure
and weighed the mountains in scales
and the hills in a balance?[30]

This passage goes on to mock the gods of the nations for being impotent
idols, but returns soon afterwards to the image of the heavenly council.[31]
Like the psalmists, Second Isaiah draws attention to other gods in order
to show that there is really no God like Yahweh. This sort of theology,
known as henotheism, represents an intermediate stage between polytheism and monotheism and has been described as the belief that while
other gods might exist, only one God really matters.[32] In other words,
the one and the many are acknowledged, while simultaneously exalting
the One. It may well be that Celtic Christianity also had a henotheistic
stage, as clergy and laity alike adjusted their world-view from polytheism
to monotheism. They knew, or believed, that their ancestors had worshipped the elements.[33] And though they no longer called them gods,
many Christians continued to regard them in some way as spiritual
powers.

OATHS BY THE ELEMENTS

In the personalised universe of primal religions (19) human beings are
surrounded on all sides by friendly and unfriendly transcendent beings.
While there is no way of proving that the idea of the elements as personal
powers and legal guarantors comes to Celtic Christianity from Celtic
primal religion this is certainly how some Celtic Christians presented the
world-view of their ancestors, when they began to write about it in sagas

and mythological histories from about the ninth century onwards. The following example comes from the twelfth-century collection *Lebor na hUidre / Book of the Dun Cow*, but earlier versions of the story do exist and the poem at the end may be ninth-century in origin. The story tells how Loegaire king of Tara swore by the elements and subsequently broke his promise, with fatal results:

> Loegaire went on a hosting to Leinster, to exact the cattle tribute from them. The Lagin [the people of Leinster] assembled and gave battle to him and Loegaire was defeated in battle, i.e. in the battle of Ath Dara. Loegaire was captured in this battle and pledges were given to the Lagin; i.e. the sun and the moon, water and air, day and night, sea and land, that he would not demand the tribute during his life. Thereupon he was released.
>
> Now this had been foretold to Loegaire, that it would be between Ireland and Alba that he would find his death, and hence he never went on a naval expedition. Loegaire then went on a hosting to exact the cattle tribute from them. He did not however bear the pledges in mind. When he came to Grelach Da Phil on the side of Casse in the plain of Liffey, between the two hills which are called Ériu and Albu, he died there of the sun and of the wind and of the other pledges; for at that time no one dared break faith with them. So that hence the poet said:
>
>> Loegaire Mac Néill died on the side of Casse, in the green land.
>> The elements of God which he invoked as a pledge brought
>>   the fatal encounter to the king.
>> The battle of Ath Dara the Swift was that in which
>> Loegaire Mac Néill was captured
>> The just sanction of the elements of God, it is this which
>>   killed Loegaire.[34]

We can only guess at the exact meaning of 'he died there of the sun and of the wind and of the other pledges'. Our scientific world-view calls for an explanation involving sun-stroke or perhaps a falling tree, but even if this were a historical account of Loegaire's death, it is difficult to imagine him dying simultaneously from eight different causes, all of them due to the elements. There is in Irish story-telling a motif known as 'the three-fold death' whereby people die of a combination of wounding, burning and drowning, but it seems more likely that in this instance Loegaire dies by the will and decision of the elements rather than by their direct intervention. Another phrase from the same tale – 'they passed a judgement of death on the king' – sounds more like rulers or magistrates than executioners. As for the treaty with the Lagin, the fact that the elements are invoked as pledges in such an important transaction as the ransoming of a king, gives some indication of the status in which they were believed to have been held. They appear here as the guardians of cosmic order, and since kingly misrule was one of the traditional causes of cosmic disorder, it comes as no surprise to find them carrying out 'just sanctions' against an unjust king.[35] The author's quiet approval of the situation suggests that he understood and perhaps shared this traditional world-view, though he is careful to indicate that the elements are not independent spiritual powers, but the *Duli Dé*, the elements of God. Other writers preferred to see the saints as mediators of divine judgement, and in one version of the story the role of the elements is played down and Loegaire dies after being cursed by Patrick.[36]

It would be easy to multiply examples of swearing by the elements. The 'unfree people' end their unsuccessful revolt with an oath – by the sky, the earth, the moon and the bright sun – to return to their subject status.[37] Sun and moon, sea and land are demanded as sureties before one of the single combats in the *Táin*, and the sureties of sea and wind, sun, ether and firmament bring about the death of Aed Ruad when he defrauds one of his champions and drowns in the rapids at the mouth of the river Erne, 'by a miracle of sea and mighty wind.'[38] Oaths by the elements also appear in Classical texts which could possibly have influenced the saga-writers. But they could hardly have influenced the framing of Adamnán's Law.[39] This would seem to be another example of the way in which the primal imagination shapes similar beliefs in unrelated cultures.

A STORM WOMAN

When Muirchertach son of Muiredach, son of Eogan, king of Ireland, was in the House of Cletech, beyond the Boyne of the Brugh – and he had a wife, Duaibsech, daughter of Duach Brazentongue, king of Connacht – the king came out one day to hunt on the border of the Brugh, and his hunting companions left him alone on his hunting mound.

He had not been there long when he noticed a solitary young woman, shapely and fine, fair-headed, bright-skinned, with a green mantle about her, sitting near him on the mound; and it seemed to him that of womankind he had never seen her equal for beauty and refinement. So that all his body and nature filled with love for her, for gazing at her it seemed to him that he would give the whole of Ireland for one night's loan of her, so utterly did he love her at first sight. And he welcomed her as if he knew her and asked her for news.

'I will tell you', she said. 'I am the sweetheart of Muirchertach
mac Erca, king of Ireland, and I have come here to look for him.'

That pleased Muirchertach and he said to her: 'Do you know
who I am, girl? he says.

'I do,' she answers, 'for I know more secret places than this, and
I know you and the other men of Ireland as well.'

'Will you come with me, girl?' says Muirchertach.

'I would,' she answers, 'if you rewarded me well.'

'I will give you power over me, girl,' says Mac Erca.

'Your word on that,' says the girl, and he gave it at once...

'I will give you a hundred of every herd and a hundred drinking-
horns, and a hundred cups and a hundred gold rings and a feast
every other night in the House of Cletach.'

'No,' says the girl, 'Not that. But you must never utter my name,
and Duaibsech the mother of your children shall not be in my
presence, and the clerics must never enter the same house as me.'

'You shall have all this,' says the king, 'for I gave you my word,
but it would be easier for me to give you half of Ireland. And tell
me truly,' says the king, 'what your name is, so that I can avoid
saying it.'

And she said, 'Sigh, Sough, Storm, Rough wind, Winter night,
Cry, Wail, Groan.'[40]

So begins the death-tale of Muirchertach mac Erca. Muirchertach was a
sixth-century king of Tara, but apart from that little is known about him
historically. His mother, Erc daughter of Loarn, came from Lorn in
Scotland, according to one eleventh-century poem. The same source
says that the young Muirchertach committed murder in his own country
and was exiled to his mother's people. Once there, he murdered his
grandfather, Loarn, and was exiled again – this time to the land of the
Britons, whence he returned to Ireland.[41] Some of these episodes are
mentioned in the confession which he eventually makes to St Cairnech.

Muirchertach takes the beautiful young woman home and puts his
wife and children out of the house. When Cairnech hears of this, he goes
to the king's fort on the Hill of Cletach and curses it: 'May neither its
corn nor its milk be good'. Meanwhile Muirchertach's mysterious sweetheart, whose principal name is Sín (meaning 'Storm'), is seeking justice
for an older wrong. Muirchertach does not know this, but her courtship
of him is an act of vengeance for the death of her family and all the old
tribes of Tara whom he had murdered. She presides at his feasts but
serves him poisonous wine and 'druidical meat' which deprive him of his

strength. She then conjures up enemies from stones and clods of earth, and he is unable to defeat them.

The clerics find him hacking away at the ground and release him from his delusions, teaching him to make the sign of the cross in front of his eyes. They also advise him to build a church to the 'Great Lord of the Elements'. He does so, makes his confession and receives communion, but as soon as he returns to Sín he relapses. One winter's night she summons up snow and gales, and he carelessly pronounces some of her forbidden names. He begins to have prophetic nightmares, including one of being burnt alive in a house full of demons. This comes horribly true when Sín burns the house down round him and he dies. His rejected wife keens for him and dies of grief. So does the hauntingly beautiful Sín, after making her confession to St Cairnech.

This powerful tale of obsession and revenge appeals to us today mainly for its grand emotions and its conflicting values. This may not be so very different from the response of its original listeners, but the story also touches on dynastic politics and on the relationship of Christianity to primal religion. Contemporary listeners would have recognised in Sín some of the characteristics of the pre-christian goddesses. Like a 'war goddess' (29) she robs Muirchertach of his strength; like a 'sovereignty goddess' (32–4) she serves him food and drink. We are even told that Muirchertach thought of her as 'a goddess of great power', though this is pointedly presented as one of his delusions. Her rivalry with the Creator and her ability to turn water into wine are clearly intended to be blasphemous – but she is also made to profess her own mortality and even her faith in God.

The author clearly wants us to think of Sín as a human being whose power is due to druidry rather than divinity. However, the release which Muirchertach obtains by dedicating a church to 'The Great Lord of the Elements', together with her strange names and her residual goddess features, suggests that somewhere in the background to this tale there might once have been an elemental deity of storms and winds, or some other more familiar deity whose power over the weather is not usually described in quite such dramatic terms. In another version of the tale, she is 'Sín daughter of Sige of the *síd* mounds' – without doubt, an Otherworld figure.[42]

The present text belongs to the period of late-middle / early-modern Irish and therefore represents a much later stage in the tradition from Blathmac's poetry, the Law of Adamnán and 'St Patrick's Breastplate', none of which contain any reference to Otherworld beings. There is no doubt that Cairnech is the spiritual authority in this tale, but it is

Muirchertach rather than Sín who is the villain of the piece or, at best, the tragic hero. Sín is presented as human rather than demonic, her actions springing from family loyalty rather than from an evil nature, and when she does eventually salute the clerics and receives their salutation in return, the moment is almost one of mutual respect. This will not be enough for readers who regret the passing of the old goddesses and feminine divine imagery in general. As for Muirchertach, he is eventually released from hell through the prayers of St Cairnech who, we are told, could save even the worst person who ever lived.

THE COSMIC CHRIST

A rather different view of the elements appears in the Irish biblical apocryphon known as *Tenga Bhith-Nua Annso Sis / The Evernew Tongue Here Below*. In its present form, this text was probably composed in Ireland during the tenth century, but it may be based on Latin or Greek sources.[43] It is basically a cosmological treatise, presented as a question-and-answer session between the apostle Philip, who appears from heaven especially for the purpose, and a large number of Hebrew sages assembled on Mount Zion. Suddenly they see a dazzling light in the sky and a clear friendly voice speaks to them in the language of the angels – a universal language which birds and animals also understand. The voice belongs to the apostle Philip, who introduces himself as 'the Evernew Tongue', this being a sort of heavenly nickname. He has been sent, he tells them, to explain all about creation:

> For that tale [the Genesis story] tells of the making of heaven and earth ... and of the formation of the world, which has been brought about by Christ's resurrection from the dead on this eve of Easter. For every material and every element and every nature which is seen in the world were all combined in the body in which Christ arose, that is in the body of every human person.
>
> Firstly, there is the matter of wind and air. This is how respiration came about in human bodies. Then there is the matter of heat and boiling from fire. This is what makes the red heat of blood in bodies. Then there is the matter of the sun and the other stars of heaven, and this is what makes the lustre and light in people's eyes. Then there is the matter of bitterness and saltness; and this is what makes the bitterness of tears and the gall of the liver and much anger in human hearts. Then there is the matter of the stones and clay of the earth; and this is what joins together to form flesh and bone and limbs in human beings. Then there is the matter of the flowers and

beautiful colours of earth; and this is what makes the different complexions and whiteness of faces and colour in cheeks.

All the world arose with him, for the nature of all the elements was in the body which Jesus assumed. For unless the Lord had suffered on behalf of Adam's race, and unless he had risen after death, the whole world, together with Adam's race, would be destroyed at the coming of doom; and no creature of sea or of land would be reborn, but the heavens, as far as the third heaven would blaze. None would remain unburnt except for the three heavens of the great Heavenly Kingdom. There would be neither earth nor kindred, alive or dead, in the world, only hell and heaven, had not the Lord come to ransom them. All would have perished in this way without renewal.[44]

There is a sense of delight in this text – a delight at explaining things, and a delight at the ingenuity of God and the intricacy of creation. The elements are intimately present here as part of the human frame, the raw materials of our physical and emotional make-up. They are our breath, blood, tears, bones and beauty. The sense of kinship with nature could hardly be more powerfully expressed – and not just kinship, but dependence as well. This is the language of poetry rather than anatomy, but it is ecologically exact in its insight that human beings are not a separate creation but very much part of nature. In the Hebrew Bible, the first human is made from the dust of the earth, brought to life by the breath or Spirit of God. This tradition was certainly known in Ireland, from Genesis and from apocryphal works like 2 Enoch and the Irish *Creation of Adam* which is closely related to it and describes Adam's breath as 'the light of the world, namely the Holy Spirit'.[45] If these texts deal mainly with Creation, *The Evernew Tongue* focuses on a different moment of intimacy between God and nature – the Incarnation.

In *The Evernew Tongue*'s version of this mystery, God becomes one with creation, with fire, air, stones, bitterness and flowers, at the same time as becoming one with human flesh, 'for the nature of all the elements dwelt in the body which Jesus assumed'. It is not humans alone who become a new creation through his risen body, but the elements, all the raw materials of creation, are saved as well. There are parallels here with Irenaeus's doctrine of recapitulation which teaches that Christ came into the world as a second Adam, to overcome death and restore all things to fullness of life in God.[46] Irenaeus, a second-century bishop in Celtic Gaul, was writing to refute the gnostic idea that only spiritual realities have any value. He argued that the material world is also blessed and sanctified, since God became one with it in the Incarnation, and through the Resurrection re-opened the way to life for the whole creation. This is also the case in *The Evernew Tongue,* where the whole created order – human bodies, the elements, even sea creatures and land-animals – are saved by the resurrection of Christ. The elements are not gods here, or guarantors, or members of the heavenly host. Neither are they the forces of chaos, though they do contribute bitterness to our bodies as well as beauty. They are building blocks of the creation, indispensable and bound for glory in a way which western theology has never really come to terms with.

THE DOCTRINE OF CREATION

In the beginning God created the heaven and the earth etc. The High-king of the world who is mightier than any king, higher than any power, fiercer than any dragon, gentler than any child, brighter than suns, holier than any saint, more vengeful than men, more loving than any mother, the only Son of God the Father has given to the many tribes of the world this account of the form and creation of the universe. Since the shape that everything visible in the universe possesses was unknown save only to God: since for Adam's race it was 'a head in a bag' and 'being in a dark house' never having known what shape was on the world, nor who created it, until this account came from heaven to open the sense and intellect of all, so that the way of life and salvation might be ascertained and found by souls.

For everything was obscure to the eyes of Adam's race, except that they used to see the course of the stars, to wit, of the moon and sun and the other stars, which used to go round every day continually without resting. So they used to see the world's wells and rivers flowing without cessation always at every time. So they used to see the sadness of the earth, and the trance and sleep of the light and the fruits at the coming of winter. So they used to see the resurrection of the world, with its warmth and light, with its flowers and fruits at the rearising of summer. Still they knew not who made it until there came the story of the creation of the world with its shapes and services as God had arranged them. Obscure then, was all this until this tale was set forth, until it was revealed by the Evernew Tongue who spoke from the roof of heaven above the assembly of Mount Zion.[47]

The story of Creation was told and retold many times in Celtic Christianity. One of its oldest Latin hymns, the *Altus Prosator* ascribed to

Colum Cille, praises the Creator and describes his work.[48] The tenth-century Irish Adam and Eve story known as *Saltair na Rann / The Psalter of Quatrains* retells the Genesis narrative in detail, and the extract above comes from the opening lines of *The Evernew Tongue*.

It is often said that there was no Creation myth in Irish primal religion. This may or may not be true, but few cultures are without a myth of origins. Fragments of such a myth may be embedded in texts like the birth-tale of Conn Cétchathach – Conn of the Hundred Battles – where in a single night Ireland is provided with a king, and a number of famous trees, rivers, loughs and even roads. Towards the end of the *Táin*, there is an episode in which the Donn of Cuailgne and another great bull tear each other to pieces and their bodies become features of the landscape. This is reminiscent of Babylonian and Indian mythology where the earth is formed from the dismembered bodies of Tiamat and Purusha. Other origin myths use the imagery of hatching, begetting or giving birth. Sometimes the first existents are simply there without explanation, as God is in the opening chapters of Genesis. Creation is only one of a number of ways of thinking about the beginning, but if the idea did come to Ireland with Christianity, there are signs that it received an enthusiastic response.

Muirchú tells the story of Monesan, an Anglo-Saxon princess whose intuitive understanding of the doctrine of Creation leads to her conversion. Passionately interested in the world around her and not satisfied with simply seeing the sun in the sky, she wants to know who made it. On learning that it was made by 'he whose seat is in heaven' she becomes so intent on seeing God that her bewildered parents take her to Ireland to meet Patrick, who questions her, recognises her as a believer, and baptises her at once.[49] Here, the doctrine of creation forms the principal threshold between primal religion and Christianity.

In *The Evernew Tongue*, Creation comes literally as a revelation. Heaven opens, and suddenly people understand things which had puzzled them before. Significantly, the phenomena which are singled out for attention include elements and aspects of nature which were probably focal points of primal religion in pre-christian times: sun, moon and stars, wells and rivers, the earth. The implication would seem to be that before they heard about the Creator, people simply did not understand what they were seeing. According to St Paul, it has always been possible to perceive God's invisible nature in creation. He gives the Romans a tongue-lashing for seeing it and not acting on it.[50] *The Evernew Tongue* is slightly gentler, presenting their condition as a kind of imprisonment – 'head in a bag' and 'in a dark house' – from which they are now set free.

There can be little doubt that the doctrine of Creation was enjoyed in
early Christian Ireland, but it is more difficult to be sure that it resulted
in a greater appreciation of nature. As we have seen, a sense of kinship
with nature and of the sacramental universe are common features of
primal religions throughout the world, so much so that they used to be
referred to as 'nature religions' or 'fertility cults'. It seems unlikely that
Celtic primal religion was entirely unlike other primal religions in this
respect. The Christians of medieval Ireland certainly believed that
nature had been a focus of worship for their ancestors, and many features
of their own outdoor spirituality are more credibly explained by a selec-
tive and creative continuity with the past, rather than through the sole
influence of the Bible or missionary teaching. True, there is a freshness
and a joy in some of the monastic nature poems which is difficult to
match in the sagas, but *Finn's poem on Mayday* (122) breathes a similar
spirit, earlier, and with no obvious christian references at all.

Could it be that people felt safer with the elements, once they could
envisage them under the control of a benevolent Creator – the God of
the Elements? [51] Instead of an array of powerful energies of more or less
equal weight, did they now see the elements as taking their place, like
local kings and chieftains, under the authority of the High King of
Heaven? Such a move would mirror changes in Irish society during the
early medieval period. Unfortunately, we do not know enough about
Celtic primal religion to map out the changing cosmology quite so pre-
cisely, but it seems that while the term *Dia dúilech* can certainly be
rendered 'Creator God', the adjective *dúilech* suggests something imbu-
ing the elements and creatures, rather than shaping them like an artisan. [52] This 'something' – which we may glimpse in the Amairgen poem
'I am wind on sea ...' – would already have given some sense of unity to
nature, so the doctrine of creation did not necessarily provide this for the
first time. It is interesting to speculate about why the idea proved so
popular. There must have been something new and different about it, but
unless it also had some point of contact with something which people
already recognised and valued, they could never have received it at all.

With the arrival of the Creator, the old gods and goddesses gradually
disappeared into the landscapes and elements which were once their
homes, to emerge only in disguise or with new identities, as strange
people from long ago, and perhaps as that curious but respected group,
'the elements of God'. Even today there are people who regret their
disappearance. The planet is felt to be more vulnerable without them
and there is a nostalgia for their presence. This reawakening of the
primal signals a disaffection with the modern Western mind-set, but it

also often includes a rejection of Christianity which, in its dominant forms, appears to care little for the earth and its creatures and even stands accused of colluding with those who harm it.[53] Celtic Christianity took shape in a different world, where the main environmental challenges were from floods, fires and pestilences rather than from men and women. Not all of its insights are of value today, but its strong sense of intimacy, on many levels, between God, nature and human beings, offers a traditional but neglected christian cosmology which may well have something to offer.

Chapter 10

Signs of Life

We have heard from Patrick in his own words remembering how, as a young man, he found God in the forests and on the mountain, in all weathers. We have heard about the mythologised Patrick, who also prays on a mountain and meets an angel there, founds a church in the wood of Fochloth and another by a sacred tree, celebrates the resurrection with fire and baptises people in   springs. The traditions of other saints are similar: Colum Cille founds churches in woods, blesses a healing well, and converses with angels on a little hill. Brigit's church at Kildare was famous for its oak tree, its leafy altar-base and its perpetual flame. Clearly, there was an outdoor spirituality in Irish and Hebridean Christianity from earliest times. The churches, when they were built, remained close to nature, with natural symbols both inside and out.

From the first centuries of vernacular poetry, Irish poets chose to write about nature, observing it and celebrating it. They also retained an emotional connection with their subject, even when dealing with complex poetical forms. Nature was a place of prayer for many of them, a place of healing and inspiration. Hardship was an acknowledged part of this experience, indeed it sometimes seems to have been deliberately sought out so that nature became a place of challenge and transformation in the face of something greater than themselves. Saints are sometimes portrayed as being in harmony with nature in an extraordinary way, either because of their friendship with the wild creatures or through a God-given alliance with the elements. Metaphors like 'sun of women' and 'the salmon of the well of mercy' draw clear lines of connection between nature and the saints or Christ, indicating through language a continuing sense of the sacramental universe.

Nature also appears frequently in writings about the pre-christian past. In the place-lore tradition for example, rivers and loughs, hills, mountains and plains are often named after extraordinary men and women of the past, many of whom are probably the euhemerised local deities of Irish primal religion. There are tales of Otherworld beings encountered unexpectedly in the midst of nature or deliberately courted or sought out, at certain times of year and in certain places. Nature provided many of the symbols of sacred kingship, particularly the tree and the branch of kingship. The fertility of the land was traditionally linked with the king's wisdom and justice and his relationship with the Otherworld powers. The various Celtic paradises were imagined first and foremost as places of great natural beauty, rather than as heavenly assemblies or celestial cities. Nature also provided access to the Otherworld through wells, caves and *síd* mounds, the journey to it being by land or water, rather than through the air. The benefits of the Otherworld were traditionally believed to be available in this world through certain persons and objects, and also through trees and rivers. The Boyne and the Shannon, for example, were said to flow from the well of wisdom and knowledge in the Otherworld.

There is a certain amount of overlap between stories of the pre-christian past and more obviously ecclesiastical texts like hymns, martyrologies and Lives of saints. Both pre-christian figures and saints climb mountains and perform 'sunwise circuits' and miracles at holy wells. The 'litany' of the Yew of Ross contains a handful of christian epithets, and many which are obscure and possibly derived ultimately from pre-christian forms of worship. The staff of Jesus probably owes at least as much to the native 'branch of peace' as it does to the staffs of Moses or Aaron. Mixed traditions like these may well mark the transition from primal religion to a strongly-enculturated Christianity. This transition was not accomplished overnight: centuries after the event, people were still sifting and re-evaluating the past, retelling traditional stories for contemporary purposes, as well as parts of the Bible in their own words. Some primal beliefs about nature were probably carried over quite unconsciously, as part of a generalised world-view. Others were consciously adapted and interwoven with christian sources.

Nature is an area in which the overlap between Celtic Christianity and primal religion is particularly obvious. This is a source of anxiety to some people, particularly when it comes to the use of natural symbols in prayer and worship. It is easy to lose sight of the fact that many of the great figures of the judeo-christian tradition stand against a mythological background of sacred trees, holy mountains and sacred waters, and that usually these are presented as places of theophany and blessing. True, there was a stage in which nature sanctuaries were condemned by the prophets. The 'abominations' said to have taken place on the 'high places' and 'beneath every spreading tree' have left behind a legacy of fear which has more to do with unacceptable religous rites than with nature itself. The prophets also denounced idolatry, though this can affect any symbol or doctrine. A centralising tendency in favour of the Temple in Jerusalem is also evident, though Jerusalem also stands on a holy mountain. The prophets found themselves unable to dispense with the language of nature when speaking about God: as the fountain of life, an evergreen cypress, a fiery brightness in a storm cloud and so on. In other parts of the tradition, nature sanctuaries are deliberately claimed as hebrew and later christian holy places – the oaks of Mamre, the well at Beersheba, Sinai and Carmel, the river Jordan, the pool of Siloam, Jacob's well, Tabor, Calvary. We also find visionary landscapes in the Bible, and metaphors drawn from nature are used repeatedly to express the power and presence of God.

Whatever the doctrinal differences between the faiths, the christian experience of nature can never be radically separated from the experience of people from other religions and other periods of history, because of our common humanity. For the same reason, there will also be shared perceptions between religious people and unbelievers. Nature is life to us, in a most basic and essential way, so that in the primal religions it is regarded with a mixture of joy and dread. The author of *The Evernew Tongue* presents nature as the place where the ancestors could have found the Creator, in the continual movement of the sun and stars, the ever-flowing waters, the cycle of the seasons. We are very close here to the most basic level of religious experience, with the realisation that the universe has a rhythm of its own and is governed by visible and invisible energies on which we are ultimately dependent. Here, at the junction of the practical and the mystical, it is easy to see why nature so easily generates signs of the Sacred, both in primal religions and in the world religions which build on them or develop out of them.

Natural phenomena can be used to symbolise invisible as well as visible necessities. In both Irish and biblical literature, water is associated with wisdom and trees with kingship. Natural symbols are also found in Irish myths of justice and peace, education and the arts, all of which were seen as essential and life-giving to the community. Most of these symbols are attractive: the fruitful tree, the salmon of wisdom, the fire in the hearth. But they also acknowledged the destructive side of nature, either as the elements in an angry mood, or as strange chaotic forces like the water monster or the fiery dragon. Some of what seems to us today to be harshness, was probably understood at the time simply as the right response to injustice, as when the elements pass a death sentence on Loegaire for breaking his treaty with the Lagin. As for the water monster and the dragon, they lie in wait for anyone and only people of unusual courage and character can put them in their place and then only with divine or Otherworld assistance. This ambivalence towards nature is mirrored to some extent in the Bible, where the waters of peace are also the waters of the Flood.

The christian message that nature was ultimately in the hands of a single Creator or divine craftsman, seems to have been welcomed in Ireland. Certainly, the theme of Creation was popular with Irish writers, as were titles like 'King of cloudy heaven' and 'God of the Elements'. The christian God does not appear in person in the midst of the land-scape – despite precedents in Genesis – but the distance between this world and the next was constantly bridged by saints and angels. Often, places where this was believed to have happened were also natural fea-tures, so that God, though hidden, was still approachable through nature and could even be spoken to quite boldly at times. Some texts, following New Testament and other sources, envisage an even closer relationship between nature and the Creator through the incarnation and resurrection of Christ. People also believed that the landscapes before their eyes were not the only landscapes; that there were other levels of reality where one might see the Tree of Life, meet with biblical characters, visit paradise islands, and converse with angels or human souls in the form of birds.

Finally, it is important to recognise that the Celtic experience of nature which we have been describing, goes beyond what is socially and materially useful. There is little to be gained, socially or materially, from gazing out to sea or listening to birdsong in a wood.Yet there is some-thing going on in these poems, which seems to me to be absolutely essential. We may find it hard to articulate what it is. We may even be unwilling to take it seriously, and certainly there are other claims on our attention – other needs, other kinds of beauty; but without nature we are literally nowhere and nothing, at least as far as this world is concerned; and if there is another, nature is the way to it, according to Celtic tradition.

> The God who made the world and all the things in it, being ruler of heaven and earth, does not live in shrines made by human beings, nor is he served by human hands, as though he needed anything, since he himself gives life and breath and everything to all creatures ... Yet he is not far from each of us, for indeed as some of your own poets have said: In him we live and move and have our being.
>
> St Paul to the Athenians, Acts 17:24–5, 27b–28

Notes

CHAPTER ONE

1. See K. Hughes and A. Hamlin, *The Modern Traveller to the Early Irish Church*, London, 1977, 54–79.
2. R. Sharpe, *Adomnán of Iona: Life of Saint Columba*, London, 1995, III. 17. 219 and 369.
3. See p. 41. Hereafter, cross-references to other parts of the book simply appear as nos in brackets.
4. Journals include *Ériu*, *Éigse*, *Revue Celtique (RC)*, *Cambrian (formerly Cambridge) Medieval Celtic Studies (CMCS)*, *Zeitschrift für Celtisches Philologie (ZCP)*, *Études Celtiques (EC)*, *Studia Hibernica (Stud. Hib.)*, *Peritia*, *Celtica* and the folklore journals *Béaloideas* and *Folklore*. Most of them are available for consultation in University libraries and other specialist centres.
5. On the question of gender, there is little to suggest that women were commonly engaged in religious writing in medieval Ireland. We do hear occasionally of a woman poet (Liadin of Corkaguiney, for example: Meyer *AIP*, 65–6; Murphy, *EIL* 82–5) so the idea of a literary woman was not unthinkable, though few if any of the surviving texts can be ascribed definitely to women. However, given the small amount of research in this area to date, and the large number of anonymous texts which exist, the possibility of female authorship cannot be dismissed entirely. Awaiting further research, I will therefore occasionally refer to scribes/editors/authors as 'he or she', though there can be little doubt that we are dealing with a predominantly masculine tradition.
6. Meyer, *AIP* 3; extracts from this tale are also found in Jackson, *CM*, 173–5; T. P. Cross and C. H. Slover, *Ancient Irish Tales*, London, 1973, 588–95; and Murphy, *EIL*, 92–101. For the full text, see *The Voyage of Bran, Son of Febal*, ed. A. Nutt and K. Meyer, London, 1895.
7. See, for example, the section on Iona's library in T. O. Clancy and G. Márkus, *Iona: The earliest poetry of a Celtic Monastery*, Edinburgh, 1995, 211–2.
8. H. P. Oskamp, *The Voyage of Máel Dúin*, Groningen, 1970. *The Voyage of the Úi Corra*, ed. W. Stokes, *RC* 14, 1893, 22–69. Jackson prints extracts from both in *CM*, 152–62.
9. Cf. *The Voyage of St Brendan*, trans. J. F. Webb, in *The Age of Bede*, rev. edn, 1988, 211–45.
10. See 43–5. For further reading, see J. Carey, 'The location of the Otherworld

192 Celtic Christianity and Nature

in Irish Tradition', *Éigse* 19, 1982–3, 36–43; P. Sims-Williams, 'Some Celtic
Otherworld Terms', in *Celtic Language, Celtic Culture*, ed. A. T. E. Matonis
and D. F. Melia, Van Nuys, 1990.
11. See p. 113–14. For Judas Iscariot, see *The Voyage of St Brendan* §25, in
   Webb and Farmer, *The Age of Bede*, 239–40.
12. G. Murphy, 'The origin of Irish nature poetry', *Studies* 20, 1931, 87–101.
13. See J. G. Frazer, *The Golden Bough*, abridged edition, London, 1922, 48–52.
   Cf. V. Flint, *The Rise of Magic in Early Medieval Europe*, Princeton, 1991, 3–
   8. For further discussion, see J. P. Mackey, 'Magic in Celtic primal religion',
   ZCP 45, 1992, 66–84.
14. Rev. 21:11,25; 22:12.
15. *The Voyage of St Brendan*, trans. Webb, 245, 212.
16. Murphy, 'The origin', 87–101.
17. *Lebor Gabála Érenn / The Book of the Takings of Ireland* [commonly abbre-
   viated *LG* and also known as *The Book of Conquests*] part 5, ITS 44, ed. R.
   A. S. Macalister, Dublin, 1956, 110–13.
18. Macalister, *LG*.
19. Ex. 3:14; Jn 6:41; 8:12, 58; 10:7; 14:6; 15:5.
20. *Bhagavad Gita*, 10:30–31.
21. Murphy, 'The origin', 87–101.
22. *The Táin*, ed. T. Kinsella, Oxford, 1970, 101–2. The *Táin* is one of a number
   of Irish texts which retain their Irish titles even in translation.
23. Ibid., 111.
24. J. Gantz, *EIMS*, London, 1981, 103–4.
25. *Félire*, 56. A more accessible edition is 'The Bird's Lament for Molua', ed.
   Jackson, 296 in *CM*, 296.
26. See 111. Jonas's 7th cent. *Life of Columbanus* I, §8, 15, 17, cited by Murphy
   in 'The origin', together with similar traditions about Ciarán of Saighir,
   Cainneach, Moling, and Coemgen, from C. Plummer, *VSH*.
27. The fullest work on the *Céli Dé* is probably that of P. O'Dwyer, *CD*.
28. '"The two eyes of Ireland": religion and literature in Ireland in the eighth
   and ninth centuries', in *The Church of Ireland AD 432–1932: the report of the
   Church of Ireland Conference held in Dublin, 11th–14th October, 1932*, ed. W.
   Bell and N. D. Emerson, Dublin, 1932, 73. *The Irish Tradition*, Oxford,
   1947, 47
29. For example, by Seamus Heaney in 'The God in the Tree', *Pleasures of
   Gaelic Poetry*, ed. Seán Mac Réamoinn, London, 1982, 25.
30. See below, introduction to chapter seven, 'Poetry of the Woods and Seasons'.
31. D. Ó Corráin, 'Early Irish Hermit Poetry?', in *SSS*, 251–67.
32. 'Three Legends from the Brussels Manuscript 5100–4', ed. Stokes, *RC* 26,
   372–7; Plummer, *op. cit.* II, 122–4.
33. A scribal note in Latin at the end of the Book of Leinster version of the *Táin*
   reads: 'I who have copied down this story, or more accurately fantasy, do not
   credit the details of the story or fantasy. Some things in it are devilish lies
   and others poetical figments; some seem possible and others not; some are
   for the enjoyment of idiots.' *Táin*, 283. A note in Irish above it invokes a
   blessing on anyone who will memorise it faithfully in its existing form and
   not change it in any way.

34. G. S. Mac Eoin, 'Orality and literacy in some middle-Irish king-tales', in S. N. Tranter and L. C. Tristram (eds), *Early Irish Literature – Media and Communication*, Tübingen, 1992, 149–83.
35. J. V. Taylor, *The Primal Vision: Christian presence and African Religion*, London, 1965, 203–4; Noel O'Donoghue, 'St Patrick's Breastplate', in *An Introduction to Celtic Christianity*, ed. J. P. Mackey, Edinburgh, 1989, 46–54. O'Donoghue cites P. L. Henry, *Saoithiulacht na Sean-Ghaeilge*, Dublin, 1978, 137.
36. For the full text see *The Irish Liber Hymnorum* II, ed. J. H. Bernard and R. Atkinson, HBS 14, London, 1898, 49–51; the translation used here is that of Meyer, *AIP*, 25–7 but there are several others, e.g. in *GT*, 30–1 and in *TP* II, 354–8.
37. G. S. Mac Eoin, 'The invocation of nature in the loricae', *Stud. Hib.* 2, 1962, 212–17. For more on the *Benedicite*, see pp. 173–5.
38. 'Invocation of the Graces', in *CG* I, 6–7. 'Bathing Prayer' 60–3. 'Invocation for Justice' 52–9.
39. 'The Primal Religions of the world and their study', in *Australian Essays in World Religions*, ed. V. Hayes, Bedford Park, 1977, 32; Turner, ibid., 28.
40. Based on Turner, op. cit., 32.
41. Taylor, *Primal Vision;* Andrew Walls, 'Primal Religious Traditions in Today's World', in *Religion in Today's World*, ed. F. Whaling, Edinburgh, 1987, 250–78; Kwame Bediako, 'The primal imagination and the opportunity for a new theological idiom', Duff Lectures, 1990, New College, Edinburgh (awaiting publication).

CHAPTER TWO

1. I have followed Georóid Mac Eoin's guide to the different periods of the Irish language. These are roughly as follows: C5–7 Ogam script, C7 Archaic Irish, C8–9 Old Irish, C10–12 Middle Irish, C13–16 Early Modern Irish, C17f. Modern Irish. For details, see G. Mac Eoin, in *The Celtic Languages*, ed. M. J. Ball with J. Fife, London, 1993, 102. On sacred kingship see F. J. Byrne, *Irish Kings and High Kings*, London, 1973, 159, 256; on the continuing potency of myth in medieval and early-modern Ireland, see J. Mackey, 'Primal past and christian present: Religions of the Celts and the Koories', paper presented at the 1st Australian Conference of Celtic Studies, Sydney, 1992, and 'Mythical past and political present', paper presented at the 3rd Colloquium of the Russian Association of Celtic Studies, St Petersburg, 1994.
2. Based on *LG*, 34–7. Readers who require an exact literal translation of the texts in this book should consult the scholarly editions referred to in the footnotes. The versions given here are closely based on these, but without some of the awkward turns of phrase and deliberate archaisms which were sometimes introduced to give the texts a more historical-literary flavour.
3. *Rennes, RC* 16, 1895, 44–6.
4. Kilbride XVI copy of the *Dindshenchas* of Ard Macha, in 'The Edinburgh Dindshenchas', ed. W. Stokes, *Folklore* 4, 1893, 480–1.
5. For another version of this story, see *Táin*, ed. Kinsella, 6–8.
6. *Rennes, RC* 16, 1895, 279–83.
7. See 43–5. J. Carey discusses all the Macha traditions in detail in his 'Notes on the Irish war goddess', *Eigse* 19, 1982–3, 263–75.

8. *MD* III, 2–25. A shorter prose version may be found in *Rennes, RC* 15, lines 311–15.
9. *MD* III, 18–19, lines 217–18.
10. *The Wooing of Emer / Tochmarc Émire, RC* 11, 442–3. See also M. MacNeill, *The Festival of Lughnasad,* Dublin, 1962, I, 7.
11. *MD* III, 10–11, 14–15, lines 109–10 and 165–6.
12. *MD* IV, 146–163.
13. *Rennes, RC* 15, 277–9.
14. See D. A. Binchy, 'The fair of Tailtiu and the feast of Tara', *Ériu* 18–19, 1958, 127–36.
15. *Rennes, RC* 16, 61.
16. *On the Fitness of Names / Cóir Anmann,* ed. W. Stokes, *IT* 3, eds. Windisch and Stokes, Leipzig, 1891, 403.
17. Stokes, *RC* 24, 173, 178–9, §7. For more on Samain and the other festivals, see D. O hOgain, *Myth, Legend and Romance,* London, 1990, 402–4, and K. Danaher, 'Irish folk tradition and the Celtic calendar', in *Celtic Consciousness,* ed. R. O'Driscoll, Edinburgh, 1982, 217–25.
18. For more details on the traditional fairs, see K. Simms, *From Kings to Warlords,* Woodbridge, 1987, 62–3.
19. See *Rennes, RC* 15, 315.
20. K. Meyer, *The Triads of Ireland,* Dublin, 1906, §35.
21. Simms, *From Kings to Warlords,* 24–6.
22. From *The Fitness of Names / Cóir Anmann,* ed. Stokes, *IT* 3, 318–23.
23. *The Journey of the sons of Eochaid Macmedóin / Echtra mac nEchach Muigmedóin,* ed. M. Joynt, *Ériu* 4, 1910, 91–111 and W. Stokes, *RC* 24, 1903, 190 –203. The former is in verse, the latter is a prose version. Joynt and Stokes both identify parallels to the transformation scene in English and French medieval romance, eg. the *Marriage of Sir Gawain,* the story of Floren from Gower's *Confessio Amantis,* in *'The Wife of Bath's Tale'* by Chaucer, and in the story of Percival by Chrestien de Troyes. See also A. K. Coomaraswamy, 'The Loathly Bride', *Speculum* 20, October 1945.
24. E. O'Curry, *Lectures on the Manuscript Materials of Ancient Irish History,* Dublin, 1861, 620–1. There is also a paraphrase by M. Dillon in his *Early Irish Literature,* London, 1948, 107–9.
25. See 'Medb Cruachna', *ZCP* 17, 1927, 129–46.
26. *The Battle of Mag Mucrama / Cath Maige Mucrama,* ITS 50, ed. M. O'Daly, §34–7.
27. *The Cattle Raid of Fraích / Táin Bo Fraích* ed. Gantz, *EIMS,* 121–2. For further references and notes on Cruachu, see J. Waddell, 'The royal site in Connacht', *JIA* 1, 1983, 21–46. M. Herrity, 'A survey of the royal site of Cruachain in Connacht', *JRSAI* 113, 1983, 121–30.
28. Prologue to *Félire,* 28, §177. See also *GT,* 64–5.
29. For further reading on 'the Sovereignty goddess' see R. A. Breatnach, 'The Lady and the King', *Studies* 42, 1953, 321–6; P. Mac Cana, 'Aspects of the theme of King and Goddess', *EC* 7, 1955–6, 76–114, 356–413 and *EC* 8, 1958–9, 59–65; M. Breatnach, 'The Sovereignty Goddess as Goddess of death', *ZCP* 39, 1982, 243–60, and M. Herbert, 'Goddess and King: the sacred marriage in early Ireland', in *Women and Sovereignty,* ed. L. Fradenburg, Edinburgh, 1992.

30. *Audacht Morainn*, ed. F. Kelly, Dublin, 1976.
31. M. Breatnach, op. cit., 243–60.
32. In another version of the story, it is his mother who is an Otherworld being. See *De Síl Chonairi Móir*, ed. L. Gwynn, *Ériu* 6, 130–43.
33. *The Destruction of Da Derga's Hostel*, ed. Gantz, *EIMS*, 77–8.
34. See K. McCone, 'Werewolves, cyclopes, *díberga* and *fianna:* juvenile delinquency in early Ireland', *CMCS* 12, 1–22.
35. From the ninth-century text, *The Battle of Mag Mucrama / Cath Maige Mucrama*, ed. M. O'Daly, ITS 50, Dublin, 1975, §66. See also *The Death of Muirchertach Mac Erca* 177–80.
36. Ps. 95:4–5.
37. Gen. 28:19; 32:27; 32:20.
38. Ps. 72:1–3.
39. Am. 4, passim.
40. Joel 3:18a.
41. J. Gibson, *Canaanite Myths and Legends*, Edinburgh, 1978, 4.
42. Heb. 11:9,
43. *Cormac's Adventure in the Land of Promise / Echtra Cormaic i Tír Tairngiri*, ed. Stokes, *IT* 3 (1), Leipzig, 1891, §34–6, 213–14. See also *AIT*, 503f.

CHAPTER THREE

1. *Conf.* §16, ed. A. B. E. Hood, 44.
2. I acknowledge a debt throughout this section to Noel O'Donoghue – in particular to his work on St Patrick, *Aristocracy of Soul*, London, 1987. Also *The Holy Mountain*, Dublin, 1983 and his unpublished lectures on the prayer of Jesus in the Gospels.
3. *The Patrician Texts in the Book of Armagh*, ed. L. Bieler, Dublin, 1979, 2–20.
4. I.e. before he escaped from slavery and undertook his priestly training on the continent.
5. Muirchú's *Life of Patrick*, II, 15 (13) 1–4; Bieler, *Patrician Texts*, 80–3.
6. *Conf.* §23, ed. Hood, 45.
7. Tírechán's *Life of Patrick*, I, 50; Bieler, *Patrician Texts,*, 124–5, 162–3.
8. Skerry Church is three miles from Broughshane near Ballymena.
9. Based on 'The Boyish Exploits of Finn' – *Macgímartha Find* – ed. K. Meyer, *Ériu* I, 1904–5, 187–9. For other translations see J. F. Nagy, *The Wisdom of the Outlaw*, Berkeley, 1985, 216–17; also *AIT*, Dublin, 1969.
10. S. O'Grady, *Silva Gadelica* II, Dublin, 1892, 120–1.
11. J. O'Donovan and W. Stokes, *Cormac's Glossary*, Calcutta, 1868, 4.
12. See 26–32.
13. Gwynn, *MD* III, 348.
14. Eg. Stokes, *Trip.* I, clviii. And (without necessarily accepting that Donn, Nuadu and the Dagda are identical) O'Rahilly, *EIHM*, 283, 466–7, 484. In the *Tripartite Life*, the daughters of Loegaire clearly distinguish between the *Síde* and the gods. *Trip.* 100. Cf. *Trip.* II, 315.
15. Cf. the following passage from *The Intoxication of the Ulaid*: 'The *Túatha Dé Danann* went into the hills – the region of the *Síde* – then, and they submitted to the *Síde* under the ground.' Gantz, *EIMS*, 190. See also a note in *The Book of Conquests* which states that the *Tuatha Dé Danann* were not *síd* folk, ITS, 41, 165, §353.

16. T. Ó Cathasaigh, 'The semantics of *síd*', *Éigse* 17, 1977–9, 135–54. For an alternative etymology of *síd*, see E. Hamp, 'Irish *síd* "tumulus" and Irish *síd* "peace"', *EC* 19, 141.
17. Mk 9:2–8
18. R. De Vaux, *Ancient Israel: Its Life and Institutions*, London, 1973, 274–88.
19. S. Sandmel, *The Hebrew Scriptures*, New York, 1978, 27–8.
20. Deut. 4:10–15.
21. 1 Kgs 19:8.
22. Ex. 19 and 24.
23. De Vaux, *AI*, 280–1
24. Ibid., 284–5.
25. Ibid., 285–7. Gen. 28:18.
26. 1 Kgs 19:8.
27. Mt. 17:1; Mk 9:2–10; Lk. 9:28–37; De Vaux, *AI*, 280.
28. Mt. 14:23 and parallels. Lk. 6:12; 22:39–41 and parallels.
29. De Vaux, *AI*, 280–1.
30. Mk 14:26–51 and parallels. Mt. 27:54.
31. For more about margins and liminality, see A. and B. Rees, *Celtic Heritage*, London, 1961, 83–94. Also *WO*, 35–7.
32. *Adamnán's Life of St Columba*, ed. Reeves, III, xvii, 121–2. Reeves's edition is used here for copyright reasons, but see also R. Sharpe, *Adomnán of Iona: Life of St Columba*, London, 1995 with introduction and detailed notes. Also A. O. and M. O. Anderson, *Adomnan's Life of Columba*, Edinburgh, 1961; 2nd edn, Oxford, 1991. There are slight variations in paragraph numbering between Sharpe and Reeves. The current paragraph in Sharpe's edition, for example, is III, 16, 217–19.
33. Sharpe, *Adomnán of Iona*, 368; for Reeves's map, see *Adamnán's Life*, 4–5.
34. J. Dawson, 'Calvinism and the Gaidhealtacht in Scotland', *Calvinism in Europe*, A. Pettigree, A. Duke and G. Lewis (eds), Cambridge, 1994, 251.
35. Tírechán §38, Bieler, *Patrician Texts*, 152–3.
36. The *Lebar Brecc Homily on St Patrick* provides yet another version. See *Trip.* II, 475–9.
37. This is the name of the bell, which was obviously known to contemporary listeners.
38. F. Kelly, *A Guide to Early Irish Law*, Dublin, 1988, 182.
39. See 169. *The Law of Adamnán / Cáin Adamnáin*, ed. K. Meyer, Oxford, 4–5, §6–15.
40. Lk. 18:1–8.
41. Tírechán invents a new meaning for some of these stones, saying that they mark the grave of Patrick's charioteer. Bieler, *Patrician Texts*, 152–3.
42. 'Colum Cille's Greeting to Ireland', ed. K. Meyer, *AIP*, 85, 114; cf. Jackson, *CM*, §20, 71.
43. Sharpe, *Adomnán*, I, iii, 115–117.
44. *The Hiding of the Hill of Howth / Uath Beinn Etair*, ed. K. Meyer, *RC* 11, 125. For another edition, see *AIT*, 422–3; Kinsella, *Táin*, 13; *MD* III, 104–119.
45. Based on *Life of Brenainn*, ed. Stokes, *Lismore*, 252.
46. Deut. 34:1–5.
47. Athanasius, *Life of Antony*, §2–3.

48. For more on Skellig Michael, see L. and M. de Paor, *Early Christian Ireland,* London, 1958, 54–6. K. Hughes and A. Hamlin, *The Modern Traveller to the Early Irish Church,* London, 1977, 19–21, 39. Des Lavelle, *Skellig: Island Outpost of Europe,* Dublin, 1976.
49. Hughes and Hamlin, op. cit., 21.
50. See for example, N. D. O'Donoghue, *The Mountain Behind the Mountain,* Edinburgh, 1993.

CHAPTER FOUR

1. M. Mac Neill, *The Festival of Lughnasad,* Oxford, 1962, 607; W. G. Wood Martin, *Traces of the Elder Faiths in Ireland,* ii, 82, 100–4.
2. P. D. Hardy, *The Holy Wells of Ireland,* Dublin, 1836, 38–42.
3. Ibid. Also J. and C. Bord, citing an unidentified 18th cent. source, in *Sacred Waters, holy wells and water lore in Britain and Ireland,* London, 2nd edn, 1986, 248.
4. V. Flint, *The Rise of Magic in Early Medieval Europe,* Princeton, 1991, 71–81.
5. Based on *Adamnán's Life of St Columba,* ed. Reeves, II, 11, 78; Sharpe, *Adomnán,* 162–3.
6. Tírechán §39, Bieler, *Patrician Texts,* 152–5. Cf. *Trip.,* ed. Stokes, II, 323.
7. B. Raftery, *Pagan Celtic Ireland,* London, 1994, 183–5.
8. Plummer, *VSH,* I, CXLIX.
9. The most accessible of these stories is perhaps 'Ruadh in the land under the wave', ed. Jackson, *CM,* 150–1. See also the adventure of Colman Mac Luachain mentioned by Plummer in *VSH* I. cxlviii, and 'The Adventure of Laeghaire mac Crimhthainn', ed. Jackson, *Speculum* 17, 282–3. For further references and a discussion, see John Carey, 'The location of the Otherworld in Irish Tradition', *Éigse* 19, 1982–3, 36–43.
10. *The Colloquy with the Ancients,* ed. O'Grady, *SG II,* 103–4.
11. See 67 and 33. G. Ó Crualaoich, 'Continuity and adaptation in legends of the *cailleach bhéarra',* *Béaloideas* 56, 1988, 153–78.
12. *Colloquy,* ed. O'Grady, *SG II,* 161.
13. *Trip.,* ed. Stokes, I, 90–1, and 106–7. Cf. *Colloquy,* ed. O'Grady, *SG II,* 133. For other wells in *Trip.,* see 8–9, 84–5, 108–11.
14. Tírechán §26.1, Bieler, *Patrician Texts,* 142–3.
15. Hood, *Conf.,* 51, 52.
16. Ed. Stokes, *IT* 3 (2), 392–3.
17. *The Tale of Macc Da Thó's Pig / Scéla Muicce Meic Da Thó, EIMS,* ed. Gantz, 186. See also *Bricriu's Feast / Fled Bricrenn,* ibid., 221–55.
18. Other figures who are conceived when their mothers swallow a tiny creature in a drink of water include Étaín (*The Wooing of Étaín / Tochmarc Étaín,* ed. Gantz, *EIMS,* 47), Conchobar (*The Conception of Conchobar / Compert Conchobuir,* ed. Meyer, *RC* 6, 180) and Cú Chulainn (*Táin,* ed. Kinsella, 23).
19. *The Evernew Tongue,* ed. Stokes, *Ériu* 2, 112–13, §37.
20. *On the Fitness of Names,* ed. Stokes, 342–5, §133.
21. E. Hull, 'Pagan Baptism in the West', in *Folklore,* Dec. 1932, 410–18.
22. W. Stokes, 'The Gaelic Maundeville', *ZCP* II, 1899, 52–5.
23. Hull, 'Pagan Baptism', 412, citing *The Courtship of Monera / Tochmarc Monera, with The Battle of Magh Leana,* ed. Curry, in *Celtic Society Publications,* 1855, 164–5.

24. *CG* I, 114–15, 60–3.
25. *Cath Maige Tuired*, ed. E. Grey, ITS 52, London, 1982, §84.
26. *Táin*, ed. Kinsella, 132–5.
27. *LG* 5, ed. Macalister, ITS 44, 30–3, §386–8.
28. Cf. Gen. 9:22–3.
29. See 33. *The Wooing of Étaín / Tochmarc Étaín*, ed. Gantz, *EIMS*, 45.
30. W. Y. E. Wentz, *The Fairy Faith in Celtic Countries*, Gerrard's Cross, 1977, 79, n. 1. The original edition was published in Oxford in 1911. For mermaids in the medieval tradition see, for example, the strange story of Líbán who was caught in a net in Lough Neagh by one of St Comgall's fishermen. *Félire*, ed. Stokes, 52–5. Also *AU* for the year 1118.
31. H. Morris, 'The holy wells of Donegal', *Béaloideas*, IML, VI, 1936, 148–9. Cf. the last days of the Hag of Beare in her famous Lament, where she reluctantly takes the veil. Meyer, *AIP*, 90–3.
32. Plummer, *VSH* I, cxlvii–cxlviii.
33. *Rennes*, ed. Stokes, *RC* 15, 456–7.
34. For example, *The Cauldron of Poesy*, ed. L. Breatnach, *Ériu* 32, 1981, 45–9, §11 (dated to the second half of the ninth century by Breatnach, earlier by P. L. Henry); *Cormac's Adventure in the Land of Promise / Echtra Cormaic*, ed. Stokes, *IT* 3(1), §34–6, 213–14; *MD* III, ed. Gwynn, 286–95; and *The Colloquy of the Two Sages / Imacallam in dá Thúarad*, ed. Stokes, *RC* 26, 1905, 457.
35. From a gloss in the Book of Leinster cited by E. Hull in *The Poem Book of the Gael*, London, 1912, 52. The gloss actually refers to the sea-shore, but it has been applied to other watery margins as well. Cf. K. Meyer, *Ériu* I, 1904–5, 185 n. 4.
36. 'Cináed Úa Hartacáin's poem on Brugh na Bóinne', ed. L. Gwynn, *Ériu* 7, 229, 236.
37. See K. Simms, 'Satire in later Medieval Ireland', paper delivered at the IXth International Conference of Celtic Studies, Paris, 1991.
38. *MD* III, ed. Gwynn, 26–33. Boand's marital relationships vary within the tradition itself, but in the *Dindshenchas* she is married to Nechtan.
39. See 122–4. *Boyish Exploits*, ed. Meyer, *Ériu* I, §18–19.
40. Prov. 18:4, 13:14. Cf. 10:11, 16:22.
41. *MD* III, ed. Gwynn, 294–5.
42. Gen. 2:10–14.
43. Gen. 16:7–14. There is another version of this story in Gen. 21: 14–19.
44. Gen. 24:62–7. Cf. 25:11.
45. Gen. 26:17–33. Cf. 21:25–34.
46. *Adamnán's Life of St Columba*, ed. Reeves, II, 9, 77; Sharpe, *Adomnán*, II, 10, 161–2.
47. Ex. 17:7; Num. 20:1–13; Deut. 1:46; Jdg. 11:16–17. G. Von Rad, *Old Testament Theology*, Edinburgh, 1962, I, 11. G. Fohrer, *History of the Israelite Religion*, London, 1973, 44 and 72. For other holy wells, see De Vaux, *AI*, 277–8 .
48. 1 Kgs 1:33–40; De Vaux, *AI*, 278, 102; Gen. 2:10–13.
49. Ezek. 47:1–12; Cf. Zech. 14:8.
50. Ps. 1:1.
51. Is. 44:3–4; Joel 2:28.

52. Ps. 36:8–9; Prov. 16:22; 10:11; 13:14; 18:4. Cf. Jn 7:37–8.
53. Jer. 17:13.
54. Jn 10:10.
55. Jn 4:7–26; 5:1–9; 9:7.
56. J. Jeremias, *Jerusalem in the Time of Jesus*, London, 1969, 118.
57. Sandmel, *The Hebrew Scriptures*, 90. n. 4; Jerusalem Bible (Standard edition), note to Jn 9:7.
58. Gen. 6–8; Ex. 14:21–28; cf. Ps. 124:4; Is. 8:5–8.
59. Rom. 6:3–4.
60. Ps. 42:7.
61. *Adamnán's Life*, ed. Reeves, II, 28, 88–9; Sharpe, *Adomnán*, II, 27, 175–6.
62. Stokes, *RC* 20, 257, §60.
63. See 59. *Colloquy, SG* II, 163.
64. *MD* III, ed. Gwynn, 104–7; *Life of Brigit*, ed. Stokes, *Lives of Saints from the Book of Lismore*, Oxford, 1890, line 1728. Cf. *The Evernew Tongue*, ed. M. Herbert and M. McNamara, *IBA*, 116, §34–5.
65. *Rennes*, ed. Stokes, *RC* 15, 441–2. A similar story is told of St Finbar at Lough Gouganebarra, Co. Cork, near the source of the river Lee. Cf. Rev. 12:3–17 and the deutero-canonical story of Bel and the Dragon. Daniel 14 in the Vulgate.
66. T. O. Clancy and G. Márkus, *Iona: the earliest poetry of a Celtic Monastery*, 86–8.
67. Cf. Rahab, the sea-monster, Job 26:13; Ps. 89:10; Is. 51:9. Ovid, *Metamorphoses*, trans. M. M. Innes, Harmondsworth, 1984, Book 4, lines 724ff, pp. 112–13.
68. E.g. the destructive pigs in *The Battle of Mag Mucrime*, ed. Stokes, *RC* 13, 448–50. See also 'The Magic Pigs of Cruachu', ed. Jackson, *CM*, 159.
69. *Duanaire Finn / Book of the Lays of Finn* II, ed. G. Murphy, ITS 28, Dublin, 1933, 35, 90/206. Dating by Murphy from *DF* III.
70. Ibid., 60/235.
71. *DF* I, ed. E. Mac Neill, ITS 7, London, 1908, 24, 78–80 / 191–3.
72. *DF* III, ed. Murphy, ITS 43, Dublin, 1953, 140.
73. Jn 9.
74. Wood-Martin, *Traces*, II, 112.
75. *Oxford Dictionary of the Christian Church*, 2nd edn, ed. F. L. Cross and E. A. Livingstone, Oxford, 1984, 51. s.v. 'Fish'.
76. Ibid., 111–14.
77. J. F. Nagy, 'Otter, salmon and eel in traditional Gaelic narrative', *Stud. Celt.* 20, 1985–6, 123–44.
78. O'Rahilly, *EIHM*, 319–20.
79. Logan, *The Holy Wells of Ireland*, Gerrard's Cross, 1980, 121–2. Cf. 'The Song of Wandering Aengus', W. B. Yeats, *Selected Poetry*, ed. N. Jeffares, London, 1967.
80. *Aithdioghluim Dána*, ed. L. McKenna, ITS 37 and 40, Dublin 1939 and 40, no. 49.
81. Ibid., §20. Cf. no. 70, §12 – 'the child, the Salmon, ever adorable.' And no. 89, §7 – 'the salmon of the ocean, their warmest friend.'

CHAPTER FIVE

1. A. T. Lucas, 'Sacred Trees of Ireland', *Journal of the Cork Historical and Archaeological Society* 68, 16–54.
2. Tacitus, *Annals*, 14, §30.
3. Pharsalia I, 4, 50–8; Strabo 12, 52.
4. Maximus, *Logoi*, 8, 8.
5. For illustrations, see R. Cook, *The Tree of Life*, London, 1988.
6. Lucas, 'Sacred Trees', 42, 16.
7. Mac Neill, *DF* I, 34–6, 135–7. Macalister, *LG* 4, 131.
8. Rennes, ed. Stokes, *RC* 15, 428–31.
9. Lucas, 'Sacred Trees', 20–6.
10. J. Vendryes, *Airne Fíngein*, Dublin, 1953, §111; L. McKenna, *Aith.Dán.*, 4, §6; 9, §1.
11. Jud. 9:6–15.
12. Ezek. 31; Dan. 4:4–27; Is. 11:1, 10; Jer. 23:5; 33:15; Zech. 3:8.
13. Mt. 21:8; Jn 12:13.
14. *Conf.* §23. Cf. Muirchú, ed. Bieler, *Patrician Texts*, I, 7 (6), 70–3.
15. Bieler, *Patrician Texts*, 134–5, §14. According to Bieler, the Wood of Fochloth was at Killala in North Mayo. Ibid., 219.
16. Ibid., 156–9, §42–3. For other Patrician churches by sacred trees, see 136–7. §16, 162–3, §51. Also *Trip.* ed. Stokes, I, 157.
17. *Annals of Ulster*, ed. Hennessy, I, 503. S. Mac Airt and G. MacNiocaill in their recent edition, 426–7, translate the same word as 'wooden sanctuary', but without explanation.
18. 'Cogitosus: Life of Brigit', ed. S. Connolly and J.-M. Picard, *Journal of the Royal Society of Antiquaries of Ireland* 117, 1987, 14, §2(3).
19. *Félire*, ed. Stokes, 11.
20. *Chronicum Scotorum*, ed. W. Hennessy, 257; *Annals of the Four Masters*, ed. J. O'Donovan, II, p. 1147 for year 1162; *Annals of Ulster*, ed. Mac Airt and MacNiocaill, 493; *Lismore*, ed. Stokes, 176.
21. This poem comes from a manuscript which was in the library of a Munster bishop who died in 958. Its ultimate provenance is unknown. Translations by Jackson, *ECNP*, 10, §7; and Ó Corráin, 'Hermit Poetry?', *SSS*, ed. Ó Corráin et al., 256.
22. A. B. E. Hood, *St Patrick: his writings and Muirchú's Life*, London, 1978, 96–7, §27. See also Bieler, *Patrician Texts*, 98–101, §I, 27 (26) = B, II, 1.
23. Gen. 15:5–21.
24. Gen. 18:1–3. Cf. 12:6–7 and Jubilees 14:2.
25. De Vaux, *AI*, 292–3
26. *Life of St Coemgen*, ed. Plummer, *VSH* I, 253.
27. *De Locis Sanctis*, ed. Denis Meehan, Dublin, 1983, II, 11, 82–3. Cf. Bede, *Ecclesiastical History of the English People*, trans. L. Sherley-Price, V, 17, 297.
28. S. Sandmel, *The Hebrew Scriptures*, 345–6.
29. Gen. 21:33.
30. Gen. 12.6–7; De Vaux, *AI*, 279.
31. Ibid., 278–86; and for reference to Sozomenus in the paragraph, see p. 292.
32. Jdg. 6:11–12; 1 Kgs 19:1–19; Zech. 1:7–13.
33. Ex. 3:1–6; De Vaux, *AI*, 276.
34. Muirchú, ed. Bieler, *Patrician Texts*, II, 5, 116–17.

35. For more detail on birds and animals, see Ross, *PCB*, 234–353. There are some grounds for relating Derg Corra to Finn. See Nagy, *The Wisdom of the Outlaw*, Los Angeles, 1985, 128f.
36. *Táin*, ed. Kinsella, 127, 96.
37. McKenna, *Aith Dána*, 60, §4; 72, §5; 61, §27; 97, §26–30.
38. *Rennes*, ed. Stokes, *RC* 16, 277–9.
39. According to the *Dictionaire de Spiritualité*, the earliest portions of the litany of Loreto are found in 12th cent. manuscripts from Paris and Mainz and are probably of eastern origin. The *New Catholic Encyclopaedia* refers to an 8th cent. Marian litany in Gaelic. This is probably a reference to the *Lebar Brecc* litany of the Virgin which O'Curry dated to the 8th century, but which was later redated to the 12th. *NCE*, 790; Stokes, *Trip.* I, clxv. The Yew of Ross is said to have fallen during the 7th century.
40. *The Birth and Life of Moling*, ed. Stokes, *RC* 27, 1906, 257–312, §34.
41. Lucas claims that the saints of Ireland prayed and fasted for it to fall because they coveted its wood for church building. His source is John O'Hanlon's 19th cent. *Lives of the Irish Saints* 4, 218, but O'Hanlon does not name this tree as the Yew of Ross. Indeed it would seem to have been a tree from a different part of the country. If this story exists in earlier Lives of Molaise/ Laserian, I have been unable to find it. Lucas, 'Sacred Trees', 18. St Martin's attack on a sacred pine would have been known in Ireland through the *Life of St Martin* by Sulpicius Severus (d. 420) a copy of which was present in the early ninth-century *Book of Armagh*. For a modern edition, see *A Select Library of Nicene and Post-Nicene Fathers of the Christian Church*, second series, vol. 11, ed. H. Wace and P. Schaff, Oxford, 1894, 10, §13. In Willibald's 8th cent. *Life of St Boniface* the British-born bishop of Mainz chips a few notches out of the 'Oak of Jupiter' and is immediately aided by 'a divine blast from above' which fells the tree, splitting it into four parts. Boniface uses the timber to build a wooden oratory. Willibald, *Life of St Boniface*, ed. G. W. Robinson, Cambridge, 1906, 63–4, §6.
42. Stokes, op. cit., 420 n. 2. Cf. *The Poems of Blathmac*, ed. J. Carney, ITS 47, Dublin, 1964, 39, §100; *Félire*, ed. Stokes, 14 December, 260–1. For a more general discussion, see Ó Cathasaigh, 'The sister's son in early Irish literature', *Peritia* 5, 1986, 128–60.
43. Gwynn, *MD* IV, 241.
44. Josh. 24:1–29; Bieler, *Patrician Texts*, 162–3, §51.
45. Mircea Eliade, *Encyclopaedia of Religion*, s.v. 'Trees' and 'Axis Mundi'.
46. *Life of Moling*, ed. Stokes, *RC* 27, 1906, §34.
47. *MD* III, 147; Stokes, *RC* 15, 420.
48. See *Annals of the Four Masters* for 982, 1099 and 1111; *Annals of Clonmacnoise* for 976, *Chronicum Scotorum* for 980 and 1129; *Annals of Innisfallen* 982; for summary, see Lucas, 'Sacred Trees', 25–6.
49. Murphy, *EIL*, 68–9. There are several versions of the poem 'Full of white angels'. See also Stokes, *Lismore*, 27, and O'Kelleher and Schoepperle, *Life of Colum Cille*, Illinois, 1918, §183, 189.
50. *Life of Colum Cille*, ed. O'Kelleher & Schoepperle, 83–85. Although this compilation dates from the 16th cent., it contains 'a formidable amount' of pre-1200 Middle-Irish material, according to M. Herbert, *Iona, Kells and Derry*, Edinburgh, 1988, 9.

51. Based on *Liber Hymnorum*, ed. Bernard and Atkinson, II, 28. M. Herbert dates this Preface tentatively to the 10th or early 11th cent., op. cit., 198. Daire Calcaig was an earlier name for Derry or for one of the oakwoods there. For another version of the same story, see Stokes, *Lismore*, 305.

52. Lucas, 'Sacred Trees', 30.

53. 'The Exile of Conall Corc', ed. V. Hull, *Publications of the Modern Language Association of America* 56, 949. Hull dated this story to the 9th, or possibly 8th cent.

54. Giraldus Cambrensis, *The Topography of Ireland*, trans. T. Forester., ed. and revd by T. Wright, London, 1863, 109–10, §54. O'Meara's edition does not include this passage which occurs only in Gerald's expanded edition of the *Topography*.

55. *Life of Colum Cille*, ed. O'Kelleher and Schoepperle, 83–5.

56. Ibid.

57. Lucas, 'Sacred Trees', 40.

58. Josh. 24:1–29; De Vaux, *AI*, 291.

59. Jdg. 4:4–5; Jdg. 9:37; 1 Kgs 13:14.

60. 1 Kgs 6; 7, passim.

61. The building of a house for Baal is described in some of the Ugaritic myths. His previous home was believed to be on top of a mountain. J. Gibson, *Canaanite Myths and Legends*, Edinburgh, 1978, 8–14.

62. I. Engnell, 'Knowledge and life in the Creation story', *Vetus Testamentum Supplement* 3, 1955, 114–15.

63. *On the Settling of the Manor of Tara / Do Suidigud Tellaich Temra*, ed. R. I. Best, *Ériu* 4, 121–72. See also E. Hull, 'Fintan and the Hawk of Achill,' *Folklore*, 1932, 386–409.

64. *Airne Fingein*, ed. J. Vendryes, Dublin, 1953, §3.

65. Meyer, *AIP*, 3–4. See also Cross and Slover, *AIT*, 588–95.

66. For arguments for and against *The Voyage of Bran* being a christian allegory, see J. Carney, *Studies in Irish Literature and history*, Dublin, 1955, 280–95; Prionsias Mac Cana, 'The Sinless Otherworld of *Immram Brain*', *Ériu* 27, 1976, 95–115.

67. H. P. A. Oskamp, *EC* 14, 205–14.

68. Gantz, *EIMS*, 155–78.

69. *The Voyage of St Brendan*, trans. J. F. Webb, in *The Age of Bede*, 211–45. §§11, 18. Some scholars date the *Navigatio* to the 10th cent.

70. *The Voyage of Snedgus and MacRiagla*, ed. Stokes, *RC* 9, 1888, 14–25.

71. O'Grady, *SG* I, 342–59, II, 385–96.

72. *Studies in Irish Literature and History*, Dublin, 1955, 280–95. Cf. Mac Cana, op. cit., 95–115.

73. M. Eliade, *Patterns in Comparative Religion*, London, 1958, 276–8.

74. P. Grimal, *Dictionary of Classical Mythology*, Oxford, 1986; *The Passion of Perpetua and Felicity*, in *A Lost Tradition: women writers of the early church*, ed. P. Wilson-Kastner, Lanham, 1981, 24, §10; L. Robert, 'Une vision de Perpetue, martyre à Carthage en 203', *Comptes Rendus de l'Académie des inscriptions et Belles-Lettres*, 1982, 228–76.

75. M. Eliade, *Shamanism, Archaic Techniques of Ecstacy*, London, 1964, 168–9, 39.

76. *The Irish Adam and Eve Story* ed. D. Greene and F. Kelly, 22–3, lines 1017–

20. Cf. the flock of heavenly birds in *The Evernew Tongue / Tenga Bhith-nua*, see *IBA*, 116–18, §35–42.
77. See K. Simms, *From Kings to Warlords*, Woodbridge, 1987, 22–6 and her paper on religious role of poets, 'Satire in Medieval Ireland', *Proceedings of the IXth International Conference of Celtic Studies*, Paris, 1991. Also F. J. Byrne, *Irish Kings and High Kings*, London, 1973, 15–16, 20–2.
78. *Bricriu's Feast / Fled Bricrenn*, ed. Gantz, *EIMS*, 228.
79. *The Tidings of Conchobar Son of Ness / Scéla Conchobair Maic Nessa*, ed. Stokes, *Ériu* 4, 1910. 30–1, §21.
80. *The Violent Deaths of Goll and Garb*, ed. Stokes, *RC* 14, 426–7, §47. Cf. *The Intoxication of the Ulaid / Mesca Ulad*, ed. Gantz, *EIMS*, 193, 210. According to the 10th cent. *Colloquy of the Two Sages*, chief poets carried golden branches, middle-grade poets carried silver ones, and ordinary poets carried branches of bronze. However, Sencha carries a bronze branch though he is chief poet of Ulster, and it seems unlikely that any poet would have carried a gold branch when kings like Bran and Cormac were depicted with silver ones.
81. *AU*, ed. Mac Airt and MacNiocaill, for the years 1015, 1073, and 1113. Cf. also 950, 1013, 1102.
82. *Trip.* ed. Stokes, I, 28–31. Cf. 'Notes on Fiacc's Hymn', ibid., II, 420–1. Cf. The *Lebar Brecc Homily on St Patrick*, ibid., II, 474–5.
83. *Stair Nicoméid, the Irish Gospel of Nicodemus*, ed. I. Hughes, ITS 55, London, 1991, x–xi. For another edition of this text, see M. Herbert and M. Macnamara, *IBA*, Edinburgh, 1989, 19–88.
84. 'The Harrowing of Hell', ed. O.J. Bergin, *Ériu* 4, §7–9, 112–15.
85. Ibid., §18–22, 116–17.
86. *Gospel of Nicodemus*, ed. Herbert & Macnamara, *IBA*, 79–80, §III.19.
87. Ibid., 55.
88. Ibid., 177; Eliade, *Patterns in Comparative Religion*, London, 1958, 274–6.
89. Is. 53:2.
90. Mk 4:30–32; Lk. 13:19; Mt. 13:31–32. Cf. Ezek. 17:22–3.
91. For example, Rom. 6:1–11, 23; 1 Cor. 12:11; 2 Cor. 5:17; Col. 3:11; 1 Pet. 5:10.
92. Col. 1:15–20.

CHAPTER SIX

1. For extended discussion, see A. Ross, *PCB*, 234–96, revised ed. 302–77.
2. *Félire*, ed. Stokes, 56. A more accessible edition is 'The Bird's Lament for Molua' in *CM*, ed. Jackson, 296. 16th cent. *Life of Colum Cille*, ed. O'Kelleher and Schoepperle, 177.
3. *The Voyage of St Brendan*, in *The Age of Bede*, ed. J. F. Webb and D. H. Farmer, 220–1.
4. W. Y. E. Wentz, *The Fairy Faith in Celtic Countries*, 67, 76, 85, 105–6, 109, 113; R. Christiansen, 'Some notes on the fairies and the fairy faith', *Béaloideas* 39–41, 1971–3, 95–111.
5. *Lebor Gabhála / The Book of Conquests* III, ITS 39, 154–5, § 268.
6. For Óengus and Caer, see Gantz, *EIMS*, 112; for Mider and Étaín, op. cit., 57. Other bird transformations include Nemglan and Conaire's father in *The Destruction of Da Derga's Hostel / Togail Bruidne Da Derga*, ibid., 64–6;

Fand, wife of Manannán and her companion Lí Ban, who appear as water-birds in the later tale *The Wasting Sickness of Cú Chulainn / Serglige Con Culainn*; Also the Badb and the Morrígan, who are frequently depicted as crows.

7. Ibid., 65–6. Cf. the strange bird-flocks seen by Cromm Deróil in *The Intoxication of the Ulaid*, 199–205.

8. See 33. *The Birth of Cú Chulainn* also begins with the pursuit of a strange bird-flock. Gantz, *EIMS*, 131–2.

9. O'Donovan and Stokes, *Cormac's Glossary*, 135–8; see also P. Ford, 'The blind, the dumb and the ugly', *CMCS* 19, 1990, 30–4.

10. Based on Marie-Louise Sjoestedt, 'Le siège de Druim Damhghaire', *RC* 43, 1926, 110–13, §117.

11. Adamnán, Finn, Suibne, Moling and a number of other saints all have features in common with shamanism. See D. F. Melia, 'Law and the shaman saint', *Celtic Folklore and Christianity*, ed. P. Ford, Santa Barbara, 1983, 113–27; Nagy, *WO*, 161, and 'The Wisdom of the *Geilt*', *Éigse* 19, 44–60; B. Benes, 'Spüren von Schamanismus in der Sage *Buile Suibne*', *ZCP* 29, 1960–1, 309–34; and above (p. 163).

12. Eliade, *Shamanism, Archiac Techniques of Ecstasy*, London, 1964, 3–12, 70, 156–8, 177–9, 272. See also J. Halifax, *Shaman, the wounded healer*, London, 1982.

13. *Adamnán's Life of Saint Columba*, ed. Reeves, I, xxxv, 67–8. Cf. the poem from *CG* about Colum Cille's healing of a wounded swan from Ireland. Compendium edition, 1992, 328–30, §361.

14. *The Bodleian Amra Choluimb Chille*, ed. Stokes, *RC* 20, 1899, 40–1, 48–9. Also T. Clancy and G. Márkus, *Iona: the earliest poetry of a Celtic monastery*, Edinburgh, 1995, 96–128.

15. The curse known as *glam dicénn* (Stokes, op. cit., 41 n. 2) is further discussed by K. Simms, 'Satire in later medieval Ireland', paper delivered at the IXth International Conference of Celtic Studies, Paris, 1991. For the pose in other contexts, see *The Battle of Mag Tuired / Cath Maige Tuired*, ed. E. Grey, ITS 52, London, 1982, 58–9, §129.

16. *Eulogy of Colum Cille*, 38–41.

17. On the unpleasantness of cranes, see Ross, *PCB*, revd edn, 351–65.

18. See 42. *Trip.* ed. Stokes, II, 414–5.

19. Jackson, *CM*, 282–3, from *Lismore*, ed. Stokes, xiii–xv. Cf. the bird Michael in *The Voyage of the Uí Corra*, ed. Stokes, *RC* 14, 22–69, §14. Stokes dates the *Life of Brendan* as 10th cent., and the *Notes on Fíacc's Hymn*, as no earlier than the 11th. The extraordinary birdsongs of the roughly contemporary *Evernew Tongue* have a similar effect: *IBA*, ed. Herbert and McNamara, 116–17. See also Uainebhuidhe's music 'for which one would have abandoned the whole world's various strains' in *The Colloquy of the Ancients*, ed. O'Grady, *SG* II, 252–3.

20. *Lismore*, ed. Stokes, 260. Cf. *The Voyage of Snedgus and MacRiagla*, ed. Stokes, *RC* 9, 1888, 14–25, §17–8, 22–3 and *The Two Sorrows of the Kingdom of Heaven*, ed. Herbert and McNamara, *IBA*, 19, §2.

21. K. Müller-Lisowski, 'Contributions to a study on Irish folklore', *Béaloideas* 18, 1948, 142–99. O'Rahilly, *EIHM*, Dublin, 1947, 481–4.

22. For details of this debate, see O'Rahilly, loc. cit.

23. *Lebar Brecc Homily on St Patrick*, ed. Stokes, *Trip.* II, 474–7; *The Edinburgh Dindshenchas*, ed. Stokes, *Folklore* 4, 1893, 486; *MD*, ed. Gwynn, III, 378–9.

24. See Lives of Carthach, Finán, and Maedoc, *VSH* ed. Stokes, I, 170, §4; II, 87, 1; 141, 1. Also Cíarán and Finan in *Félire*, 86–7, 112–13. Non-ecclesiastical examples include Étaín and Cú Chulainn, *EIMS*, ed. Gantz, 47, 131–3.
25. Eliade, *Shamanism*, 272. Cf. 70.
26. Ps. 139:15–16, Jer. 1:5, Jn 1:1–18.
27. Deut. 4:17; Rom. 1:20–25.
28. Is. 31:5; Ps. 17:8; 36:7; 57:1; 61:4; 63:7; 91:4; Ruth 2:12.
29. Ex. 19:4; Deut. 32:11.
30. Mt. 23:37; Lk. 13:34; for the dove of the Spirit, see Mk 1:10; Mt. 3:16; Lk. 3:22; Jn 1:32.
31. Ex. 25:20; 27:9; I Kgs 6:7.
32. Is. 6:2; Ezek. 1 passim. Cf. Dan. 7:4–6.
33. Lev. 14.1–32; Cf. Lk. 2:24; Lev. 12:8.
34. Deut. 14:11–18; Cf. Lev. 11:13–19. Acts 10:9–15; 11:4–10.
35. Ezek. 39:17–20; Rev. 19:21–27.
36. The nesting swallows: Ps. 84:3; the great tree: Mt. 13:32; Mk 4:32; Lk. 13:19; cf. Ezek. 17:23; the two-a-penny sparrows: Mt. 10:29–31. Cf. Mt. 6:26; Lk. 12:24.
37. The cranes of Midir of Brí Léith from the *Book of Leinster* quoted by Ross, *PCB*, revd edn, 337, 352, 356.
38. Giraldus Cambrensis, *The Conquest of Ireland / Expugnatio Hibernica*, I, 33, ed. A. B. Scott, and F. X. Martin, Dublin, 1978; Ross, *PCB*, revd edn, 355; Carmichael, *CG* III, 1940, 196–7, compendium ed. 1992, 249.
39. R. I. Best, 'Prognostications of the raven and the wren', *Ériu* 8, 1916, 120–6, with the amendment of 'son' for 'boy' (*mac*) following O'Donovan, 'A poem attributed to Colum Cille', *Miscellany of the Irish Archaeological Society* I, Dublin, 1846, 12–13.
40. Divination by sneezes and bird song are mentioned by Apuleius in his *Apologia*, and condemned by Isidore of Seville (d. 638) *De Magis* and by the 7th cent. author of the *Life* of St Eligius (d. 660). See Valerie Flint, in *The Rise of Magic in Early Medieval Europe*, Princeton, 1991, 15, 50–3, 89.
41. Best, op. cit., 120–6.
42. *Martyrology of Tallaght*, ed. R. I. Best and H. J. Lawlor, HBS, 68, 94–7. Dating by P. O'Dwyer, *Céli Dé*, Dublin, 1981, 140–1.

CHAPTER SEVEN

1. Nuala Ní Dhomhnaill, *Rogha Dánta / Selected Poems*, trans. M. Hartnett, Dublin, 1988, passim, but especially 'Poem for Melissa', 136–7. Examples from Seamus Heaney would include 'In Gallarus Oratory' from *Door into the Dark*, London, 1969; also poems from *Death of a Naturalist, Station Island*, and other collections.
2. From 'The Great Hunger', *The Complete Poems*, Newbridge, 1972, 84.
3. K. Simms, 'Satire in later medieval Ireland', paper delivered at the IXth International Conference of Celtic Studies, Paris, 1991.
4. O'Donovan and Stokes, *Cormac's Glossary*, 94–5. For a more accessible account of these and other rituals, see O'Rahilly, *EIHM*, 323–40.
5. O. Bergin, *Irish Bardic Poetry*, §27, 118 and 265.
6. Meyer, *AIP*, 54–5. For other translations see Murphy, *EIL*, 156–9; Jackson, *CM*, 63–4; and Carney, 'Three Old Irish Accentual Poems', *Ériu* 22, 1971,

26–41. Cf. the later poem 'Summer has Come', Meyer, *AIP*, 53.

7. Carney, 'The dating of archaic Irish poetry', *Early Irish Literature, Media and Communication*, ed. S. Tranter and H. Tristram, Tübingen, 1989, 40.

8. Carney, op. cit., 38–40.

9. M. Tymoczko, 'Cétamon: Vision in early Irish seasonal poetry', *Eire-Ireland* 18, 1983, 17–39.

10. Meyer, *AIP*, 56. For other translations, see Stokes, *RC* 20, 258–9; Jackson, *CM*, 64, §13; Greene and O'Connor, *GTIP*, 98–9, §21. For other winter and seasonal poems in different translations, see Meyer, *AIP*, 57–8; Jackson *CM*, 64–7; Greene and O'Connor,*GTIP*, 134–43.

11. Jackson, *ECNP*, 129–33, 175.

12. Jackson, *CM*, 158–62.

13. Frazer, *GB*, 399–424.

14. Carmichael, *CG* I, 166–8; S. Ó Súilleabháin, *Irish Folk Custom and Belief*, Dublin, 1967, 21, 52; K. Danaher, 'Irish folk tradition and the Celtic calendar', in *Celtic Consciousness*, ed. R. O'Driscoll, 217; D. Ó hOgain, *Myth, Legend and Romance*, London, 1990, 64; Frazer, *GB*, 400–1, 406–9.

15. From *The Colloquy of the Two Sages*, ed. Stokes, *RC* 26, 32–5. Jackson, *Man* 34, May 1934, 67–70. The curious phrase 'wooden blades flee' appears in the *Book of Leinster* version as 'the blades with poison depart'. Jackson translates it as 'witchcraft flees'.

16. Jackson, *ECNP*, 170–1.

17. Based on *Thes. Pal.*, ed. Stokes and Strachan, II, 290. For other translations see K. Meyer, *AIP*, 99; Jackson, *ECNP*, §II; Carney, *EIP*,13; Greene and O'Connor, *GT*, 18, 84–5; and D. F. Melia, 'A Poetic Klein Bottle', *Celtic Language, Celtic Culture*, ed. A. T. E. Matonis and D. F. Melia, Van Nuys, 1990, 187–96. For further discussion, see Ó Corráin, 'Early Irish hermit poetry?', *SSS*, 257, and Melia, op. cit.

18. From the Middle-Irish poets' primer edited by R. Thurneysen (in Irish only) as *Mittelirische Verslehren* in *IT* 3, ed. Windisch and Stokes, 1–182, *MV* 3, §67. See also Jackson, *CM* 125; Murphy, *EIL* 6–7. Greene and O'Connor quote all three blackbird poems in *GT* 54, 205–7. For a free translation which captures some of the chirps and flourishes of the original, see M. C. Ó Brian, 'The role of the poet in Gaelic Society', in *The Celtic Consciousness*, ed. R. O'Driscoll, Port Laoise, 1982, 243–53. Ó Brian uses a later manuscript, hence the variant last line.

19. Jackson, *CM*, 125. Murphy dates it to the ninth century, but this is disputed by Ó Corráin in 'Hermit Poetry', *SSS*, 255.

20. Thurneysen, *MV* I, §53; *MV* 2, §75, 112, §75. See also Jackson, *ECNP* IX, and Murphy, op. cit.

21. Based on Meyer, *AIP*, 100. Dating by Ó Corráin, op.cit., 256.

22. See 49. For more on the apotropaic properties of bells, see *NCE*, 259–63, and *Encyclopaedia Britannica*, 15th edn, 14, 58d–9.

23. *The Frenzy of Suibne / Buile Suibne*, ed. J. G. O'Keeffe, ITS 12, London, 1913, 32–3, §22. Cf. the later text 'While Finn was living with the Fiana ...' *ECNP*, ed. Jackson, 21–2.

24. See also Jackson, *CM*, 72–3, §22; Murphy, *EIL*, 112–13; Stokes and Strachan, *Thes. Pal.* II, 294.

25. *Suibne*, ed. O'Keeffe, xv–xix.

26. Ibid., passim, especially §75, 137–41. See also Seamus Heaney, *Sweeney Astray*, London, 1984.
27. *Suibne*, ed. O'Keeffe, §32, 49. For the proud ivy bush, see §40, 75 and other ivy bushes in §40, 27, 31, 38 and §27, 39. For other sanctuary trees, see §§12, 20, 33, 35, 42.
28. J. Carney, 'Suibne Geilt and the children of Lir', *Éigse* 6, 1948–52, 88.
29. Meyer, *Ériu* 1, 40. For another translation, see K. Jackson, *A Celtic Miscellany*, revd edn, Harmondsworth, 1971, 280.
30. Based on Meyer, *AIP*, 47–50. For other translations, see Murphy, *EIL*, 10–19; Jackson, *ECNP*, §5, *CM*, 68–70; Carney, *Medieval Irish Lyrics*, Dublin, 1967, §27; R. Lehmann, 'Guaire and Marban', *ZCP*, 36, 1978, 96–111.
31. By way of contrast, see 'The Hermit', Jackson, *CM*. §224, 281–2, also translated by Murphy as 'A Hermit Song', *EIL* §9, 19–20.
32. Mt. 6:25–34. Lk. 12:22–32. *Life of Anthony* §3.
33. Lk. 18:28–30. Cf. Mt. 10:28–31; Mt. 19:23.
34. Ó Corráin, *SSS*, 261.
35. Is. 11:6–9.
36. Meyer, *AIP*, 87. Meyer dates it to the 12th cent.
37. *Life of Colum Cille / Betha Choluim Chille*, ed. A. O'Kelleher and G. Schoepperle, Illinois, 1918, §185, 190–1.

CHAPTER EIGHT

1. For details, see M. J. O'Kelly, *Newgrange: Archaeology, Art and Legend*, London, 1982; J. Patrick, 'Midwinter sunrise at Newgrange', *Nature* 249, 1974, 517–9. For a more personal account, see J. C. Roy, *The Road Wet, the Wind Close*, Dublin, 1986, 22–46. The passage grave at Maes Howe on Orkney is also illuminated on the winter solstice, but at sunset rather than sunrise. Stonehenge is aligned to the first rays of the sun on the summer solstice. The passage grave at Bryn Celli Ddu on Anglesey is oriented towards sunrise on May Day. M. Green, *The Sun-gods of Ancient Europe*, London, 1991, 11, 62, 31.
2. See M. Eliade, *Patterns in Comparative religion*, London, 1958, 135–41, where Eliade also gives examples from New Zealand, Oceania and Indonesia.
3. *Confession*, ed. C. H. H. Wright, §20.
4. 1 Kgs 19:9–13.
5. 1 Kgs 18:38. 2 Kgs 1:11–2.
6. See §§6, 9–12, 47.
7. For further discussion, see N. O'Donoghue, *Aristocracy of Soul*, London, 1987, 16–18.
8. *Conf.*, §59–60. Cf. Tírechán, ed. Bieler, §4, 126–7.
9. Eph. 5:14. Cf. Rev. 21:22.
10. Plummer, 'Litany of Jesus – II', *Irish Litanies*, HBS 62, London, 1925, 40–1.
11. *Lismore*, ed. Stokes, 149. This was a favourite text for Irish hagiographers. A particularly close parallel can be found in the opening lines of the 10th-cent. *Life of Adamnán*, in *Betha Adamnáin*, ed. M. Herbert and P. Ó Riain, Dublin, 1988, 46–7, §1.
12. For more detail see J. Morgenstern, 'The Gates of Righteousness', *Hebrew Union College Annual* 6, 1929, 1–37, and 'The King-God among the Western Semites and the meaning of Epiphanes', *Vetus Testamentum* 10, 1960, 138–

97. Also F. J. Hollis, 'The Sun-cult and the Temple at Jerusalem', *Myth and Ritual*, ed. S. H. Hooke, Oxford, 1933, 87–110; W. O. E. Oesterley, 'The Early Hebrew Festival Rituals', ibid., 112–46; A. R. Johnson, 'The Role of the King in the Jerusalem Cultus', *The Labyrinth*, ed. S. H. Hooke, London, 1935, 71–111; H. G. May, 'Some Aspects of Solar Worship at Jerusalem', *Zeitschrift für die Alttestamentliche Wissenschaft* 55–6, 1937–8, 269–79; S. Mowinckel, *The Psalms in Israel's Worship*, vol. 1, trans. D. R. Ap-Thomas, Oxford, 1962, 94, 133; S. Terrien, 'The Omphalos Myth and Hebrew Religion', *Vetus Testamentum* 20, 1970, 315–38.

13. Ps. 118:19–20, 24, 27. See Morgenstern, 'The Gates of Righteousness', 15.

14. Ibid., 36.

15. Later, Elyon would be one of the Hebrew names of God, as in Ps. 47:2: 'Yahweh Elyon is terrible, a great king over all the earth'. For Elyon's solar characteristics and vestiges of solar worship in Jerusalem, see Johnson, 'The Role of the King', 82–3; Terrien, 'The Omphalos Myth', passim; and Sandmel, *HS*, 64. The shrine of Elyon was tended by a succession of priest-kings, one of whom, Melchizedek, appears in Gen. 14:17–20. The sun temple at Beth Shemesh ('House of the Sun') also seems to be have been taken over as a Yahweh sanctuary. See 1 Sam. 6:1–15.

16. Morgenstern, 'The King-God', 148.

17. S. Sandmel, *HS*, 64–5, 518–21.

18. 2 Kgs 23:11.

19. Ezek. 8:16.

20. *Sukkah* v.4; W. O. E. Oesterley, 'Early Hebrew Festival Rituals', 134. Cf. Ezek. 44:1–3.

21. Ezek. 1, passim. Cf. Dan. 7:9 and Rev. 1:12–16.

22. Ezek. 43:1–5. Cf. Ezek. 9:9–10:19 and 11:22–3 where the glory of the Lord leaves the temple because of the prevailing climate of violence and injustice.

23. Num. 6:25. Cf. Ps. 4:6; 31:16; 67:1; 80:3, 7, 19; 89:15; 119:135.

24. Hab. 3:4; Num. 6:25. Cf. Ps. 4:6; 31:16; 67:1; 80:3, 7, 19; 89:15; 119:135.

25. 2 Sam. 23:2–4.

26. Eg. Is. 9:1–2; 42:6–7; 51:4; 58:6; 60:1–2, 19–20.

27. Lk. 1:78–79.

28. Mt. 4:15–16. Cf. Is. 9:1–2; 12:46; Mt. 5:14; 13:43; 17:2; Rev. 1:16.

29. Jn 1:4–5, 9; 9:5; Acts 9:3–8. Cf. Acts 22:6–11; 26:12–18, where he describes the light as 'brighter than the sun'.

30. Am. 5:18–20. Sandmel, *HS*, 64–5. Johnson, 'The Role of the King', passim.

31. See Bieler, *Patrician Texts*, 203.

32. The juxtaposition of Easter with a pre-christian festival at Tara is probably a storyteller's device rather than an historical fact. Celebratory fires and festivals of kingship are described in various sources but none of them could coincide with Easter. See D. A. Binchy, 'The Fair of Tailtiu and the Feast of Tara', *Ériu* 18–19, 113–38.

33. Dan. 3.

34. Muirchú, ed. Bieler, I, 15 (14) (3–6), 84–7.

35. Ibid., I, 16 (15) (2–4) 87–9. For Tírechán's version of the story, see Bieler, 130–3, §8 (2–6).

36. Cf. the flight and fall of Simon Magus, *The Acts of Peter* II, 32(3) ed. W. Schneemelcher, London, 1965, 315–16.

37. Cf. the contest of St Rufinus and the Manichees, *Historia monachorum in Aegypto* 9, in Migne, *Patrologia Latina* 21, pp. 426–7, §165.
38. See for example Gen. 15:17; Ex. 3:1–6; Lev. 9:23–4; Acts 2:3. Also p. 143–6 above.
39. *Rennes*, ed. Stokes, *RC* 15, 297; *MD* ed. Gwynn, II, 42. Similarly in *The Battle of Moytura*, tribute is paid to the Fomorians (p. 150) for every fire or hearth in Ireland. *CMT*, ed. Grey, 28–9, §25. Elsewhere, fire plays an important part in the foundation of Eoganacht dynasty at Cashel (p. 92).
40. Muirchú, ed. Bieler, *Patrician Texts*, I, 16 (15) (2) 86–7.
41. See 70. O'Donovan and Stokes, *Cormac's Glossary*, 137–8; also Patrick Ford, 'The Blind, the dumb and the ugly', *CMCS* 19, 1990, 30–5.
42. *Life of Colum Cille*, ed. O'Kelleher and Schopperle, Illinois, 1918, 190, §186.
43. See Lives of Abban, Cronán and Molaise, ed. Plummer, *VSH* I, 32, §52, II, 29, §24; II, 133, §10. For Cathbad, see *VSH*, I, cxxxv n.5, citing the *Life of Caillin* in the *Book of Fanagh*.
44. M. Martin, *Description of the Western Islands of Scotland*, 2nd edn, 1716, republished in facsimile 1981. For churches, see 99, 248; for fishermen, 118; for the Flannan Isles, 16–17; a visiting clergyman, 20; holy wells, 140, 277; a sacred stone, 241; carrying of fires, 116–17.
45. Arbois, *The Irish Mythological Cycle*, Dublin, 1903, 8–9, 103–5, 112–14; Rhyss, *The Origin and Growth of Religion as Illustrated by Celtic Heathendom*, Hibbert Lectures 1886, London, 1888; Nutt, *The Voyage of Bran*, I, 292; Hull, *Folklore* 18, 131; Plummer, *VSH*, I, cxxxvi. Their views are summarised by O'Rahilly, *EIHM* 513–14.
46. RIA, *Dictionary of the Irish Language*, 1913–36, s.v. Lug.
47. Based on *The Fate of the Children of Tuirenn*, ed. Eugene O'Curry, *The Atlantis* 4, 1863. See also Cross and Slover, *AIT*, 50–7.
48. See Macalister, *LG*, 4, 134–7; and *The Battle of Moytura / Cath Maige Tuired*, ed. E. Grey, ITS 52, London, 1982. The spear in the *LG* version 'is plainly the lightning spear', according to O'Rahilly, *EIHM*, 311. In terms of the argument of *EIHM*, this makes it a solar weapon (p. 153).
49. See 33. For Lug's encounter with Cú Chulainn, see *Táin*, ed. Kinsella, 142–7.
50. *Cath Maige Tuired*, ed. Grey, 66–7, §145. See 110–11 for translations.
51. Ibid., 40–1, §67–8.
52. *IMC*, 113–14; cf. 8–9, 77, 122.
53. *Cath Maige Tuired,*, ed. Grey, §16. Bres, the Fomorian leader, is the child of this union. His parentage is described differently in *The Fate of the Children of Tuirenn*, where he is Bres son of Balor.
54. Ibid., §§25, 36, 37, 39, 45, 160.
55. For further discussion see E. Grey, '*Cath Maige Tuired*, Myth and Structure', *Éigse* 1982–3, 1–36, 230–62; T. Ó Cathasaigh, 'Curse and Satire,' *Éigse* 1986, 10–15. Cf. 'The First Battle of Moytura', ed. J. Fraser, *Ériu* 8, 1916, 20–1, §24.
56. See Murphy, *DF* III, lxxii – lxxxv. Also P. Mac Cána, '*Fianaigecht* in the Pre-Norman Period'; *The Heroic Process*, ed. B. Almqvist, Dun Laoghaire, 1987; cf. T. Ó Cathasaigh, '*Cath Maige Tuired* as exemplary myth', *Folio Gadelica*, ed. De Brun et al., 1983, 13.
57. *EIHM*, passim, but especially chp. III, 'The *Gaí Bulga* and its kin', 58–74,

chp. xv, 'The traveller of the heavens' 286–307, and chp. xvi 'The three gods of Craftsmanship', 308–17. O'Rahilly later expanded his argument in 'Buchet the Herdsman', *Ériu* 16–17, 1952–5, 1–20.

58. *Cath Maige Tuired*, ed. Grey, §§135, 133.
59. Murphy, *DF* iii, lxxi, quoting Tomás Ó Cillín in *Béaloideas* iv, 88, and the Ordnance Survey Letters for Donegal, 1835, 46–51, 81–97, 129–30, 229. A christian tradition of the eye of God was known in Hebrides at the end of the 19th cent., though it is not always clearly linked with the sun. See Carmichael, *CG* ii, 45, 69; iii, 57, 307; iv, 169, or *CG*, 1992, 137–45, 384–92. Carmichael's editing process is little understood and could well have included the amalgamation of fragments which did not originally belong together. Since he was also a contemporary of Arbois, Müller and others, there is a question as to how far he might have been influenced by their theories, for example in linking prayers which use sun imagery with others on the eye of God.
60. This name for Ogma appears without further explanation in a genealogy in *LG* 4, ed. Macalister, ITS 41, 188–9.
61. From a manuscript known as 'Cormac and the Badgers', cited by Stokes in *Three Old Irish Glossaries*, xliii.
62. *Dindshenchas* ii of Sliab n-Echtga, ed. Gwynn, *MD* iii, 306–7.
63. For *Láir Derg* see 'The Laud Genealogies and tribal histories', ed. Meyer, *ZCP* 8, 307, and 'Conall Corc and the kingdom of Cashel', ed. V. Hull, *ZCP* 18, 420–1. For the horse called Grian, see *Dindshenchas* of Loch Dá Gabar, *MD*, ed. Gwynn, iv, 182–3.
64. *The Wooing of Étaín / Tochmarc Étaín*, ed. Bergin and Best, *Ériu* 12, 148–9, 156–7. Gantz's edition, *EIMS* 46–7, translates *granián* simply as 'bower'.
65. Gerald of Wales: *The History and Topography of Ireland*, ed. O'Meara, §102, 109–10; Simms, *From Kings to Warlords*, 21–3.
66. See 67. *The Battle of Mag Mucrama / Cath Maige Mucrama*, ed. M. O'Daly, ITS 50, 1975, §3–5.
67. See 44. See M. Mac Neill, *The Festival of Lughnasad*, Oxford, 1962, 412–3; G. Ó Crualaoich, 'Continuity and Adaptation in Legends of Cailleach Bhéarra', *Béaloideas* 56, 1988, 153–8. In the folk tradition, Áine is sometimes identified with the Hag of Beare, and with Anu, from the Paps of Anu in Co. Kerry.
68. *EIHM*, 286–94. Áine's family connections vary with the sources, so we may well be dealing with more than one Áine. References include O'Donovan and Stokes, *Cormac's Glossary*, §60; Stokes, 'The Battle of Mag Mucrime', *RC* 13, 434–8, §3–5; O'Grady, *SG* ii, 179–80, 196–7, 347–8, 575; Gwynn, *Dindshenchas* of Bend Etair ii, *MD* iii, 114–15; Thurneysen, *MV*, 83; Meyer, *Cath Finntrágha / The Battle of Ventry*, *Anecdota Oxoniensia*, Medieval and Modern Series 1(1), Oxford, 1882, 74.
69. D. Fitzgerald, 'Popular Tales of Ireland,' *RC* 4, 1879–80, 185–92. Cf. the carrying of fires in the 18th-cent. Hebridean tradition, p. 150 above.
70. *The Poems of Blathmac*, ed. Carney, ITS 47, Dublin, 1964, 47–9, §138–9. Cf. §161.
71. Ibid., §§143, 150.
72. *Aithdioghluim Dána*, ed. L. McKenna, ITS 40, Dublin, 1939–40, 191, §12; 168, §§5, 11; 219, §29. Also 'a sun-bright graceful maid', 192, §26; *The Poems of Philip Bocht Ó Huiginn*, ed. McKenna, Dublin, 1931, no.2, §§13, 24, 11a §4. Also 'bright heaven's sun' no.2 §1.

73. *Philip Bocht Ó Huiginn*, ed. McKenna, no.2, §§22–4, 32.
74. *Gerald of Wales: the History and Topography of Ireland*, ed. J. O'Meara, §67–9, 81–2. Cf. §77, 88.
75. O'Grady, 'The Life of St Magnenn of Kilmainham', *SG* II, 41.
76. Plummer, *VSH* I, 230–1, §32.
77. Cf. The Hebridean folk tradition that Bride would visit the house during the night on the eve of Bride's Day, leaving the imprint of her staff or her foot in the ashes of the hearth. Carmichael, *CG* I, 168. This is also mentioned in Martin's earlier *Description of the Western Islands*, 119.
78. See R. A. S. Macalistair, *Proceedings of the Royal Irish Academy*, 34C (1919), 340–1. Three centuries before Gerald, the author of *Cormac's Glossary* had been aware of Hestia and had identified her with an Irish 'goddess of fire' whom he calls Aed: 'to wit, *dea*, which means 'goddess', the goddess in question being Vesta, goddess of fire.' The etymology may be fanciful, but the identification of an Irish 'fire goddess' with Hestia is intriguing. *Cormac's Glossary*, trans. O'Donovan, 5.
79. O'Donovan and Stokes, *Cormac's Glossary*, 23.
80. McCone, *PPCP*, 166. For an extended discussion of fire and the arts, see 161–78.
81. O'Donovan and Stokes, *Cormac's Glossary*, 94–5.
82. McCone, *PPCP*, 162, citing *CIH*, ed. D. A. Binchy, 1978, 377, 26 and 380, 14–15. For another hospitaller, see p. 81–2.
83. Carmichael, *CG* I, 232–3, 236–7, 240–1.
84. 'Cogitosus's Life of Saint Brigit', ed. S. Connolly and J.-M. Picard, *JRSAI* 117, 1987, 12–27, §26, 31, 6.
85. *Bethu Brigte*, ed. D. Ó hAondha, Dublin, 1978, §1, 3, 18, 19.
86. The story of the child in the burning house and the column of flame, occur frequently in the Lives of other saints. See Plummer, *VSH* I, Buite §iii; *VSH* II, Ita §2, Mochoemog §vii, Fechin §iv; Heist, *Codex Salamanticensis*, Daig §2; Also Colum Cille, see p. 160–1.
87. Stokes, *Lismore*, Life of Brigit, 184, lines 1212–4.
88. Attributed to Ultán of Ardbraccan. See Stokes and Strachan, *Thes. Pal.* II, 325; Also *Lismore*, Life of Brigit, 199.
89. Reeves, *Adamnán's Life*, III, 24, 132–133. Sharpe, *Adomnán*, III, 23.230–1.
90. Ibid., III, 4, 112–13. *Táin*, ed. Kinsella, 77, 153.
91. The term 'soldier of Christ' is frequently used by Adamnán, e.g. Sharpe, *Adomnán*, I, 20, 127; I, 49, 151; III, 23, 230.
92. Reeves, *Adamnán's Life*, III, 19, 123–4. Sharpe, *Adomnán*, III, 18, 219–20. Cf. III, 17, 119–21, 219–23; III, 2, 206.
93. Sharpe, *Adomnán*, 306–8.
94. *The Destruction of Da Derga's Hostel*, ed. Gantz, 77; O'Donovan and Stokes, *Cormac's Glossary*, 94–5.
95. Jn 14:26, 16:12.
96. Most of the following examples are taken from Plummer's two-volume collection, *VSH*, which contains a selection of undated Latin Lives, all of them later than the 7th century. For phenomena of light and fire, see *VSH* I: Brendan §3; Carthach §4; *VSH* II: Comgall §4; Finan §1; Maedoc §3.
97. *VSH* II: Fechin §4; Ita §2; Mochoemog §7; Also Daig, see *Codex Salamanticensis*, ed. Heist, Brussels, 1965, 389, §2.

98. *VSH* I: Buite §3; Carthach §8.
99. *VSH* I: Brendan §5; *VSH* II: Comgall §7; Ita §2; Maedoc §39.
100. Muirchú's *Life of Patrick*, ed. Hood, 97, §28; same passage ed. Bieler, *Patrician Texts*, 100–3, I, 28(27); Plummer, *VSH* I: Buite §7; Brendan §83; Cíarán of Saigir §29; Coemgen §35; *VSH* II: Comgall §§8, 46; Fechin §17; Lasrén/Molaise §§12, 24.
101. *VSH* II: Comgall §15; Fintan §16.
102. *VSH* I: Ailbe §40, Coemgen §5; Cíarán of Saigir §33; *VSH* II: Comgall §39; Finan §§5, 26 n. 9; Lugaid/Molua §17; also Daig, see Heist, *Codex Salamanticensis*, 389, §16.
103. *VSH* I: Buite §19; Cíarán of Saigir §32; *VSH* II: Comgall §43–4; Lasrén/ Molaise §7; Mochoemog §3.
104. Muirchú's *Life of Patrick*, ed. Bieler, *Patrician Texts*, II, 8 (7), 118–19 with an appeal to scripture. Also *VSH* II: Fechin §20, Colman §24, Molaise §11, Lugaid/Molua §39.
105. *VSH* I: Cainnech §27, Carthach §28.
106. *VSH* I: Buite §19, Cainnech §35, Coemgen §18 n. 18.); also Patrick, *Trip.* I, cxxxviii, n. 7.
107. *VSH* I: Cíarán of Saigir §19, Carthach §4; *VSH* II: Mochoemog §7, Ita §23, Fechin §13.
108. *VSH* I: Brendan §5; *VSH* II: Maedoc §39, Fintan §16.
109. Josh. 10:12–14, Dan. 3. Cf. Is. 43:2: 'When you walk through fire you shall not be burned, and the flame shall not consume you.'
110. Hab. 3:4. The Desert tradition is cited, without references, by Thomas Merton in his anthology *The Wisdom of the Desert*, London, 1961, 50.
111. *VSH* II: Finan §1, Comgal §19 n. 1.
112. *Táin*, ed. Kinsella, 92. Cf. Muirchú's *Life of Patrick*, ed. Hood, 97, §28; also Bieler, *Patrician Texts*, 100–3, I, 28 (27). For cold water ascetics of the East, see N. Chadwick, *The Age of the Saints in the Early Celtic Church*, London, 1961, 104–5.
113. V. Flint, *The Rise of Magic in Medieval Europe*, Princeton, 1991, 59–84.
114. For the *Life of Daig*, see Heist, *Codex Salamanticensis*.
115. P. Ó Riain, 'Traces of Lug in the early Irish hagiographical tradition', *ZCP* 36, 1978, 138–56.

CHAPTER NINE

1. J. Gibson, 'The theology of the Ugaritic Baal Cycle', *Orientalia* 53, fasc.2, 1984, 218–9.
2. W. F. Wakeman, *A Survey of the Antiquarian Remains on the Island of Inismurray*, London, 1893, xii.
3. Ibid., 126.
4. Sharpe, *Adomnán*, II, 34, 182–4; cf. I, 1, 109; for examples of other weather-working episodes in Lives of Saints, see Plummer, *VSH* I, 48, §6 (Ailbe); *VSH* II, 92, §18 (Finan); 133, §11 (Lasrén / Molaise of Devenish); 179, §29 (Mochoemog)' and 213, §35, 53 (Lugaid).
5. See 10. *LG* 5, ed. Macalister, 38–9, 54–7, 114–17.
6. *Cáin Adamnáin, an Old-Irish treatise on the Law of Adamnán*, ed. K. Meyer, *Anecdota Oxoniensia*, Oxford, 1905, §45; *St Patrick: his writings and Muirchú's Life*, ed. A. B. E. Hood, London, 1978, 93–4, §23. For another edition, see

Bieler, *Patrician Texts*, I, 23(22) = B II, 4. 102–7. For further discussion, P.
   L. Henry, *The Early English and Celtic Lyric*, London, 1966, 181–94.

 7. *Voyage of Snedgus and MacRiagla*, ed. Stokes, *RC* 9, 1888, 14–25, §§7–10,
    21–3.
 8. Columbanus, *Sermon V*, ed. G. S. M. Walker, *Sancti Columbani Opera*,
    Dublin, 1957, 85–7; *The Cambrai Homily*, ed. Stokes and Strachan, *Thes.
    Pal.* II, 244–7.
 9. Sharpe, *Adomnán*, I, 7, 118; Stokes, *Lismore*, 170, line 730. The precise
    reasons for Colum Cille's removal to Iona have never been fully established.
    For discussion, see M. Herbert, *Iona, Kells and Derry*, Edinburgh, 1988, 10–
    30. Sharpe also summarises the various traditions, op. cit., 12–15.
10. Meyer, *The Law of Adamnán / Cáin Adamnáin*, §23–4. For what follows, cf.
    SG II, 264–5.
11. G. MacEoin identifies two further examples: the so-called 'Leyden lorica'
    which is actually a prayer to obtain a lover, is a Latin work from around the
    seventh century. The 'Litany of Creation' is a protection prayer in Irish,
    from around the eleventh century. 'Invocation of nature in the *loricae*', *Stud.
    Hib.*, 2, 1962, 212–17.
12. Gal. 4:8–11; 2 Pet. 3:10–11 also refers to the *stoicheia*.
13. Mt. 27:45, 51; Lk 23:44–45.
14. *The Poems of Blathmac*, ed. Carney, 23–5, §61–70.
15. Ibid., 124. Carney draws attention to an apocalyptic passage in 2 Esdras 5:5
    – 'blood shall drip from wood,' and to an Anglo-Saxon poem by Cynewulf
    in which trees shed tears of blood.
16. Meyer, *AIP*, 17; R. Bromwich, 'The keen for Art O'Leary', *Éigse* 5, 1945–7,
    248–9. My thanks to Professor Ó Madagáin for this. For more on keening,
    see his 'Irish vocal music of lament and syllabic verse', *The Celtic Conscious-
    ness*, ed. O'Driscoll, Edinburgh, 1982, 311–31.
17. Carney's alternative translation: 'had the good elements known about it, and
    the sky had not fallen on them ... they would have been open to severe
    reproaches,' implies that it would have been a dereliction of duty for the
    elements not to punish the offenders. Op. cit., 125
18. The Byzantine mystic St Simeon the New Theologian would later write
    about the Fall in similar terms: 'the heaven prepared to fall on him and the
    earth did not wish to bear him. But God ... did not allow the elements to
    unleash themselves immediately upon man.' Quoted by P. Evdokimov in his
    article 'Nature', *Scottish Journal of Theology* 18, 1965, 11.
19. Cf. Ps. 104:4, '... who makest the winds thy messengers, fire and flame thy
    ministers.'
20. §191–6, 226–9. Cf. Mk 4:39–41; Lk 8:24; Mt. 8:26.
21. §236–58.
22. 'Old Irish Homily', ed. Strachan, *Ériu* 3, 8–10.
23. For the whole Canticle, see Dan. 3:51–90. Bibles of the Reformed tradition
    usually conclude Dan. 3 at verse 30. Sources for the rest of the chapter
    include the Jerusalem Bible, the Roman Breviary, the Book of Common
    Prayer, and the Apocrypha as included in some editions of the Revised
    Standard Version. The *Benedicite* is also known as 'The Song of the Three
    Young Men', 'The Song of the Three Children', and 'The Canticle of
    Daniel'.

24. See 13. *LRCC*, 2nd edn, 1987, 111, 190–1; O'Dwyer, *CD*, 184.
25. Curran, *AB*, 680–91.
26. Evdokimov, art. cit., 7.
27. Ps. 82:1–2. Cf. Ps. 89:6–7.
28. Ps. 82:6–7; Ps. 103:19–20.
29. Ps. 135:5; cf. Ps. 95:3; Ex. 15:11.
30. Is. 40:12.
31. Is. 40:18–20. Cf. 41:21–24.
32. J. Gibson, 'Language about God in the Old Testament', *Polytheistic Systems*, ed. G. Davies, Edinburgh, 1989, 43. This whole section is based on work by Professor Gibson.
33. 'They used to carve on (their altars) the forms of the elements they adored there.' O'Donovan and Stokes, *Cormac's Glossary*, 94.
34. 'The conversion of Loegaire and his death', ed. Plummer, in 'Irish Miscellanies', *RC* 6, 165–8. For dates, see G. Mac Eoin, 'The mysterious death of Lóegaire mac Néill', *Stud. Hib.* 8, 27.
35. For an extended discussion of the elements as guardians of cosmic order, see W. Sayers, '*Mani Maidi an Nem ... ':* ringing changes on a cosmic motif', *Ériu* 37, 1986, 99–117.
36. Mac Eoin, 'The mysterious death', 32, citing Macalister, *LG* 5, ITS 44, 540ff, poem cxxxvi, §7.
37. 'Das sind die Bürgen die sie dazu stellten: der Himmel, die Erde, der Mond, die schöne Sonne ...' [These are the sureties which they offered for it: the sky, the earth, the moon, the beautiful sun], Thurneysen, 'Morands Fürstenspiegel', *ZCP* 11, 58, §11. O'Kelly's edition of *The Testament of Morann* does not include this passage, but for a summary of the story see D. Hyde, *Literary History of Ireland*, 1967, 27–9.
38. Fer Diad's demands occur only in the Book of Leinster version of the *Táin*, ed. O'Rahilly, 212. For Aed Ruad, see *Rennes*, ed. Stokes, 31–3. Also Donn's oath by sea, sky and earth in *DF*, ed. Mac Eoin, I, 30/131 and Conchobar's oath in *Táin*, ed. O'Rahilly, 217.
39. E.g. Calypso's oath by the earth, the sky and the river Styx. *Odyssey*, trans. E. V. Rieu, Harmondsworth, 1946, v, 92. In the *Iliad*, Agamemnon calls on Zeus, the sun, the rivers, the earth, and those who live under the earth, to witness a crucial agreement between the Greeks and the Trojans. *Iliad*, trans. Robert Fagles, London, 1990, III, lines 228–334.
40. Based on Stokes, *The Death of Muirchertach Mac Erca*, *RC* 23, 396–400, §1–4.
41. D. Ó hOgain, *Myth, Legend and Romance*, 310–11.
42. Macalister, *LG* 5, 1956, 362–3, 534–5.
43. *IBA*, 182–3.
44. Based on *Tenga Bhith-Nua Annso Sis / The Evernew Tongue Here Below*, ed. Stokes, *Ériu* 2, 98–9, §11–13 with help from M. Herbert's translation, Herbert and McNamara, *IBA*, 109–18.
45. Ibid., I, 163–4.
46. Cf. 1 Cor. 15 passim; Cf. Col. 1:15–20, Rom. 8.18–23. Other influences on the text may include Greek and Latin apocrypha and biblical commentaries. Herbert and McNamara, *IBA*, 182–3
47. *The Evernew Tongue*, ed. Stokes, §1–3.

48. Clancy and Markus, *Iona: the Earliest Poetry*, 39–68.
49. *St Patrick: his writings and Muirchú's Life*, ed. Hood, 96–7, §27. See also Bieler, *Patrician Texts*, 98–101, §1, 27 (26) = B II, 1.
50. Rom. 1:18–20.
51. Titles like this had a lasting appeal in Celtic Christianity. One 10th-cent. prayer addresses God repeatedly as *A Dé Dulig* – 'Oh God of the elements / creatures / everything'. Eight centuries later, the God of the elements was still invoked in Hebridean spirituality as *A Dhe nan dul* – 'Oh God of the elements' or 'God of All' in Carmichael's translation. See P. Ó Neill, 'Airbertach Mac Cosse's Poem on the Psalter', *Éigse* 17, 19–46, §1, 36, 40; Murphy, *EIL*, 36–7; B. Ó Cuív, 'Some early devotional verse in Irish', *Ériu* 19, 1–24, II, §7, III, §16; Carmichael, *CG* I, 14 (in the prayer translated as 'God be with us') and 18 (in the prayer 'Jesu, thou son of Mary').
52. Conversation with T. Ó Cathasaigh, April 1989, University College, Dublin.
53. L. White, 'The historical roots of our ecologic crisis', *Science* 155, 3767, 10.3.67, 1204–7.

Abbreviations

AB	*Antiphonary of Bangor*, ed. Warren; Curran
Amra	*Amra Choluimb Chille*, ed. Stokes; Clancy and Márkus
AI	*Ancient Israel*, De Vaux
AIP	*Selections from Ancient Irish Poetry*, ed. Meyer
AIT	*Ancient Irish Tales*, ed. Cross and Slover
Aith. Dán.	*Aithdioghluim Dána*, ed. McKenna
AU	*The Annals of Ulster*, ed. Hennessy; Mac Airt and MacNiocaill
CC	*The Celtic Consciousness*, ed. O'Driscoll
CD	*Céli Dé*, O'Dwyer
CG	*Carmina Gadelica*, ed. Carmichael
CH	*Celtic Heritage*, Rees and Rees
CIH	*Corpus Iuris Hibernici*, ed. Binchy
CM	*A Celtic Miscellany*, ed. Jackson
CMCS	*Cambrian* (formerly *Cambridge*) *Medieval Celtic Studies*
DF	*Duanaire Finn*, ed. Murphy, L. G.; MacNeill, E.
EC	*Etudes Celtiques*
ECNP	*Studies in Early Celtic Nature Poetry*, Jackson
EECL	*The Early English and Celtic Lyric*, Henry
EIL	*Early Irish Lyrics*, ed. Murphy
EIHM	*Early Irish History and Mythology*, O'Rahilly, T. F.
EIMS	*Early Irish Myths and Sagas*, ed. Gantz
EIP	*Early Irish Poetry*, ed. Carney
Félire	*Félire Óengusso Céli Dé*, ed. Stokes
FL	*The Festival of Lughnasad*, MacNeill, M.
FM	*Annals of the Four Masters*, ed. O'Donovan
GHC	*Gods and Heroes of the Celts*, Sjoestedt
GB	*The Golden Bough*, abridged edn, Frazer
GT	*A Golden Treasury of Irish Poetry*, Greene and O'Connor
HBS	Henry Bradshaw Society
HS	*The Hebrew Scriptures*, Sandmel
IBA	*Irish Biblical Apocrypha*, ed. Herbert and Macnamara
IT	*Irische Texte*, ed. Windisch and Stokes
I. Trad.	*The Irish Tradition*, Flower
ITS	Irish Texts Society
JIA	*Journal of Irish Archeology*
JRSAI	*Journal of the Royal Society of Antiquaries of Ireland*

LG	*Lebor Gabála Érenn*, ed. Macalister
Lismore	*Lives of Saints from the Book of Lismore*, ed. Stokes
LL	*Book of Leinster*
LRCC	*Liturgy and Ritual of the Celtic Church*, ed.Warren
LU	*Lebor na hUidre*
MD	*Metrical Dindshenchas*, ed. Gwynn, E. J.
MV	*Mittelirische Verslehren*, ed. Windisch and Stokes
NCE	*New Catholic Encyclopaedia*
ODCC	*Oxford Dictionary of the Christian Church*
PCB	*Pagan Celtic Britain*, Ross
PPCP	*Pagan Past, Christian Present*, McCone
RC	*Revue Celtique*
Rennes	*Rennes Dindshenchas*, ed. Stokes
RIA	Royal Irish Academy
RV	Rig Veda
Saltair	*Saltair na Rann*, ed. Greene, Kelly and Murdoch
SG	*Silva Gadelica*, ed. O'Grady
SSS	*Sages, Saints and Storytellers*, ed. Ó Corráin, Breatnach and McCone
Stud. Celt.	*Studia Celtica*
Stud. Hib.	*Studia Hibernica*
Táin	*Táin Bó Cúailgne*, Kinsella; O'Rahilly, C.
Thes. Pal.	*Thesaurus Palaeohibernicus*, ed. Stokes and Strachan
TLS	Todd Lectures Series
Trip.	*The Tripartite Life of Patrick*, ed. Stokes
VSH	*Vitae Sanctorum Hiberniae*, ed. Plummer
WO	*The Wisdom of the Outlaw*, Nagy
YBL	*Yellow Book of Lecan*
ZCP	*Zeitschrift für Celtisches Philologie*

NOTE ON IRISH PRONUNCIATION

The pronunciation of Irish words and names can be daunting to newcomers and outsiders. Kenneth Jackson provides a useful 'Pronouncing Index' in *A Celtic Miscellany*, rev. edn, Harmondsworth, 1971, pp.325–43, as does Daithi Ó hOgain in his encyclopaedia of the folk tradition, *Myth, Legend and Romance, an Encyclopaedia of the Irish Folk Tradition*, London 1990, pp.7–15. Old and Middle Irish are not pronounced in exactly the same way as Modern Irish and spelling also varies.

Bibliography

In order to help non-specialists to find their way to the primary sources more easily, some texts are listed here under English titles together with the name of the editor. Where there is a choice of editions, this is indicated by semi-colons. For example, 'Adamnán, *Life of St Columba*, see Anderson; Reeves; Sharpe', indicates three separate editions. Full details are given under the editor's name.

PRIMARY SOURCES FOR NON-SPECIALISTS

Jackson, K., *A Celtic Miscellany*
Meyer, K., *Selections from Ancient Irish Poetry*
Greene, D. and O'Connor, F., *A Golden Treasury of Irish Poetry*
Gantz, J., *Early Irish Myths and Sagas*
Sharpe, R., *Adomnán of Iona: Life of St Columba*
Farmer, D. H. and Webb, J. F., *Voyage of St Brendan*
Heaney, S., *Sweeney Astray*

GENERAL BIBLIOGRAPHY

Adamnán, *Life of St Columba*, see Reeves; Anderson; Sharpe.
——, *On the Holy Places*, see Meehan.
Anderson, A. and M., *Adomnan's Life of Columba*, Edinburgh,1961.
——, Second edition, Oxford, 1991.
Annals of the Four Masters, see O'Donovan.
Annals of Tigernach, see Skene.
Annals of Ulster, see Hennessy; Mac Airt and MacNiocaill.
Antiphonary of Bangor, see Warren; Curran.
Battle of Mag Tuired, see Grey.
Battle of Mag Rath, see O'Donovan; Marstrander.
Baylis, P., *An Introduction to Primal Religions*, Edinburgh, 1988.
Bediako, K., *Christianity in Africa: the renewal of a non-western Religion*, Edinburgh, 1995.
Benes, B., 'Spüren von Schamanismus in der Sage Buile Suibne', *ZCP* 29, 1960-1, 309-34.
Bergin, O., 'The Harrowing of Hell', *Ériu* 4, 1910, 113-19.
——, *Irish Bardic Poetry*, ed. Greene, D., and Kelly, F., Dublin, 1970.
Bernard, J. H., and Atkinson, R., *The Irish Liber Hymnorum*, 2 vols., Henry Bradshaw Society 14, London, 1897-8.

Best, R., 'On the Settling of the Manor of Tara', *Ériu* 4, 1910, 121–72.
——, 'Prognostications of the raven and the wren', *Ériu* 8, 120–6.
Best, R. and Bergin, O., 'The Wooing of Étaín', *Ériu* 12, 1938, 137–96.
Best, R. and Lawlor, H., *Martyrology of Tallaght*, Henry Bradshaw Society 68, London, 1931.
Bhreatnach, M., 'The sovereignty goddess as goddess of death?', *ZCP* 39, 1982, 243–60.
Bieler, L., *The Works of St Patrick*, London, 1953.
——, *Ireland, Harbinger of the Middle Ages*, Oxford,1963.
——, *The Patrician Texts in the Book of Armagh*, Dublin, 1979.
Binchy, D.A., 'The fair of Tailtiu and the feast of Tara', *Ériu* 18–19, 1958, 113–38.
——, 'The passing of the old order: the impact of the Scandinavian invasions on the Celtic-speaking peoples *c.* 800–1100 AD', *Proceedings of the International Congress of Celtic Studies*, ed. B. O Cuív, Dublin, 1962, 119–32.
——, *Corpus Iuris Hibernici*, Dublin, 1978.
Birth of Cú Chulainn, see Gantz, *EIMS*.
Blathmac, see Carney.
Book of Conquests, see Macalister.
Book of the Lays of Finn, see Mac Neill; Murphy.
Boyish Exploits of Finn, see Meyer; Nagy, *WO*.
Bord, J.and C., *Sacred Waters, holy wells and water lore in Britain and Ireland*, London, 2nd edn, 1986.
Bradley, I., *God is Green*, London, 1990.
——, *The Celtic Way*, London, 1993.
Breatnach, L., 'The cauldron of poesy', *Ériu* 32, 1981, 45–94.
——, *Uraicecht na Ríar, the Poetic Grades in Early Irish Law*, Dublin, 1987.
——, 'An edition of *Amra Senáin*', in *Sages, Saints and Storytellers*, Ó Corráin, Breatnach and McCone, Maynooth, 1989.
Breatnach, R. A., 'The lady and the king', *Studies* 42, 1953, 321–6.
Bricriu's Feast, see Gantz, *EIMS*.
Bromwich, R., 'The keen for Art O'Leary', *Éigse* 5, 1945–7.
Byrne, F. J., *Irish Kings and High Kings*, London, 1973.
Calder, G., *Auraicept na n-Éces*, Edinburgh, 1917.
Carey, J., 'Notes on the Irish war goddess', *Éigse* 19, 1982–3, 263–75.
——, 'The location of the Otherworld in Irish Tradition', *Éigse* 19, 1982–3, 36–43.
Carmichael, A., *Carmina Gadelica*, 6 vols, 2nd edn, Edinburgh, 1928.
——, Compendium edition with introduction by MacInnes, J., Edinburgh, 1992.
Carney, J., 'Suibne Geilt and the children of Lir', *Éigse* 6, 1948–52, 83–110.
——, *Studies in Irish Literature and History*, Dublin,1955.
——, *The Poems of Blathmac*, Irish Texts Society 47, Dublin, 1964.
——, *Early Irish Poetry*, Cork, 1965.
——, 'Three Old Irish Accentual Poems', *Ériu* 22, 1971, 26–41.
——, 'The dating of archaic Irish poetry', *Early Irish Literature – Media and Communication*, ed. Tranter, S., and Tristram, H., Tübingen, 1989.
Cattle Raid of Cooley, see Kinsella (*Táin*); O'Rahilly, C.
Cattle Raid of Fraích, see Gantz, *EIMS*.

Cauldron of Poesy, see Henry; Breatnach.

Chadwick, N., 'Geilt', *Scottish Gaelic Studies* 5, 1941, 106–53.

——, *Poetry and Prophecy*, Cambridge, 1942.

——, *The Age of the Saints in the early Celtic Church*, London, 1961.

Chronicum Scotorum, see Hennessy.

Clancy, T. and Márkus, G., *Iona: the Earliest Poetry of a Celtic Monastery*, Edinburgh, 1995.

Cogitosus, *Life of Brigit*, see S. Connolly and J.-M. Picard.

Colloquy of the Ancients, see O'Grady, *SG*.

Colloquy of the Two Sages, see Stokes.

Condla's Journey, see Oskamp.

Connolly, S., and Picard J.-M., 'Cogitosus: Life of Brigit', *JRSAI* 117, 1987, 11–27.

Cook, R., *The Tree of Life*, London, 1974.

Cormac's Glossary / Sanas Cormaic, see O'Donovan.

Cross, T. P. and Slover, C. H., *Ancient Irish Tales*, London,1937.

Curran, M., 'Early Irish Monasticism', in *Irish Spirituality*, ed. Maher, M., Dublin, 1981, 11–19.

——, *Antiphonary of Bangor*, Dublin, 1984.

Danaher, K., 'Irish folk tradition and the Celtic calendar', in *Celtic Consciousness*, ed. O'Driscoll, R., Edinburgh, 1982, 217–25.

Davidson, H. E., *Myths and Symbols of Pagan Europe*, Manchester, 1988.

Dawson, J., 'Calvinism and the Ghaidhealtacht in Scotland', in *Calvinism in Europe*, Pettigree, A., Duke, A., and Lewis, G., (eds) Cambridge, 1994.

Death of Muirchertach meic Erca, see Stokes.

De Paor, L. and M., *Early Christian Ireland*, London, 1958.

Destruction of Da Derga's Hostel, see Stokes; Gantz, J., *EIMS*.

De Vaux, R., *Ancient Israel, its life and institutions*, trans. John McHugh, 2nd edn.London, 1965.

De Vries, J., *La Religion des Celtes*, Paris, 1963.

Dillon, M., *The Cycles of the Kings*, London, 1946.

——, *Early Irish Literature*, London, 1948, repr.1972.

Dillon, M. and Chadwick, N., *The Celtic Realms*, London, 1967.

Dream of Óengus, see Jackson, *CM*; Gantz, *EIMS*.

Duanaire Finn, see Mac Neill; Murphy.

Eliade, M., *Rites and Symbols of Initiation*, New York, 1958.

——, *Patterns in Comparative Religion*, London, 1958.

——, *Shamanism, Archaic Techniques of Ecstasy*, London, 1964.

——, *Encyclopaedia of Religion*, London, 1987.

Engnell, I., 'Life and knowledge in the creation story', *Vetus Testamentum Supplement* 3, 1955.

Evdokimov, P., 'Nature', *Scottish Journal of Theology* 18, 1965.

Evernew Tongue, see Stokes; Herbert and MacNamara, *IBA*.

Félire Óengusso, see Stokes.

Fitzgerald, D., 'Popular Tales of Ireland', *Ériu* 4, 185–92.

Flint, V., *The Rise of Magic in Early Medieval Europe*, Princeton, 1991.

Flower, R., *The Irish Tradition*, Oxford, 1947.

——, '"The two eyes of Ireland": religion and literature in Ireland in the eighth and ninth centuries', *The Church of Ireland AD 432–1932: the report*

of the Church of Ireland conference held in Dublin, 11th–14th October, 1932, ed. W. Bell and N. D. Emerson, Dublin, 1932, 66–75
Ford, P. (ed.), *Celtic Folklore and Christianity*, Santa Barbara, 1983.
——, 'The blind, the dumb and the ugly', *CMCS* 19,1990, 30–4.
Forester, T., and Wright, T., *Giraldus Cambrensis: The Topography of Ireland*, London, 1863, 109–10, §54.
Fraser, J., 'The first battle of Moytura', *Ériu* 8, 1916, 1–63.
Frazer, J. G., *The Golden Bough*, abridged edn, 1922, reprinted, London, 1990.
Frenzy of Suibne, see O'Keeffe.
Gantz, J., *Early Irish Myths and Sagas*, London, 1981.
Gibson, J., *Canaanite Myths and Legends*, Edinburgh, 1978.
——, 'The theology of the Ugaritic Baal cycle', in *Orientalia* 53, Fasc. 2, 1984, 202–19.
——, 'Language about God in the Old Testament', in *Polytheistic Systems*, ed. G. Davies, Edinburgh, 1989.
Giraldus Cambrensis (Gerald of Wales), see O'Meara; Forester and Wright; Scott and Martin.
Gougaud, L., *Les Chrétientés Celtiques*, Paris, 1911.
Grant, M., *Myths of the Greeks and Romans*, London, 1989.
Gray, E., *Cath Maige Tuired / The Battle of Mag Tuired*, Irish Texts Society 52, London, 1982.
——, 'Cath Maige Tuired, myth and structure', *Éigse* 19,1982–3, 1–36, 230–262.
Green, M., *The Gods of the Celts*, Stroud, 1986.
——, *The Sun-gods of Ancient Europe*, London, 1991.
Greene, D., Kelly, F. and Murdoch, B., *The Irish Adam and Eve Story from Saltair na Rann*, 2 vols., Dublin, 1976.
Greene, D. and O'Connor, F., *A Golden Treasury of Irish Poetry*, London, 1967.
Grimal, P., *The Dictionary of Classical Mythology*, Oxford, 1986.
Gwynn, E.J., *The Metrical Dindshenchas*, 5 vols, Todd Lectures Series 8–12, Dublin, 1903–35.
Gwynn, L., 'Cináed Úa Hartacáin's poem on Brugh na Bóinne', *Ériu* 7, 1914, 210–38.
Hamp, E., 'Irish *síd* "tumulus" and Irish *síd* "peace"', *EC* 19, 141.
Hardy, P. D., *The Holy Wells of Ireland*, Dublin, 1836.
Haren, M. and Pontfarcy, Y. de, *The Medieval Pilgrimage to St Patrick's Purgatory*, Enniskillen, 1988.
Heaney, S., *Door into the Dark*, London, 1969.
——, 'The God in the Tree', in *Pleasures of Gaelic Poetry*, ed. MacRéamoinn, S., 25–34, London, 1982.
——, *Sweeney Astray*, London, 1984.
——, *Station Island*, London, 1984.
Heist, W. W., *Vitae Sanctorum Hiberniae ex codice olim Salmanticensi nunc Bruxellensi*, (*Codex Salamanticensis*), Brussels, 1965.
Hennessy, W. M., *Chronicum Scotorum*, London, 1866.
——, *Annals of Ulster*, Dublin, 1887.
Henry, P. L., *The Early English and Celtic Lyric*, London, 1966.

——, 'The cauldron of poesy', *Studia Celtica* 14–15, 1979–80, 114–21.
Herbert, M., *Iona, Kells and Derry*, Edinburgh, 1988.
——, 'Goddess and King: the sacred marriage in early Ireland' in *Women and Sovereignty*, ed. Fradenburg, L., Edinburgh, 1992.
Herbert, M. and Ó Riain, P., *Beatha Adamnáin / Life of Adamnán*, Dublin, 1988.
Herbert, M. and Macnamara, M., *Irish Biblical Apocrypha*, Edinburgh, 1989.
Herity, M., 'A survey of the royal site of Cruachain in Connacht', *JRSAI* 113, 1983, 121–30.
Herity, M., and Eogan, G., *Ireland in Pre-history*, London, 1977.
Herren, M., *Hisperica Famina*, Toronto, 1974.
Hiding of the Hill of Howth, see Meyer.
Hollis, F., 'The sun-cult and the Temple at Jerusalem', in *Myth and Ritual*, ed. Hooke, S., Oxford, 1933, 87–110.
Hood, A. B. E., *St Patrick: his writings and Muirchú's Life*, London, 1978.
Hughes, K., *The Church in Early Irish Society*, London, 1961.
Hughes, K. and Hamlin, A., *The Modern Traveller to the Early Irish Church*, London, 1977.
Hull, E., 'The silver bough in Irish legend', *Folklore* 12, 1901, 431–45.
——, *The Poem Book of the Gael*, London, 1912.
——, 'Fintan and the hawk of Achill, or the legend of the oldest animals', *Folklore* 43, 1932, 386–409.
——, 'Pagan baptism in the West', *Folklore* 43, 1932, 410–18.
Hull, V., 'The Exile of Conall Corc', *Publications of the Modern Langauge Association of America* 56.
Hyde, D., *A Literary History of Ireland*, London, 1899.
Intoxication of the Ulaid, see Gantz, *EIMS*.
Jackson, K. H., 'Tradition in early Irish prophecy', *Man* 34, 1934, 67–70.
——, 'The Adventure of Laeghaire mac Crimhthainn', *Speculum* 17, 377–87.
——, *Studies in Early Celtic Nature Poetry*, Cambridge, 1935.
——, 'The motive of threefold death in the story of Suibhne Geilt', in *Essays and Studies presented to Professor Eoin Mac Neill*, ed. Ryan, J., Dublin, 1940, 535–50.
——, 'A further note on Suibne Geilt and Merlin', *Éigse* 7, 1953, 112–116.
——, *The Oldest Irish Tradition: a window on the iron age*, Cambridge, 1964.
——, *A Celtic Miscellany*, revised edn, Harmondsworth, 1971.
Jeremias, J., *Jerusalem in the Time of Jesus*, London, 1969.
Journey of Cormac in the Land of Promise, see Stokes.
Journey of Nerae, see Meyer.
Journey of the Sons of Eochaid Macmedóin, see Joynt; Stokes.
Journey of Tadhg mac Céin, see O'Grady, *SG*.
Joynt, M., 'The journey of the sons of Eochaid Macmedóin', *Ériu* 4, 1910, 91–111.
Kavanagh, P., *The Complete Poems*, Newbridge, 1972.
Kelly, F., *Audacht Morainn / The Testament of Morann*, Dublin, 1976.
——, 'The Old Irish Tree List from the law tract *Bretha Comaithchesa*', *Celtica* 11–12, 1976–7, 107–24.
——, *A Guide to Early Irish Law*, Dublin, 1988.
Kinsella, T., *The Táin, translated from the Irish epic Táin Bó Cuailgne*, Oxford, 1970.

Law of Adamnán, see Meyer.
Lebar Brecc Homily on St Patrick, see Stokes, *Trip.*
Lehmann, R., 'Guaire and Marbhán', *ZCP* 36, 1978, 96–111.
Lincoln, B., *Priests, Warriors and Cattle*, Berkeley, 1980.
Löffler, C., *The Voyage to the Otherworld Island in Early Irish Literature*, Salzburg, 1983.
Logan, P., *The Holy Wells of Ireland*, Gerrards Cross, 1980.
Lucas, A.T., 'Sacred trees of Ireland', *Journal of the Cork Historical and Archeological Society* 68, 16–54.
Mac Airt, S. and MacNiocaill, G., *Annals of Ulster*, Dublin, 1983.
Macalister, R. A. S., *Lebor Gabála Érenn, the Book of the Taking of Ireland*, [=*The Book of Conquests*] 5 vols., *Irish Texts Society* 34–5, 39, 41, 44, 1938–56.
Mac Cana, P., 'Aspects of the theme of king and goddess in Irish literature', *Etudes Celtiques* 7, 1955–6, 76–114, 356–413 and *EC* 8, 1958–9, 59–65.
——, 'Conservation and innovation in early Celtic literature', *EC* 13, 1972–3, 61–119.
——, 'The sinless Otherworld of *Immram Brain*', *Ériu* 27, 1976, 95–115.
——, *Celtic Mythology*, London, 1970; 2nd ed. Dublin,1983.
——, '*Fianaigecht* in the pre-norman period', in *The Heroic Process*, ed. Almqvist, B., Dun Laoghaire, 1987.
McCone, K., 'Werewolves, cyclopes, *díberga* and *fianna*: juvenile delinquency in early Ireland', *CMCS* 12, 1986, 1–22.
——, 'A tale of two ditties: poet and satirist in *Cath Maige Tuired*', in *Sages, Saints and Storytellers*, ed. Ó Coráinn, Breatnach and McCone, Maynooth, 1989.
——, *Pagan Past, Christian Present*, Maynooth, 1990.
Mac Eoin, G. S., 'The invocation of nature in the loricae', *Studia Hibernica* 2, 1962, 212–7.
——, 'The mysterious death of Loegaire mac Néill', *Studia Hibernica* 8, 1968, 21– 48.
——, 'Orality and literacy in some middle-Irish king tales', in *Early Irish Literature – Media and Communication*, ed. S. Tranter and Tristram, Tübingen, 1992.
Mackey, J. P. (ed.), *An Introduction to Celtic Christianity*, Edinburgh, 1989.
——, 'Christian past and primal present', paper delivered at IXth International Congress of Celtic Studies, Paris, 1991.
——, 'Magic and Celtic primal religion', *ZCP* 45, 1992, 66–84.
McKenna, L., *The Poems of Philip Bocht Ó Huiginn*, Dublin, 1931.
——, *Aithdioghluim Dána*, Irish Texts Society 37 and 40, Dublin, 1939–40.
Mac Mathuna L., 'On the expression and concept of blindness in Irish', *Studia Hibernica* 19, 1979, 26–62.
Mac Neill, E., *Duanaire Finn / Book of the Lays of Finn*, vol.1, Irish Texts Society 43, Dublin, 1953.
MacNeill, M., *The Festival of Lughnasad*, 2 vols, Oxford,1962.
Mac Réamoinn, S., *The Pleasures of Gaelic Poetry*, London, 1982.
Maher, M., *Irish Spirituality*, Dublin, 1981.
Martin, M., *A Description of the Western Islands of Scotland*, 2nd edn, 1716, repr. Edinburgh, 1981.

Marstrander, C., 'A New Version of the Battle of Mag Rath', *Ériu* 5, 1911, 226–31.
Martyrology of Tallaght, see Best and Lawlor.
Martyrology of Óengus, see Stokes.
May, H., 'Some aspects of solar worship at Jerusalem', *Zeitschrift für Alttestamentliche Wissenschaft* 55–6, 1937–8, 269–79.
Meehan, D., *Adamnán's De Locis Sanctis / On the Holy Places*, Dublin, 1983.
Melia, D. F., 'Law and the shaman saint', in *Celtic Folklore and Christianity*, ed. Ford, P., Santa Barbara, 1983, 113–27.
——, 'A Poetic Klein Bottle', in *Celtic Language, Celtic Culture*, Matonis, A. and Melia, D., Van Nuys, 1990, 187–96.
Meyer, K., 'The conversion of Loegaire and his death', *RC* 6, 1885, 162–72.
——, 'The Conception of Conchobar', *RC* 6, 1885, 173–82.
——, 'Nerae's Journey' / *Echtra Nerai*, *RC* 10, 1889, 212–28.
——, 'The Hiding of the Hill of Howth', *RC* 11, 1890, 125–34.
——, 'Finn and the man in the tree', *RC* 25, 1904, 344–49.
——, 'The boyish exploits of Finn', *Ériu* 1, 1904–5, 180–90.
——, *The Law of Adamnán / Cáin Adamnáin*, Oxford, 1905.
——, *The Triads of Ireland*, Todd Lectures Series 14, Dublin,1906.
——, 'Death tales of the Ulster heroes', Todd Lectures Series 14, Dublin, 1906.
——, *Selections from Ancient Irish Poetry*, London, 1911.
——, *Miscellany presented to John MacDonald Mackay*, Liverpool, 1914.
Moore, C., *Daniel, Esther and Jeremiah, the Additions*, New York, 1977.
Morgenstern, J., 'The Gates of Righteousness', *Hebrew Union College Annual* 6, 1929, 1–37.
——, 'The King-God among the Western Semites and the meaning of Epiphanes', *Vetus Testamentum* 10, 1960, 138–97.
Morris, H., 'The holy wells of Donegal', *Béaloideas*, IML VI, 1936, 143–162.
Murphy, G., *Duanaire Finn / Book of the Lays of Finn*, vol. 2, Irish Texts Society 28, Dublin, 1933.
——, 'The origin of Irish nature poetry', *Studies* 20, 1939, 87–101.
——, *Duanaire Finn*, vol. 3, Irish Texts Society 43, Dublin, 1953.
——, *Early Irish Lyrics*, Oxford, 1956.
Muirchú, *Life of Patrick*, see Bieler (*Patrician Texts*); Hood.
Müller, M., *Natural Religion*, London, 1889.
Müller-Lisowski, K., 'Contributions to a study on Irish Folklore', *Béaloideas* 18, 1948, 142–99.
Nagy, J. F., 'The Wisdom of the *Geilt* ', *Éigse* 19, 1982–3, 44–60.
——, *The Wisdom of the Outlaw*, Berkeley, 1985.
——, 'Otter, salmon and eel in traditional Gaelic narrative', *Studia Celtica* 20–1, 1985–6, 123–44.
Nielsen, K., *There is Hope for a Tree*, Sheffield, 1985.
Nutt, A. and Meyer K. (eds), *The Voyage of Bran, son of Febal*, London, 1895.
Ó Brien, M. C., 'The role of the poet in Gaelic society', *Celtic Consciousness*, ed. O'Driscoll, R., Edinburgh, 1982.
Ó Cathasaigh, T., *The Heroic Biography of Cormac Mac Airt*, Dublin, 1977.
——, 'The semantics of *síd* ', *Éigse* 17, 1977–9, 135–54.
——, '*Cath Maige Tuired* as exemplary myth', *Folio Gadelica: essays presented to R. A. Breatnach*, de Brún, P., Ó Coileáin, S. and Ó Riain, P., Cork,

1983, 1–19.
——, 'The sister's son in early Irish literature', *Peritia* 5, 1986, 120–60.
——, 'Curse and satire', *Éigse* 21, 1986, 10–15.
——, 'The eponym of Cnogba', *Éigse* 21, 1987, 27–38.
Ó Corráin, D., *Ireland before the Normans*, Dublin, 1972.
——, 'Early Irish hermit poetry?', in *Sages, Saints and Storytellers*, eds., O
  Corráin, Breatnach and McCone, 251–67, Maynooth, 1989.
Ó Corráin, D., Breatnach L. and McCone K., *Sages, Saints and Storytellers,
  Celtic studies in honour of Professor James Carney* (eds.), Maynooth, 1989.
Ó Crualaoich, G., 'Continuity and adaptation in legends of the *cailleach
  bhéarra,*' *Béaloideas* 56, 1988, 153–78.
Ó Cuív, B., 'The romance of Mis and Dubh Ruis', *Celtica* 2, 1952–4.
——, 'Some early devotional verse in Irish', *Ériu* 19, 1–24.
——, *Seven Centuries of Irish Learning, 1000–1700*, Dublin, 1961.
O'Curry, E., 'The Vision of the Phantom' / *Baile in Scáil*, in *Lectures on the
  Manuscript Materials of Ancient Irish History*, Dublin, 1861.
——, 'The Fate of the Children of Tuirenn', *The Atlantis* 4, 1863.
O'Daly, M., *The Battle of Mag Mucrama* / *Cath Maige Mucrama*, Irish Texts
  Society 50, Dublin, 1975.
O'Donoghue, N., *The Holy Mountain*, Dublin, 1983.
——, *Aristocracy of Soul, Patrick of Ireland*, London, 1987.
——, 'St Patrick's breastplate', in *An Introduction to Celtic Christianity*, ed.
  Mackey, J. P., 45–63, Edinburgh, 1989.
——, *The Mountain Behind the Mountain*, Edinburgh, 1993.
O'Donohue, J., *Echoes of Memory*, Dublin, 1994.
——, *Stone as the Tabernacle of Memory*, Inverin, 1994.
O'Donovan, J., *The Banquet of Dun n-Gedh and the Battle of Magh Rath*,
  Dublin, 1842.
——, *Annals of the Four Masters*, 1851.
——, *Cormac's Glossary* (trans.) with Stokes, W. (ed.), Calcutta, 1868.
O'Driscoll, R., *Celtic Consciousness*, Edinburgh, 1982.
O'Dwyer, P., *Céli Dé, spiritual reform in Ireland 750–900*, 2nd edn, Dublin, 1981.
O'Grady, S., *Silva Gadelica*, 2 vols, Dublin, 1892.
Ó hAodha, D., *Bethu Brigte*, Dublin, 1978.
Ó hOgain, D., *Myth, Legend and Romance, an encyclopaedia of the Irish folk
  tradition*, London, 1990.
O'Keeffe, J. G., 'Mac Dá Cherda and Cummaine Foda', *Ériu* 5, 1911, 18–44.
——, *Buile Suibne*, Irish Texts Society 12, Dublin, 1913.
O'Kelleher A. and Schoepperle, G., *Betha Choluim Chille* / *Life of Columcille*,
  compiled by M. O'Donnell, 1532, Illinois, 1918.
O'Kelly, M., *Newgrange: Archeology, Art and Legend*, London, 1982.
Ó Laoghaire, D., 'Mary in Irish Spirituality', in *Irish Spirituality*, ed. Maher,
  M., Dublin, 1981, 49–56.
Ó Maille, T., 'Medb Chruachna', *ZCP* 17, 1927, 129–46.
O'Meara, J., *Gerald of Wales: The History and Topography of Ireland*, London,
  1982.
Ó Neill, P., 'Airbertach Mac Cosse's poem on the Psalter', *Éigse* 17, 19–46.
O'Rahilly, C., *Táin Bó Cúailgne* / *The Cattle Raid of Cooley*, Recension I,
  Dublin, 1976.

O'Rahilly, T. F. (ed.), *Measgra Dánta* I–II, Dublin, 1927.
——, *Early Irish History and Mythology*, Dublin, 1947.
——, 'Buchet the Herdsman', *Ériu* 16, 1952, 7–20.
Ó Riain, P., 'Traces of Lug in the early Irish hagiographical tradition', *ZCP*
    36, 1978, 138–56.
Ó Suilleabháin, S., *A Handbook of Irish Folklore*, Dublin,1942.
——, *Irish Folk Custom and Belief / Nósanna agus piseoga na nGael*, Dublin, 1967.
Oesterley, W., 'The early Hebrew festival rituals', in *Myth and Ritual*, ed.
    Hooke, S., Oxford, 1933, 112–46.
Oskamp, H. P., *The Voyage of Máel Dúin: a study in early Irish voyage
    literature*, Groningen, 1970.
——, 'Condla's Journey', *Études Celtiques* 14, 1976, 205–14.
Oxford Dictionary of the Christian Church, 2nd edn, Cross, F. L. and
    Livingstone, E. A. (eds.) 1984, Oxford.
On the Fitness of Names, see Windisch and Stokes.
Patrick, *Confession*, see Bieler; Hood.
Plummer C., 'The Conversion of Loegaire and his death', *RC* 6, 1885, 165–8.
——, *Vitae Sanctorum Hiberniae*, 2 vols, Oxford, 1910.
——, *Irish Litanies*, Henry Bradshaw Society 62, London,1925.
——, *Bethada náem nÉrenn / Lives of Irish Saints*, 2 vols, Oxford, 1922.
Raftery, B., *Pagan Celtic Ireland*, London, 1994.
Rees, A. and B., *Celtic Heritage, ancient tradition in Ireland and Wales*,
    London, 1961.
Reeves, W., *Adamnán's Life of St Columba*, Lampeter, 1988, reprinted from
    Historians of Scotland, Edmonston and Douglas, 1874.
Rennes Dindshenchas, see Stokes.
Rig Veda, an anthology, trans. W.D. O'Flaherty, London, 1981.
Ross, A., *Pagan Celtic Britain*, London, 1967.
——, rev. edn, 1992.
Roy, J., *The Road Wet, The Wind Close*, Dublin, 1986.
Ryan, J., *Irish Monasticism*, London, 1931 and 1972.
——, *Essays and Studies Presented to Prof. Eoin MacNeill*, Dublin, 1940.
Saltair na Rann, see Greene, Kelly and Murdoch.
Sanders, N. K., *Poems of Heaven and Hell from Ancient Mesopotamia*, London,
    1971.
Sandmel, S., *The Hebrew Scriptures*, Oxford, 1978.
Sayers, W., 'Mani, maidi an Nem...'; ringing changes on a cosmic motif', *Ériu*
    37, 1986, 99–117.
Scott, A. B. and Martin, F. X., *Giraldus Cambrensis: Expugnatio Hibernica /
    The Conquest of Ireland*, Dublin, 1978.
Scowcroft, R. M., '*Leabhar Gabhála*, part I: the growth of the text', *Ériu* 38,
    1987, 81–142.
——, '*Leabhar Gabhála*, part II: the growth of the tradition', *Ériu* 39, 1988, 1–66.
Sharpe, R., *Adomnán of Iona: Life of Saint Columba*, London, 1995.
Sherley-Price, L. (trans.) *Bede: Ecclesiastical History of the English People*,
    Farmer, D. H. (ed.), rev. edn, London, 1990.
Simms, K., *From Kings to Warlords*, Woodbridge, 1987.
——, 'Satire in later medieval Ireland', paper delivered at IXth International
    Conference of Celtic Studies, Paris, 1991.

Simms-Williams, P., 'Some Celtic Otherworld terms', in *Celtic Language, Celtic Culture*, ed. Matonis, A. and Melia, D., Van Nuys, 1990, 57–81.

Sjoestedt, M.-L., 'Le siège de Druim Damhghaire', *RC* 43, 1926, 1–147.

——, *Gods and Heroes of the Celts*, trans. Dillon, M., London, 1949.

Skene, W. F., *Annals of Tigernach*, in *Chronicles of the Picts and Scots*, Edinburgh, 1867, 66–78.

Smyth, M., 'The physical world in seventh century hiberno-latin texts', *Peritia* 5, 1986, 201–34.

Stancliffe, C., 'The miracle stories in seventh-century Irish saints' Lives', in *The Seventh Century, Change and Continuity*, Fontaine, J., and Hillgarth, J. N. (eds), London, 1992, 87–115.

Stokes, W., *Three Irish Glossaries*, London, 1862.

——, *Tripartite Life of Patrick*, 2 vols, London, 1887.

——, 'The voyage of Snedgus and MacRiagla', *RC* 9, 1888, 14–25.

——, *Lives of the Saints from the Book of Lismore*, Oxford, 1890.

——, 'Cormac's Adventure in the land of Promise' in *Irische Texte* 3(1), ed. Windisch and Stokes, Leipzig, 1891.

——, 'The Battle of Mac Mucrime', *RC* 13, 1892, 426–74.

——, 'The Voyage of the Uí Corra', *RC* 14, 1893, 22–69.

——, 'The Edinburgh Dindshenchas', *Folklore* 4, 1893, 471–97.

——, 'The Violent Deaths of Goll and Garb', *RC* 14, 1893, 398–449.

——, 'The Rennes *Dindshenchas*', *RC* 15, 1894, 272–336; *RC* 16, 1895, 31–83.

——, 'The Bodleian *Amra Choluimb Chille*', *RC* 20, 1899, 30–55, 132–83, 248–89, 400–37.

——, 'The Destruction of Da Derga's Hostel', *RC* 22, 1901, 9–61, 165–215, 282–329, 390–437.

——, 'The Death of Muirchertach meic Erca', *RC* 23, 1902, 395–431.

——, 'The journey of the sons of Eochaid Muigmedóin', *RC* 24, 1903, 190–203.

——, 'The Death of Crimthann', *RC* 24, 1903, 174–87.

——, 'Three Legends from the Brussels Manuscript 5100–4, *RC* 26, 1905, 372–7.

——, *Félire Óengusso Céli Dé / The Martyrology of Óengus the Culdee*, Henry Bradshaw Society 29, London, 1905.

——, 'The Evernew Tongue here below', *Ériu* 2, 1905, 96–147.

——, 'The Colloquy of the Two Sages', *RC* 26, 1905, 4–64.

——, 'The Birth and Life of St Moling', *RC* 27, 1906, 257–312.

——, 'The Tidings of Conchobar, Son of Ness', *Ériu* 4, 1910, 22–38.

Stokes, W., and Strachan, J., *Thesaurus Palaeohibernicus*, 2 vols., Cambridge, 1901–3.

Strachan, J., 'An Old Irish homily', *Ériu* 3, 1907, 1–10.

Taylor, J. V., *The Primal Vision: Christian Presence and African Religion*, London, 1965.

—— (ed.), *Primal World Views, Christian Dialogue with traditional thought forms*, World Council of Churches, Ibadan, 1976.

Terrien, S., 'The Omphalos Myth in Hebrew Religion', *Vetus Testamentum* 20, 1970, 315–38.

Thurneysen, R., 'Mittelirische Verslehren', *Irische Texte* 3(1), ed. Windisch, E. and Stokes, W., Leipzig, 1891, 1–182.

——, 'Tuirill Bricenn und seine Kinder', *ZCP* 12, 1918, 237–54.

Tírechán, see Bieler, *Patrician Texts*.

Tripartite Life of Partick, see Stokes.

Turner, H. W., 'The primal religions of the world and their study', in *Australian Essays in World Religions*, ed. Hayes, V., Bedford Park, 1977, 27–37.

Tymoczko, M., '*Cétamon*: vision in early Irish seasonal poetry', *Éire–Ireland* 18, 1983, 17–39.

Vendryes, J., 'Sur un nom ancien de l'arbre', *RC* 44, 1927, 313–19.

——, 'Manannán mac Lir', *EC* 6, 1952–4, 239–54.

——, *Airne Fíngein*, Dublin, 1953.

Vision of the Phantom, see O'Curry.

Voyage of Bran, see Nutt and Meyer.

Voyage of St Brendan, see Webb and Farmer, *Age of Bede*.

Voyage of Snedgus and MacRiagla, see Stokes.

Voyage of the Uí Corra, see Stokes.

Waddell, J., 'The royal site in Connacht', *JIA* 1, 1983, 21–46.

Wakeman, W., *A Survey of the Antiquarian Remains on the Island of Inismurray*, London, 1894.

Walls, A.F., 'Africa and Christian Identity', *Mission Focus* 5, 1978.

——, 'Primal religious traditions in today's world', in *Religion in Today's World*, ed. Whaling, F., Edinburgh, 1987, 250–78.

——, 'The translation principle in Christian history', in *Bible Translation and the Spread of the Church*, ed. Stine, P. C., Leiden, 1990, 24–39.

Warren, F. E., *The Liturgy and Ritual of the Celtic Church*, Oxford, 1881, re-edited Stevenson, J., Oxford, 1987.

——, *Antiphonary of Bangor*, Henry Bradshaw Society 10, 2 vols., London, 1895.

Wasting Sickness of Cú Chulainn, see Gantz, *EIMS*.

Watson, A., 'The king, the poet and the sacred tree', *EC* 18, 1981, 165–80.

Webb, J. F. and Farmer, D. H., *The Age of Bede*, rev. edn, 1988, 211–45.

Wentz, W. Y. E., *The Fairy Faith in Celtic Countries*, Oxford, 1911, 2nd edn, 1977.

Williams, N. J. A., *The Poems of Giolla Brighde Mac Con Midhe*, Dublin, 1980.

Windisch E. and Stokes, W., 'On the Fitness of Names', *Irische Texte* 3(2), Leipzig, 1897, 285–444.

Wood-Martin, W. G., *Traces of the Elder Faiths of Ireland*, 2 vols, London, 1902.

Wooing of Étaín / Tochmarc Étaíne, see Best and Bergin; Gantz, *EIMS*.

Wright, T., *The Historical Works of Giraldus Cambrensis*, trans. Forester, T., London, 1863.

Index